D1732976

Under the Stars

ESSAYS ON LABOR RELATIONS

IN ARTS AND ENTERTAINMENT

EDITED BY

Lois S. Gray and Ronald L. Seeber

ILR PRESS AN IMPRINT OF

CORNELL UNIVERSITY PRESS

ITHACA AND LONDON

Copyright © 1996 by Cornell University

All rights reserved. Except for brief quotations in a review, this book, or parts thereof, must not be reproduced in any form without permission in writing from the publisher. For information, address Cornell University Press, Sage House, 512 East State Street, Ithaca, New York 14850.

First published 1996 by ILR Press/Cornell University Press.

Printed in the United States of America

Library of Congress Cataloging-in-Publication Data

Gray, Lois S., 1950–
    Under the stars : essays on labor relations in arts and
entertainment / Lois S. Gray and Ronald L. Seeber.
        p.   cm.
    Includes bibliographical references and index.
    ISBN 0-87546-350-9 (cloth : alk. paper). — ISBN 0-87546-349-5
(pbk. : alk. paper)
    1. Motion picture industry—Economic aspects—United States.
    2. Television broadcasting—Economic aspects—United States.
    3. Trade unions—Motion picture industry—United States—History.
    4. Industrial relations—United States.   I. Seeber, Ronald Leroy.
    II. Title.
    PN1993.5.U6G65   1995
    384′.83′0973—dc20   95-18628

♾ The paper in this book meets the minimum requirements
of the American National Standard for Information Sciences—
Permanence of Paper for Printed Library Materials, ANSI Z39.48-1984.

Contents

Foreword   vii
J. Nicholas Counter III
Jack Golodner

Acknowledgments   xiii

Introduction   1

1. The Industry and the Unions: An Overview   15
   Lois Gray and Ronald Seeber

2. Technology Transforms   50
   Les Brown

3. Flexibility and Adaptation in Industrial Relations:
   The Exceptional Case of the U.S. Media
   Entertainment Industries   86
   Susan Christopherson

4. The Transformation of Industrial Relations
   in the Motion Picture and Television Industries:
   Craft and Production   113
   John Amman

5. The Transformation of Industrial Relations
in the Motion Picture and Television Industries:
Talent Sector   156
Alan Paul and Archie Kleingartner

6. Looking Ahead   181
Lois Gray and Ronald Seeber

Bibliography   193

Contributors   201

Index   203

Foreword

Key Issues Facing Producers and Distributors in the Motion Picture and Television Industry

J. Nicholas Counter III, President,
Alliance of Motion Picture and Television Producers

Technological advances in the delivery of motion pictures and television programs to the consumer continue to frame the most important issues facing producers and distributors in the 1990s. While the past is not necessarily a prologue for the future, it is evident that technological advances have fundamentally changed the economic landscape for the survival of the motion picture and television industry.

In the early days there was only one marketplace for movies—the local theater. In the 1940s, movie attendance was over twice the admissions today (with less than half of the present population). Producers and distributors could depend upon the theatrical box office to cover their costs and earn a profit for development of the next picture. With the advent of free television, pay television, basic cable, and videocassettes, theatrical box office revenues now cover less than forty percent of the cost of production and distribution. Thus, it is imperative for producers and distributors to have unimpeded access to those after-theatrical markets in order for the industry to survive.

A similar sea change in the economics of the television business has taken place. During the 1970s, network television dominated the television sets of the American audience. In that environment producers of dramatic programs and situation comedies were able to cover their costs of production with the license fees paid by the networks for those programs. That economic model was turned on its head in the 1980s with the expansion of independent television stations, basic cable television, pay television, and VCRs. The result is that in the 1990s producers of those programs face ever-increasing deficits (the difference between production cost and license fee paid by the networks) and are dependent upon other markets such as foreign and domestic syndication in order to survive.

The impact of these technological changes on collective bargaining in the industry is well documented. The producers insisted that the collective agreements should not impede their access to these new markets. In turn, the guilds and unions were faced with demands from their membership for their fair share of the revenues from these new markets. These tensions led to numerous strikes in the industry: in 1960, over movies exhibited on free television; in 1973, over movies exhibited on pay television; in 1980–81, regarding movies and other programs made for pay television exhibition; and in 1985, as regards movies exhibited by means of videocassettes.

There are new technological advancements on the horizon that may create similar tensions in the bargaining process. The satellite delivery of movies to the theaters and directly to homes will further complicate the economics of the business. Digital technology will reduce the cost of production and may return productions from locations to the studios. The interface of computer technology with compact discs will lead to uses not yet understood. The bargaining parties will be forced to seek accommodations that will allow these technological advancements to expand rather than contract the future markets for movies and television programs.

On the international front, producers and distributors of movies and television programs are under attack. Foreign governments are imposing quotas on American products. The European community is considering directives that would deprive U.S. copyright holders of proper economic remuneration on numerous fronts. Producers and distributors thus face substantial erosion of foreign markets upon which they became so dependent in the 1980s. It is vital that labor and management unite against this frontal assault by foreign governments on the copyright system.

While the industry needs the intervention of the U.S. government in order to combat foreign barriers to the full dissemination of U.S. works, government should not interfere with the bargaining relationships of the parties here in the United States. Government intrusion in the bargaining process has proven to be ineffective if not detrimental in other industries. Those failures should not be repeated in the entertainment industry.

In the end, cooperation between labor and management is essential for the survival of the entertainment industry. Confrontation and disruption of production has resulted in losses which have never been recouped. The bargaining parties should learn from the past so that the industry will not wither but instead continue to be a world leader.

Unions View the Challenges Facing the Arts, Entertainment, and Mass Media Industry

Jack Golodner, President
Department for Professional Employees, AFL-CIO

When experts talk and write of the future of American industry, terms like "contingent work force," "high value added products," "agile management," and "global competition" are used with increasing frequency. They are today's buzzwords that describe an environment to which, it is claimed, American industry and American workers must adapt if they are not to suffer decline.

Because the arts, entertainment, and mass electronic media industry in the United States has coped with just such an environment throughout its history, it offers valuable lessons which have been mined by the authors of this book. Among them is that adaptation to rapidly changing competitive situations requires the best thinking of both management and union leaders and is best achieved when they work as true partners. The need to adapt to changes in technology, global conditions, and consumer taste does not confront management alone or unions alone. The solutions, therefore, cannot be found by either working alone but only by working together.

In the arts, entertainment, and mass media industry, agile management requires not only an agile work force but a dependable, highly skilled, and talented one as well. Unions were a response by employees to the instability created when management sought a work force on an "as needed" basis. But by serving their members' needs for a measure of certainty, stability, equity, and a fair share of the rewards, unions also helped the industry attract and retain a flexible, mobile, highly skilled, dedicated work force that has proven to be more than a match for world competitors. For an industry dependent on the availability of a contingent work force possessing the ability to produce extremely high value-added products, this is no small contribution. It is extremely doubtful that management, operating from its own short-term, bottom-line perspective, could accomplish this alone—without the input and insistence of union organizations.

Looking into the future, the arts, entertainment, and mass media industry—like so many others—must continue to face the challenges brought about by rapid technological change and a shifting competitive situation which is shaped not only by market forces but by government policies worldwide. These challenges confront the unions of this industry as well.

Technology is a theme that surfaces on each page of this book and with good reason. In less than a generation crystal sets were displaced by high fidelity transmission and reception of not only sound but color images over the air and then via cable, satellite, and now, telephone lines. Concurrently, new technologies were introduced for recording, storing, and reproducing sound and image on tape or film. Linked to new advanced transmission/distribution systems, these recordings feed directly into low-cost, high-quality consumer-operated copying devices. Soon, thanks to digital high-definition television and audio transmissions, every home, restaurant, and public space can be transformed into a lyceum, a theater, a concert hall, a stadium. Obviously such radical changes require a radical rethinking of the relationship between the creators of the programming, the producers and distributors of the product, and the consumer. And should advances in the synthesization of sound, the human voice, and even the human image continue apace, new definitions will be needed to describe the vast array of revised or wholly new occupations. Will the theater (film and live) exist as we now know it? How will sound and image performances be marketed? Who should be compensated and how? How and where does a new work force for this industry receive the knowledge and training required for the new roles it is to perform? Who should pay for such training?

These are some of the questions being raised with increasing frequency at the collective bargaining table. Only through full cooperation and a sincere acceptance of the collective bargaining process will workable solutions be found.

Clearly, government action and inaction affects the environment surrounding the union-management relationship and cannot be ignored. Government purchases the products of the industry in all its many manifestations; government sometimes subsidizes the product for the benefit of the general public; government initiates and administers copyright laws to protect the creative efforts upon which this industry rests; government regulates the means by which programming is distributed via the airwaves, the phone lines, and cable; and government oversees the laws that govern the flow of workers, products, and services across national boundaries.

As the demand for greater access to entertainment and information grows and as technology changes to accommodate this demand, new pressures to adapt are applied to the people who comprise this industry. The strains and stresses grow. Some will be confronted and resolved by the people involved through their unions and employing organizations. Others can only be addressed by informed government action.

Government, technology, and the changing size and scope of the organizations that employ and distribute the work of performers, communicators, craft people, and technicians are major concerns confronting all who participate in labor-management relations in the arts, entertainment, and mass media industry. These concerns can be addressed satisfactorily only through the collective bargaining process and by unions and management together insisting on government policy that is sensitive and responsible to this important sector. The analysis and insights provided in this book will help immeasurably in stimulating the thinking of all the parties and encouraging them to seek the kind of cooperative relationships that are so necessary to achieving constructive solutions.

Acknowledgments

The original study upon which this book is based was made possible by a grant from the U.S. Department of Labor, Bureau of Labor-Management Relations and Cooperative Programs. Leon Lunden, the director of that division, was particularly helpful with support, encouragement, and advice. Lois Gray and Ron Seeber could not have coordinated and guided this study without the assistance of many talented individuals. Melissa Harrington, Theresa Woodhouse, and Alphena Clark provided administrative and typing services. In addition, Melissa Harrington provided overall organizational skills to the project. Howard Byck, research assistant, contributed valuable ideas and time to the project. Alice Beamsderfer edited some of the papers and made many important substantive suggestions. Individual authors attacked their projects with an intellectual vigor and curiosity that is reflected in their final products.

This project would have been impossible without the assistance and cooperation of the management and union leaders who served on the advisory committee, allowed themselves to be interviewed, gave their candid views on the future of the industry, and commented on the papers. We would particularly like to thank the members of the advisory committee.

Advisory Committee

James S. Berman
Recording Industry Association of America

J. Nicholas Counter III
Alliance of Motion Picture and Television Producers

Alfred W. DiTolla
International Alliance of Theatrical and Stage Employees

Alan Eisenberg
Actors Equity Association

Martin Emerson
American Federation of Musicians

Reggie Gilliam
International Brotherhood of Electrical Workers

Jack Golodner
Department for Professional Employees, AFL-CIO

John Hall
American Federation of Television and Radio Artists

Harry C. Katz
Cornell University

Day Krolik III
NBC

Leon Lunden
U.S. Department of Labor

Eugene McGuire
NBC

John McGuire
Screen Actors Guild

Kenneth Moffett
National Association of Broadcast Employees and Technicians

Michael Moskow
Premark International, Inc.

Jeffrey Ruthizer
ABC

Gerald Schoenfeld
New York League of Theaters

Richard Shore
U.S. Department of Labor

James F. Sirmons
CBS

Sanford I. Wolff
American Guild of Musical Artists

L. S. G.
R. L. S.

Introduction

Lois Gray and Ronald Seeber

The entertainment industry is now the driving force for new technology, as defense used to be.

—*Business Week,* March 14, 1994

There is perhaps no more visible segment of the American economy than the arts and entertainment sector. When the Writers Guild engaged its members in a strike against the Alliance of Motion Picture and Television Producers in 1988, the popular culture of the vast majority of the American public was deeply affected. New television shows were delayed and the networks scrambled to find replacement programming. Virtually everyone was aware of the labor-management conflict, though probably not of its cause, and conscious of its impact on their lives. It could be argued that strikes in any of a half-dozen industries over the course of that year had less impact on the average American life, even though many times the number of workers were affected.

No other product so universally affects us as the combined output of this sector of the economy. Whether it be film, television, music, or the live arts, everyone is a consumer of this industry. Everyone has opinions, not necessarily informed or well conceived, about this industry. These simple universalities would seem to make this sector of the economy worthy of much more attention than it has received in the past. While a voluminous bibliography could be constructed of books, articles, and popular press devoted to the artistic side of this industry, almost no attention has been paid to the people who work in it, finance it, and profit from it. We know very little about the union-management relationships in this industry, which receive scant popular notice save when something like the 1988 writers' strike occurs.

This is a significant and important gap in knowledge, given the scope of change that has occurred in the industry over the past few decades. For not only does the product of this industry wield enormous influence over us, but some of the most important and far-reaching technological changes of our times have taken place in the workplaces of Hollywood, New York, and the other emerging entertainment production centers. It is this intersection of economics, labor relations, and technological change that will be addressed in this volume. Technological change has produced a dazzling array of new products and media for the enjoyment of entertainment. Technological change has also produced a difficult set of challenges for unions, workers, and managers in this industry. And technological change has influenced the economic structure of production and distribution throughout the industry. Within this volume, we will focus our attention on technological change and its impact on those institutions and individuals. Our future is dramatically influenced by these events and a deeper understanding of these changes is necessary for all of us.

Definition of the AEEM Industry

In this study, the arts, entertainment, and electronic media (AEEM) industry is defined as including four sectors: live performing arts, recordings, motion pictures, and television and radio. While some might argue that this definition is either too broadly or too narrowly drawn (for example, it excludes sports, gambling, and theme parks), it works for the purposes of studying industrial relations because of the commonality of the work performed, the product produced, and the structure of collective bargaining and management.

The live performing arts sector consists of live theater (plays, musicals, and variety shows), performed primarily in larger cities and occasionally taken to smaller metropolitan areas through touring companies to be performed by local and regional theatrical companies; live music, which includes orchestras, opera, and concerts, including jazz, pop, and rock and roll; and dance, notably ballet companies based in major cities.

The recording sector is composed of several major record companies and many smaller ones, all of which produce and distribute vinyl records, cassette tapes, and compact disks (CDs). The motion picture sector includes companies that produce and distribute films and the networks of theaters that exhibit them.

The broadcast sector of the AEEM industry, like the film sector, includes both production and distribution. Producers of television films are mostly the same companies that produce motion pictures, except for news, sports, and game shows, which are produced by departments within the television networks. Four major networks and a host of minor ones distribute the television product over the air waves or through cable systems.

Reasons for Studying This Industry

Many industrial relations scholars are finding that studies focusing on specific industries or sectors in the economy are the best way to understand current developments in industrial and labor relations (Lipsky and Donn, 1987). The era of theories of conflict and convergence in collective bargaining that can be broadly applied to all industries is more in question than it ever was. Different sectors of the economy have diverged in terms of both the employment problems they face and their approaches to industrial relations. Thus, each sector's industrial relations can be understood best by examining the specific economic and organizational context in which it occurs.

There are compelling reasons for studying the AEEM industry in particular.

1. The AEEM industry is a prime example of high technology development and application. Indeed, technology has been the driving force behind change in the industry, and understanding its effects could help to anticipate and resolve future problems in other rapidly changing industries. Leading spokespersons from both labor and management have stated that the rapid pace of technological change is the single most important influence on labor-management

relations and is at the root of most labor-management disputes in the industry (Counter and Chassman interviews).

2. The AEEM industry, while small in comparison to, say, the automobile industry, is a highly visible and thus important sector of the economy. When a few thousand television writers go on strike, the economic activity affected is relatively small in the total economy, but because of the public's familiarity with the product involved (i.e., television programs), the strike has a significant effect on public consciousness and can change consumers' behavior patterns in a way that almost no other kind of industrial conflict can.

3. The AEEM industry, unlike most of the American economy, is a major net exporter of product and as such is one of a recently dwindling set of industries that contribute positively to the U.S. balance of trade. The export of American films alone contributes well over a billion dollars to the balance of trade (Stevenson, 1989b). When television and other forms of entertainment are included, this industry becomes a significant contributor to this country's economy at a time when it is bleeding from trade deficits in nearly all other sectors. Films, television, and recordings produced in the United States set the standard for consumers around the world. No other country has a film or television industry comparable in size, and no other country exports as much of its film and television product as the United States. If we are to solve this country's balance of trade problems, we need to understand the dynamics of industries that have continued to be successful exporters.

4. At a time when unionization is in decline in the United States, the AEEM industry has continued to be heavily unionized. However, as the workforce changes and the proportion of unionized craft workers shrinks, primarily as a result of technological change, the terms and conditions of employment are becoming less and less dominated by collective bargaining. The future of the AEEM craft unions certainly could have implications for other craft unions in the United States that face obsolescence or large reductions in membership in the face of technological change.

5. The industry was influenced by conflict in the 1980s which brought strikes in creative (known as above-the-line) occupations and craft (below-the-line) occupations in the film industry. Most highly publicized have been strikes by writers and actors, but the

International Brotherhood of Teamsters and unions representing related workers and technicians have engaged in conflict too. We have also witnessed strikes at two major television networks (CBS and NBC), while negotiations at ABC have reached the brink of conflict several times in recent years. The American Federation of Musicians has been engaged in continuing disputes with employers, including symphony orchestras, night clubs, and recording companies. That this conflict has occurred in an era when many industries in the United States have had relatively peaceful relations between labor and management is of great interest to industrial relations scholars and policymakers who seek to understand the roots of conflict.

6. As a result of these conflicts and growing recognition of mutual labor-management stakes in survival of a rapidly changing industry, joint consultations are beginning to emerge in sectors of motion picture and television production, suggesting further areas for exploration with respect to the dynamics of labor-management relations. This development may have implications for other industries.

The Difficulties of Studying the AEEM Industry

Everyone knows something about this sector of the economy, because everyone is a consumer of its product. This knowledge, although widespread, is superficial. Real, in-depth knowledge or analysis of the industry is extremely scarce.

We are all aware to some extent of the technological revolution in the production and distribution of art and entertainment. Technology has allowed the production of both audio and video to be completed at a higher quality with more widely available equipment. While this equipment is not always a less costly production medium, and in many cases is significantly more costly, it has often allowed the product to be created with fewer and fewer people. This outcome is mostly invisible to the consuming public. News reports are now produced by one or two people who are able to go anywhere, rather than the previously more unwieldy and limiting three- or four-person crews. Music is recorded with the assistance of synthesized instruments and digitally sampled voices, rather than live musicians and singers.

Cable television has given many households a plethora of video alternatives, rather than the three choices of an earlier era. Even the live arts are changed by advances in lighting and sound, which enhance the performance and replace a more labor-intensive production crew.

While we are aware of these changes, we don't often think about or know much about their impact on the economics and labor relations of the production and distribution of art and entertainment product. Because the employment characteristics of the AEEM industry differ from almost all others in the economy, conventional measures of employment and earnings tell us little. We need to study the unique features of this industry.

The unusual characteristics of the employment and labor relations system include the following:

1. The AEEM industry is characterized by an exceptionally high rate of unemployment. Officials of unions representing entertainment talent estimate that as many as 90 to 95 percent of their members are unable to find work in their chosen line on any given day. For example, Actors Equity reported in 1988 that only 11.9 percent of its members were employed per week (Hummler, 1988).

2. The data on earnings and hours are notoriously unreliable. Because actors, writers, and performers often hold other jobs to sustain them while they look for work in their chosen profession, it is difficult to gather information on earnings and hours that is not contaminated by outside employment data.

3. In the AEEM industry, as in professional sports, collective bargaining defines only minimum working conditions; union members are free to and generally do negotiate individual contracts that supersede the collectively bargained minimum agreements.

4. Nearly all AEEM unions draw their membership exclusively from the AEEM sector of the economy and operate relatively isolated from other unions and bargaining. (The exceptions are the International Brotherhood of Electrical Workers [IBEW], the Teamsters, and the basic crafts from the AFL-CIO building trades.) What impact this characteristic has on bargaining and union points of view is open to speculation, but it is possible that such exclusivity in membership prevents the cross-fertilization of ideas and practices from other industries. While this is not unique to AEEM, it is particularly intense here.

5. The dominant employment model for the industry is casual employment on a project-by-project basis rather than attachment to a single employer. While this feature is not unique to the AEEM sector, it does present special bargaining problems. Workers, for example, develop loyalty to their union, their craft, and to individuals with whom they have worked rather than to their employer.

6. Many workers in the industry hold multiple union memberships, making it difficult to obtain accurate figures on the structure or extent of unionism in the industry. Typically, for example, many performing artists belong simultaneously to Actors Equity (AEA), the Screen Actors Guild (SAG), American Federation of Television and Radio Artists (AFTRA), and perhaps the American Guild of Musical Artists (AGMA) and American Guild of Variety Artists (AGVA). The sum of these unions' membership therefore does not reflect the number of performing artists who are union members, but rather a larger number that is exaggerated by the multiple union memberships.

Some of these issues have been examined but not since the early 1980s and only for members of the five performing unions (Ruttenberg et al., 1981). All these factors serve to make conventional employment data and relationships difficult to gather and analyze. The uniqueness of the sector requires further basic data collection to provide a context for the available information.

Highlights of the Chapters

The chapters in this book examine current dilemmas in labor relations presented by the dramatic technological changes that have occurred in the arts, entertainment, and electronic media industry. It has become increasingly clear in the past decade that the AEEM industry is distinct from most others, in terms of both labor relations issues and the range of possible outcomes. At times the problems facing labor relations professionals in the industry have seemed insurmountable. In many other sectors of the U.S. economy, labor-management conflict abated during the 1980s, but in the AEEM industry negotiations were increasingly characterized by the tactics of confrontation. It has been reported that the average annual number of work stoppages declined from 2,660 in the 1970s to 1,250 in the 1980s (USGAO, 1991). Visible strikes in television and film during the 1980s stand in sharp contrast to that trend. Why does conflict seem so prevalent in this industry? How does the AEEM sector fit into the dominant industrial relations themes in the United States today? The idiosyncracies of the industry's labor relations and the idea that technological change might be the factor that differentiates AEEM from other industries inspired this research project. Although there were no in-depth studies of the forces driving the industry, the researchers involved in this project believed that, in one way or another, rapid technological change played a key role in the problems that were surfacing during collective bargaining.

The first chapter by Lois Gray and Ron Seeber gives an overview of the economics of the entertainment industry as well as the unions that represent entertainment employers and their collective bargaining relationships. Here are a few of the economic highlights described in chapter 1.

With output increasing at a record rate each year, entertainment is one of our major growth industries. Americans currently spend more money on entertainment and recreation than on any other product. At the same time the explosive demand for American recordings, broadcasts, and films from consumers throughout the world gives an added impetus to growth. Entertainment products are second only to aerospace as our leading export (U.S. Department of Commerce, 1991). Although each segment of the entertainment industry has its own unique features, there are common characteristics: high capital investment, enormous marketing expenditures, and exceptional risk. Since the production process is labor intensive, labor relations play an important role in the cost structure of the industry. A few large producers dominate sales of recordings, films, and broadcasting with a trend toward integration among all market components. For example, a musical is made into a movie and shown on television with its music marketed in recordings.

American production facilities are increasingly attractive to foreign investors. While foreign ownership of television and radio is prohibited by law, five out of six major U.S.-based recording companies and four out of seven leading film studios are foreign owned, and foreign investors are increasingly a source of capital for others. As in other U.S. industries, mergers and takeovers have characterized recent economic history, bringing in new owners from outside the entertainment field. There are wide differences in profitability among industry sectors. The commercial theater and nonprofit music and dance companies, for example, struggle to stay alive while other entertainment producers have above-average profit margins.

Another distinctive characteristic of this industry is its dependence on public policy decisions. Broadcasting was created by government, which continues to exercise the power to assign air waves. The economic well-being of the film industry is challenged by the power of the Federal Communications Commission (FCC) to decide whether filmmakers or networks will dominate the production of prime time entertainment and its syndication. Exports, which are major growth sectors for films and recordings, depend on the negotiating clout of the U.S. government to break through the competitive barriers that other countries seek to impose. And given piracy as a growing threat, all sectors of the industry look to public policy decisions to protect the intellectual property of artists, writers, performers, and producers.

Chapter 1 documents that the entertainment industry, which employs about one million people, is highly unionized. Above-the-line (performer) unions have been growing while the membership of below-the-line (technician) unions has been shrinking, reflecting both technological displacement and a shift to nonunion production in some sectors of the industry. Also described is the complex structure of bargaining. In recording and film production, craft organizations negotiate agreements with multiemployer associations while one-on-one bargaining between unions and employers is characteristic of live entertainment, radio, and television. Business and labor leaders agree that technology has been the single most important influence on employment and labor relations.

Technological innovations create more jobs for actors, writers, and directors while eliminating work for musicians and technicians. Technology has also changed job content, challenged union jurisdiction over work, and raised questions about gain sharing. As a result, the entertainment industry has been racked with strife over alternative strategies for protecting jobs and advancing rates of compensation. Chapter 1 concludes with the observation that, after decades of conflict, employers and unions are beginning to explore areas of mutual interest and methods for anticipating and resolving disputes. The next two chapters analyze changes in technology and business structures and their influence on labor-management relations, particularly in film and television. Les Brown, former editor of the media section of the *New York Times* and *Television International,* points to "the end of television as we knew it" in an era of "revolutionary" changes brought about by technology and innovation, deregulation, corporate restructuring, and internationalization. Noting that technology both creates jobs and eliminates jobs, he underscores the crucial role of public and private decision making. While technology creates the opportunity for change, its implementation depends on business and public policies. The technology that created cable, videocassette recorders, and satellite dishes changed the nature of television broadcasting from "table d'hôte to à la carte," giving viewers a broader range of choice. This ended the dominance of the networks, which were locked into an old system of relationships with affiliates and advertisers, and left them in a cost squeeze with declining profit margins.

New owners, free of broadcast tradition and saddled with debt from buyouts, looked for ways to slash expenses. Automated equipment, a partial answer to rising costs, has resulted in job losses for technicians and has brought changes in their terms and conditions of employment. Growing domestic competition has encouraged the globalization of ownership and markets. Brown cites public policy decisions that could drastically change the playing field by altering financial syndication rules which open new profit-making opportunities for networks and permit local telephone companies to compete with cable. Thus he concludes that the interaction between technology and private and government policy decisions will determine the future of the television industry and predicts that changes to come will be more convulsive than ever as television is reinvented.

Susan Christopherson, professor in Cornell's Department of City and Regional Planning, deals with the changing production structure in television and moviemaking, which she views as a major challenge to the bargaining power of unions. Her chapter describes the transformation of the industry from vertical integration, which characterized the era of the studio system in motion picture production and network dominance of television (1920–59), to a vertically disintegrated system in the 1970s in which a substantial part of production was carried on by independent companies while control over financing and distribution remained in the hands of the major companies. Employment ties were loosened and unions lost much of their influence over labor supply. Nonetheless, they negotiated contracts and created institutional arrangements that made it possible to deliver to their members personnel services that had been provided in-house by employers, including health and pension benefits for technicians, a roster system to certify skill and experience, and, for performers, a system of supplementary payments which gave them property rights in their jobs.

Christopherson describes the current industrial structure in entertainment as "virtual integration" in which major firms, increasingly internationalized in both markets and ownership, are tightening their control of production in multiple markets and moving toward merger in film, television, and cable distribution. Rather than owning the facilities and hiring the personnel, the major companies are currently integrated through contract and investment. Among the industrial relations results of structural transformation coupled with technological and regulatory changes are fragmentation in terms of gender, race, and occupational identities and breakdown of traditional boundaries between labor and management. While the technician unions have stagnated or declined and the talent guilds have expanded in membership, all confront a potential weakening of bargaining power. Assessing these developments as intensifying conflict between and within work groups and undermining the fragile balance between individual recognition and common interests, Christopherson calls for new forms of collaboration among unions and between unions and management to deal with industrywide problems.

Chapter 4, written by John Amman who undertook this study as a graduate student in Cornell's School of Industrial and Labor Relations and went on to work as a business agent of Local 644 of the International Alliance of Theatrical and Stage Employees (IATSE), deals with the bargaining history and present status of craft unions in television and motion picture production, also projecting an erosion of union power. He traces the evolution of below-the-line unionism from its origin in the assembly line factory style of the Hollywood studio system in the 1920s. Through competitive struggle IATSE emerged as the dominant union in motion picture production. Like the studios, which owned theater outlets, IATSE's bargaining was reinforced by its ability to control distribution through effective organization of movie theater projectionists. IATSE assumed many personnel management functions for the industry. Its contracts specified work rules which restricted crossover of jobs. Other craft unions tended to follow the IATSE pattern in wages and benefits and all enjoyed steady employment during the studio era. Labor relations practices in television evolved from experience in radio, since ownership was under the control of the same three networks. Technicians had full-time permanent positions and were represented by three major unions—IATSE, the International Brotherhood of Electrical Workers (IBEW), and the National Association of Broadcast Employees and Technicians (NABET). The last of these was organized along industrial lines while the first two were structured by craft. Union wages and benefits reflected scarce skills translated into effective bargaining power.

Amman points out that the 1970s brought a transformation in labor-management relationships in both film and television emanating from the combined effects of deregulation, advancing technology, and changing business ownership. Like Brown, he emphasizes the role of public policy changes; the 1948 Supreme Court decision that separated moving picture production from distribution and the Federal Communications Commission decision that restricted the networks' right to make and sell their own programs opened both industries to competition. Technological changes abolished jobs and rendered some established union work rules obsolete; therefore, new owners not bound by past practices challenged existing agreements. The result has been a growth of nonunion production, spread of part-time and intermittent employment, and a decline in bargaining power for below-the-line unions. Amman highlights possible union strategies for coping with their new circumstances. These include organizing the unorganized, developing new approaches to represent freelance employees, researching production practices, providing greater flexibility in contract terms, and seeking mergers and cooperative agreement between unions.

Chapter 5 analyzes the transformation of industrial relations in the talent sector of the motion picture and television industry, complementing Chapter 4's emphasis on craft and technical workers. Written by Ph.D. candidate Alan Paul and Archie Kleingartner, professor of management and director of the Arts and Entertainment Management Program at the University of California, Los Angeles, and originally published in the *Industrial and Labor Relations Review*, this chapter affords an in-depth treatment of how performers successfully respond to changing technology and market pressures through their traditional and adversarial collective bargaining system, not only staving off concessionary demands from owners but advancing their power and influence. Paul and Kleingartner focus on the three-tier compensation system consisting of minimum pay rates, individually negotiated contracts, and an industrywide system of supplemental (residual) payments which evolved over four decades of bargaining between the talent guilds and the Alliance of Motion Picture and Television Producers.

In contrast with the craft and production unions, which have had to fight to retain the same size membership as members became a shrinking percentage of total entertainment employment after the early 1970s, talent guilds have grown in size and have retained their dominance in representation of television and movie performers.

Paul and Kleingartner attribute these results to the role that the talent guilds have played in creating and administering a compensation system that not only serves the needs of their members but places the guild in a position to monitor the business records of the producers and share in their success. While producer resistance to the spread of residuals (payment for replays) resulted in repeated strikes as distribution moved into new markets, residual payments have multiplied to a point where they equal initial compensation for performers, writers, and directors and serve as a cushion during periods of unemployment. As a result of their involvement and stake in management, talent guilds, in Paul and Kleingartner's view, have moved to a more advanced stage of labor-management relations in which they share managerial decisions.

The final chapter projects current trends as the industry confronts further technological change (for example, interactive media); regulatory decisions authorizing local telephone companies to offer video services, which promise competition from a new sector while encouraging further conglomeration of ownership; and the rise of the common market, which vastly expands the demand for U.S. products while threatening retaliatory trade restrictions. Critical issues for collective bargaining are job content, as jurisdictional lines and work divisions are rendered irrelevant; training for new work; and sharing the proceeds of new markets.

The authors conclude that facing dramatic changes in technology and government policy, both employers and unions seek new strategies and predict that collective bargaining in the arts and entertainment industry will undergo continuing analysis, experimentation, and change.

CHAPTER ONE

The Industry and the Unions: An Overview

Lois Gray and Ronald Seeber

This overview chapter provides a framework for the chapters that follow by broadly describing the arts, entertainment, and electronic media (AEEM) industry and the problems confronting it. The overview is presented in four sections focused on: first, the economic structure of the industry; second, unions and bargaining structure; third, the impact of technological changes; and fourth, historical responses on the part of unions and the labor relations system to technological change.

Economic Trends in the Entertainment Industry

Altogether Americans spend more than nine hours a day and invest eight cents of every consumption dollar on entertainment (Vogel, 1994)[1] and the rate of spending for entertainment is growing, reaching a total of $360 billion in 1994 (U.S. Department of Commerce).

Key factors influencing demand are demographics, technology,

---

[1]   Broadly defined, entertainment includes businesses devoted to all leisure activities: motion pictures, radio and television, recording, and live entertainment, which are the focus of this study, as well as sports, gambling, gardening, and other recreational pursuits.

and globalization. Both real income and life expectancy have risen steadily in the western world since World War II. This has allowed people to spend more time and money on leisure activities. Although the automobile was traditionally the top contender for consumer dollars, currently Americans spend more for entertainment, with expenditures increasing every year—even during recessions. Technological innovations such as videocassettes and compact disks have expanded the market for films and recordings and new developments like high-definition television and interactive media will further expand those markets.

Demand for entertainment has also been affected by the globalization of the U.S. economy. Indeed, one could say that America is to entertainment what South Africa is to gold, or the Saudis are to oil. Entertainment is second only to aerospace as the leading U.S. export. The privatization of television in western Europe and the changing political picture in eastern Europe are creating new markets for U.S. entertainment products, as appetite for them continues to grow in Asia, Africa, and the Middle East. After Europe, Japan is our second largest customer for movies, television programs, and records (*Economist*, 1989).

While economic structures vary among the major sectors of the entertainment industry, several characteristics are common to all of them. First *high capital costs and enormous marketing expenditures* discourage entry by new competitors, resulting in a structure of ownership in which a few large companies tend to dominate production and distribution in film, recordings, and television.

Given high capital and marketing costs, *risk* is another characteristic common to all sectors of the entertainment industry. In fact, launching any new production—whether on Broadway, in Hollywood, or in a recording or television studio—is often described as "rolling the dice." Because products and services are generally not standardized—each product has unique characteristics—production costs are difficult to project and overruns are common. Consumer tastes are notoriously unpredictable and constantly changing. Therefore, profits from a few very popular productions are required to offset losses from many others.

Globalization not only characterizes the market for American entertainment products but, increasingly, is reflected in ownership. For example, of seven major film studios, four are foreign owned.

Only one of the six dominant American-based recording companies is American owned.

Takeovers, which characterized so many American companies in the 1980s, reached gigantic proportions in the entertainment industry. In what the *Economist* (1989) termed a "feeding frenzy," $80 billion was spent on takeovers of entertainment companies in 1988–89, resulting in a snowballing of debts which add to both costs and risks. This trend continues in the 1990s.

Consolidation in entertainment ownership proceeds apace, progressing from vertical integration (in which producers gain control over distribution and sale of their products) to horizontal integration across media. The Time-Warner merger illustrates the advantages of establishing links among movies, broadcast, records, and books: one product can be sold in several different media (for example, a book can be made into a movie, with a soundtrack recording, and sold to television), greatly enhancing the potential profitability of the initial investment. Conglomerate ownership increasingly extends beyond entertainment to other industries, notably electronics. The United States is developing entertainment conglomerates that compare to Germany's Bertelsmann or Fujisaki Communications, which owns Japan's most popular television and radio networks as well as its leading record and video companies, and we are seeing a similar trend toward multimedia holdings and conglomerate ownership that joins entertainment to other industrial holdings.

Live Performing Arts

In an industry of high costs and high risks, technological innovation is a saving grace—one that can be counted on to reduce the cost of manufacturing, distributing, and receiving entertainment products and to create new markets to offset losses in the old. A partial exception to this rule is the live performing arts, which benefit from new markets created by technology but cannot expect cost reductions as a result of technological change. The creative fundamentals of theater, opera, dance, and live musical performances have remained basically unchanged for centuries. Although technology has made it possible to enhance the impact of a performance through improved sound, lighting, and staging and to transmit it to wider audiences, technological innovation has done little to reduce overall production costs.

Thus, the performing arts operate in a different economic milieu from that of other forms of entertainment. Most producing companies are nonprofit and need to be subsidized, but even those that aim for profits tend to operate in the red. The classic study of the economics of the performing arts, written by William J. Baumol and William G. Bowen in 1966, found that this market is dominated by upper-income, highly educated individuals who have both leisure time and money on their hands. The relatively limited demand for this form of entertainment is dramatized by these statistics: the average American adult spends only four hours a year on cultural events, a category which encompasses performing arts along with museum attendance and other activities—little more than one-tenth of a percent of the total time spent on all forms of entertainment. Despite talk of a "cultural explosion" in the United States, the live performing arts are barely holding their own in the stiff competition for recreation dollars. Little more than a penny of every dollar spent on entertainment goes to this sector (Vogel, 1994).

Sponsoring organizations tend to live on a financial precipice. Their potential audiences are limited both by the number of people a theater can accommodate and by the select population they attract. At the same time, costs for labor, capital, and rent have been rising faster than the general rate of inflation and faster than receipts. Live performances are, by definition, labor intensive (labor costs account for 40 to 75 percent of production costs), and, given the risky nature of the business, capital costs are also high. Compounding these problems is the fact that little can be done to offset these rising costs by increasing productivity, whether by substituting technology for labor or increasing individual output. "No one has yet succeeded in decreasing the human effort expended at a live performance of a forty-five minute Schubert quartet much below a total of three man-hours" (Baumol and Bowen, 1966). The only cushion to producers of live performing arts is the possibility of eventual sale of the product they introduce to the more profitable film and television media.

Commercial Theater

The commercial theater is largely centered in New York City. As a result of economic pressures already discussed, the number of new productions on Broadway has declined over the past thirty years from nearly sixty per season to less than twenty (Goldstein, 1995). The number of touring companies is down 90 percent from early in this century. However, box-office receipts for stage shows showed an upturn throughout the 1980s, reaching $650 million in 1990 (Vogel, 1994).

Theatrical productions begin with a producer who selects the play, raises funds, and hires a director, designer, press agent, actors, and a general manager to supervise the business end of the production. Theater owners, who share in profits or losses, provide space, box office personnel, stagehands, advertising, and sometimes musicians.

Live theatrical productions are financed much like films: producers look for investors to provide needed capital. In theater these investors, known as "angels," face long odds against ever seeing a return on their investment. When there are returns, they come mainly from ancillary rights to film, cable TV, and foreign productions, not from the run of the play itself. Producers (along with theater owners) get a percentage of gross receipts until investors are paid off and then share the income from ancillary sales. Other sources of income include concessions, program advertising, and facilities rentals.

Theatergoers complain that ticket prices have soared in recent years. Attendance is about the same today as thirty years ago, but box office gross (adjusted for inflation) has increased by almost 60 percent. Overall, the profit record for Broadway and off-Broadway productions has been poor. Vogel (1986) reports that for the decade from 1972–73 to 1982–83, there were no winning seasons on Broadway, and these seasons piled up a total deficit of $66.6 billion. In 1989, according to the *New York Times*, five out of six new Broadway productions lost money. Today a typical Broadway play costs $1.5 million to mount, and musicals $4 to $7 million (Passell, 1989). Independent producers and small investors have been squeezed out (Dunn, 1988), leaving the development of Broadway productions mainly to three theater chains. The largest investor in new plays today is the Shubert organization, a charitable trust, which currently owns roughly half the theaters on Broadway.

The problem for theaters is that costs climb faster than does revenue. Rents in the all-important New York market have risen much faster than the rate of inflation. Even though many actors are paid less for Broadway performances than for similar time investments in movies and television, star talent is expensive and wages for musicians and stagehands along with the fringe benefits and minimum crew standards required by union contracts are also costly. Technological innovations tend to increase rather than reduce costs. For example, while synthesizers are used to replace musicians elsewhere, the savings on Broadway are minimal because producers are required to employ the minimum number of musicians specified by the union contract.

Electronic and computer innovations in lighting can add to the appeal of plays and enhance the performances, but they also add to costs. Some producers and performers fear that "special effects" as in "Phantom of the Opera" and "Miss Saigon" will change audience expectations and reduce the demand for simpler theatrical performances in other settings. Most important, advertising costs, now constituting about one-third of all production costs (Vogel, 1994), have skyrocketed as theater owners have recognized the need to publicize plays through television commercials. There is a perceived lack of city support in terms of designated space for rehearsals and other auxiliary services, and the "landmark status" bestowed by the city on many theaters forbids nontheatrical use of the properties to increase revenues (Schoenfeld interview).

In contrast to Broadway, off-Broadway theater, which is growing in numbers and audience, is in effect subsidized by a differential price and cost structure. Theater costs, and all other costs, are cheaper for off-Broadway productions and those savings are passed on in the form of lower ticket prices. The form of price discrimination that is contributing to success off Broadway is currently the subject of experimentation by producers and unions as a means of salvaging little-used theaters on Broadway.

Nonprofit Organizations in the Performing Arts

Regional theaters and musical companies (opera, symphony, choral, and dance) present live performances under the aegis of not-for-profit organizations that differ in important respects from the commercial theater. In the United States, there are four major opera companies, twenty-five major orchestras, and nine major dance companies, along with scores of smaller organizations (Vogel, 1994). Each has a board of directors responsible for setting organizational objectives and hiring an artistic director and business manager. As is the case in commercial theater, costs have been rising faster than ticket prices. Even though salaries for talent tend to be lower in nonprofit organizations, labor is a major cost factor and sponsoring organizations have resisted raising ticket prices for fear of diminishing audiences. Unions question whether collectively bargained labor costs are the only force at play here and suggest that administrative costs are an escalating factor as well (Wolff interview).

To close the growing gap between box office revenues and costs, endemic in nonprofit performing arts groups, these organizations have increasingly looked to public and private donors to keep them afloat. The National Endowment for the Arts has been the major factor in the growth of regional theater, dance, and music companies and the Shubert Foundation is the leading patron of innovative off-Broadway theater. However, in recent years, grants from government and foundations have declined and corporate contributions have become more important. Now changes in the tax laws as well as mergers and consolidations among corporate sponsors threaten this funding source as well. The narrowing of financial resources for performing arts makes the producers increasingly dependent on "hits" that can be sold to television, movie, cable, and recording companies.

Recording

The recording industry, created by technology, has been on a roller coaster ride reflecting continual changes not only in musical tastes but also in the product itself and in the hardware on which it is played. The years since World War II have seen phenomenal growth in record sales along with a transformation of the product from vinyl record to cassette and compact disk. Currently, the compact disk, which stores more sound and is regarded as more accurate in transmitting it, has almost completely replaced vinyl records; but cassettes, which meet the demand for music while walking, jogging, or riding in a car, are holding their own and even growing in popularity. The rising demand for recordings is related to several demographic and cultural factors: an expanding population of teenagers and young adults; a thriving middle class that is heavily consumer-oriented; national advertising aimed at popularizing music; and improvements in audio hardware and recording technologies. Over the years, domestic sales of recorded music have skyrocketed and the contagious demand for American music has fueled a similar growth in foreign sales. In fact, sales abroad are currently growing at a faster rate than domestic sales. Worldwide consumer spending on recorded music in 1990 was estimated at $24 billion a year (*Economist,* 1991).

While sales of recordings have risen over the long term, the industry has been characterized by cyclical downturns and upswings, mostly as a result of technological innovations that threaten old markets and create new ones. For example, sales dropped precipitously from 1978 to 1983 as a result of competition from home taping, made possible by the proliferation of cassettes and videotapes. The impact of these technological changes was compounded by an economic recession and a surge in oil prices, which increased the cost of producing oil-based vinyl (Berman interview). By the mid-1980s, however, the introduction of compact disks and the inauguration of music television (MTV), which helped to popularize new recordings, came to the rescue. Record sales have boomed since then.

America dominates world markets for recordings, accounting for half of all sales. As Robert Morgado, vice president of Time Warner Communications explained, music is not as bound by language as are other forms of entertainment. About 80 percent of records sold in Germany and half of those sold in Japan are recorded in English. Britain is the largest foreign market.

Six companies (five of them foreign owned) are responsible for almost all the records produced in the United States: Warner Music (United States), Sony (Japan), BMG (Germany), Polygram (Netherlands), EMI (Britain), and MCA (Japan). These companies currently account for 84 percent of all U.S. recording sales (Hofmeister, 1994). Their dominance stems from their rosters of artists and their distribution networks. On the fringe of the industry are small alternative companies that survive by introducing unknown artists and recording new or specialized forms of musical expression. Because profit margins on sales of compact disks and cassettes have been exceeding those from vinyl records, the current trend for producers is favorable.

The future of the recording industry is clouded by uncertainty about the impact of technological changes. Among the innovations already invented but not fully implemented are sound digitalization, which can eliminate undesired noise and other recordings; digital sampling, which picks up and combines sound from other recordings; music synthesizers, computers with the ability to produce and to mix sounds; music video recordings, popularized through MTV; and recordable and erasable compact disks. The most threatening in the long run is the potential of satellite storage and broadcasting known as the "celestial juke box," which could wipe out the market for record sales (Berman interview), but the most immediate threat to record companies' sales and profits is home taping, a practice that four out of five Americans engage in, according to a congressional study. However, the study found that, while home taping displaces some sales, it can also stimulate sales by helping to advertise songs and performers (U.S. Office of Technology Assessment, 1989). Nonetheless, the study's recommendation against a government ban on home taping was contested by record producers (Wharton, 1989).

A crackdown by legal authorities has largely curbed losses from domestic counterfeiting and piracy of recorded materials (most of the copying is for personal use), but despite negotiated bilateral treaties that retaliate against countries for violating U.S. copyrights, these practices continue abroad, resulting in millions of dollars of lost revenues. The potential for piracy posed by the introduction of digital audiotapes (DAT) was blocked for four years by the refusal of record companies to license their music for the new format and by threats to sue the manufacturers of DAT. In 1991 a tentative agreement called for manufacturers to pay royalties to record companies, song writers, and music publishers on the sale of digital tape recorders and blank tapes. Congress codified this agreement by passing the Audio Home Recording Act in 1992. Still to be decided is proposed protection for performer rights (Terry, 1993).

The future offers great promise of creating new markets and stimulating the public's taste for recorded music, but the potential for unlimited access threatens the current system of control and distribution and raises age-old questions about fair compensation for performers and producers.

Motion Pictures

Since its inception early in this century, the motion picture industry has experienced steady and rapid growth. In its formative period, the motion picture industry had essentially one source of revenue—box office receipts—but over the years new outlets for films have opened up. Television, which at first challenged motion pictures for a share of viewers, quickly evolved into a new market for both new and old movies. The market expanded even more in the 1970s to include cable, pay television, and home video. Then came the foreign markets. Revenues from these ancillary markets, once labeled "secondary," currently exceed those from the original market. In the 1980s, admissions to movie theaters stagnated and box office receipts accounted for a diminishing share of total revenue, with cable and home video bringing in the lion's share of profits and foreign markets rapidly growing.

Whether these new markets have made motion picture production and distribution more profitable, however, is debatable. Nick Counter, President of the Alliance of Motion Picture and Television Producers (AMPTP), asserts that "cannibalization" of markets has led to deficits as producers are forced to wait—and pay high interest costs—for years until production expenses are offset by revenue from ancillary markets (Counter interview). On the other hand, Harold L. Vogel, a Merrill Lynch entertainment industry analyst, says that ancillary markets have had little overall impact on profit margins which, when adjusted for inflation, are about the same as they were before the introduction of the newer markets (Vogel, 1994).

The cost structure of motion picture production and distribution is extraordinarily complex. Producing the average Hollywood movie costs $26.1 million (Weintraub, 1992b), ranging up to $75 million for movies with special effects, like *Batman Returns* (Weintraub, 1992a). Production costs include story rights acquisition; preproduction expenses (e.g., script development, costume and set design, casting); expenses associated with filming; and postproduction expenses (e.g., editing, scoring, and special effects). The "entrepreneur" or producer puts all of these processes together, negotiating with agents and suppliers and generally overseeing the actors, musicians, directors, producers, writers, technicians, and laborers involved in creating the final product. With each step of the production come new negotiations with intermediaries. First, the writer sells the script through a literary agent. Next comes the search for financing. Major Hollywood studios fund their own productions or take out bank loans, while independent producers have to piece together funding from a variety of sources, sometimes including the studios themselves, which serve as bankers and distributors. Other funding possibilities include common stock offerings and limited partnerships, which became popular as tax shelters during the 1970s. Once the story and funding are in place, the sponsor turns to talent agents, some of whom put together package deals involving all of the key players. After the filming comes the postproduction process which involves still another set of organizations to mix sound and color and make prints.

Movie production costs tend to rise faster than inflation because of the unique character of each product and the need to bid for scarce talent. In addition, the use of "other people's money" sometimes leads to fiscal sloppiness and inflated costs. The total annual cost of producing feature films in the United States is estimated at approximately $4 billion. Films produced for television add another $1.6 billion, and commercials approximately $2 billion, bringing total film production costs to $7.6 billion (KMPG Peat Marwick, 1988).

Production of films is labor intensive. Above-the-line costs (talent) consume 40 percent of a typical film budget, while below-the-line costs (crew) account for another 33 percent, and postproduction labor costs are 12 percent (KMPG Peat Marwick, 1988). These labor costs reflect the scale wages specified by the union contract; actual wage rates, which normally exceed the scale and are determined by market forces; fringe benefits; and work rules specifying hours and other conditions of employment. Nonunion crews generally receive the going rate of pay but not union-specified fringe benefits. In the absence of negotiated work rules, nonunion productions also have greater flexibility in the way crews are used.

As high as the costs of production (known as "negative costs") are, they constitute less than one-third of the total cost of delivering a film to the consumer. The costs of distribution, including advertising and actually exhibiting the films, account for the remaining two-thirds of the box office dollar. The distribution network involves yet another set of players, including advertising and public relations firms, the mass media, and theater owners and their employees. Generally, films are distributed first to the market that generates the highest marginal revenue over the least amount of time and "cascade" to those with the lowest marginal revenue per time unit (Vogel, 1986). Historically, this progression has begun with theatrical release, followed by licensing to pay cable, TV networks, home video duplicators, and finally local TV syndicators, but recently home video has moved up the ladder ahead of cable. With art and specialized films, the distribution process moves in the opposite direction, "platforming" from small theaters to larger ones.

Key points in distribution are *selling* (through advertising and other promotional strategies) and *timing* to hit peak audiences. Advertising and publicity may add 50 percent or more to the cost of releasing a new feature. Like production costs, distribution costs have been rising at a rate above that of inflation.

In the early years of motion pictures, production and distribution were vertically integrated through the studios that owned films, made them, and distributed them to their own theaters, which were also horizontally integrated among the studio owners through cross-licensing. This system ended in 1948 when the U.S. Supreme Court compelled major Hollywood studios to sell their theater chains. In *United States v. Paramount,* the court ruled that the studios' vertical and horizontal combinations constituted a form of price-fixing that violated the Sherman Anti-Trust Act. When the U.S. Department of Justice in 1984 reviewed the consent decrees that had served as the basis for enforcing the Paramount decision, the decrees were nullified and Hollywood studios reentered the distribution business (Cray, 1989). Meanwhile, the structure of the industry had changed drastically, with the studio system being replaced by a more complex network of ownership and alliances that prevented a return to the old way of doing business. (See Christopherson, this book.)

Aside from the legal environment other major forces influencing the growth and profitability of the motion picture industry are technology, the availability of capital, and the recent growth of independent production and service organizations.

Technology, already discussed in terms of its impact on profits and distribution, has been the most important force for change. From the development of "talkies" in the 1920s to the special effects of today (created with the help of computer-aided designs and electronic editing and composition devices), the public has been fascinated by the advancements that made possible such movies as *Batman* and *Jurassic Park.* But, while technology has revolutionized filmmaking and distribution, it has also challenged the economic power of studios by making it possible for independent producers and services to flourish.

As capital has become increasingly important to the production, distribution, and marketing of films, financing methods have become more and more sophisticated. Since each movie is uniquely designed and packaged, financial arrangements draw on a variety of sources including the major Hollywood companies (which were originally studios but evolved into financial and distribution organizations) along with a growing assortment of small, specialized independent firms. Thus, in Hollywood, "energetic little fish often can swim with great agility and success among the giant whales, assorted sharks, and piranha" (Vogel, 1994).

Nonetheless, filmmaking continues to be dominated by the large studio conglomerates that account for 80 percent of box office receipts even though they produce fewer than one-third of the films released (*Economist*, 1989). This lead role is ensured by the studios' access to capital, the key to survival in a business where most of the costs are fixed and must be invested up front, with a long wait for payoffs and a high degree of uncertainty as to whether revenues will eventually cover sunk costs. The life cycle of *Heaven Can Wait* illustrates the need for staying power on the part of the sponsoring organization. This successful film was initially distributed for showing in U.S. theaters; in its second year it was distributed abroad and through home video and U.S. cable TV; network television began to show it in the third year and it was distributed through syndication in its sixth year.

The independents, originally competitive, are teaming up with the studios that fund and distribute their creative products. Currently the three major Hollywood studios are Paramount, Warner, and Disney, all of which have strong distribution systems and financial backing. In 1988, Paramount accounted for 22 percent and Disney and Warner 18 percent each of total box office shares (Stevenson, 1989a). However, the business of moviemaking is subject to constant change; therefore, no leadership position is ever secure. Innovations in technology—which place the distribution function in the hands of wholesalers of pay television programming, sharply reduce per-person viewing prices, and give pirates easy access to the software they produce—offer continuing challenges to the majors that have dominated this field.

According to industry sources, a small majority of films, only four out of seven, are ever profitable, even taking into account ancillary and foreign sales; so studios depend on a few big hits to wipe out losses from the failures. Even though the average film loses money,[2] the major companies are profitable. Since the heart of their business is distribution and financing, the brunt of the risks involved in marketing and production can be deflected to (and sometimes written off by) investors and producers. Smaller companies, which depend on production for their income, in contrast, have been hard hit by fluctuations in the stock market and the high risk involved in this type of enterprise.

Output of motion pictures has been subject to a long-term business cycle with fluctuations over a twenty-five-year period. However, within the cycle, this industry sector has been relatively recession resistant (Vogel, 1994) and in recent years growth of ancillary markets has dramatically increased the demand. Therefore, while costs rise at an above-average rate and competition has been increasing, major producers continue to be profitable.

Broadcasting

The broadcasting business began with radio, which was introduced and gained popularity in the 1920s. Television was introduced on an experimental basis in the 1930s and ownership of TV receivers became widespread in the 1950s. Today radio and television account for the largest share of entertainment industry revenues with television sets in nearly all American homes. The average American adult spends 1,160 hours a year listening to radio broadcasts and 1,550 hours watching television (Vogel, 1994), a time investment of more than seven hours a day.

In 1994 more than 11,500 AM and FM radio stations (up from less than 1,000 in 1946) and more than 1,500 television stations (up from six in 1946) were broadcasting in the United States. Over a thirty-

---

[2] Hollywood accounting practices with respect to profit and loss reports on individual films have been challenged in the *Buchwald v. Paramount* case (see O'Donnell and McDougal, 1992).

one-year period, advertising dollars spent for radio broadcasting rose by 62 percent annually; for television the annual growth rate was 126.4 percent. Given this explosive record, broadcasting has been projected to end the century as a $50 billion-a-year business (Vogel, 1994).

Radio and television are unique in the entertainment industry in that their revenue comes not from consumers but from advertisers. The success of a television or radio station in attracting an audience is measured in "rating points," reflecting the percentage of households able to receive its signal that are actually tuned to the signal. A station's "share" reflects what percentage of all households actually using their sets are tuned in to a specific program. These ratings, known as Nielsen ratings, named for the service that conducts the surveys and publishes the reports, are used to determine advertising rates for radio and television time. In broadcasting, ratings make the difference between profit and loss and growth or decline in the volume of business. Ratings leaders garner higher prices for advertising and have more secure relationships with their affiliates, the local stations that carry the networks. A single prime time ratings point won or lost, on a year's average, is estimated to be worth at least $80 million in revenues (Vogel, 1994). As the competition for shares of prime time audiences has intensified, the accuracy of the measurement systems, based on electronic monitoring of a sampling of households, have come under fire.

For example, in 1990 a Nielsen-reported decline in viewers threatened to cost the three networks $360 million in lost advertising revenues because commercial time is sold with a guaranteed cost per thousand viewers and, when the audience falls below the guarantee, the advertiser receives free "make good" time on other shows. Broadcasters demanded a change in the way the rating service collects data and/or an alteration in the guarantee system (Carter, 1990). But the demise of the only potential rival ensured that this unloved system will continue to determine the annual allocation of $30 billion in advertising (Carter, 1992b).

Technology has resulted in a proliferation of alternative media outlets that have increased competition for the advertising dollar. Cable television, whose prime time audience share rose from 6 percent to 20 percent between 1982 and 1989, and independent stations (up from 12 to 18) are eating away at the dominant market position of the three major networks, whose share of ad dollars dropped from 80 percent to 69 percent in 1990 (Kleinfeld, 1990). Nonetheless, the pie has continued to grow though the rate of growth is slowing (Vogel, 1994), and the vast majority of advertising dollars still go to the networks' coffers.

Further fragmentation of the home viewing audience has come from videocassettes, which now can be found in nearly all homes with television sets. On the drawing boards is delivery of television direct to home by satellite, following the example introduced by Rupert Murdoch in England (Andrews, 1992). In addition, fiber optics, another technological innovation, has encouraged telephone companies (recently unleashed by FCC ruling) to enter the home entertainment field by bringing a number of channels into the home through telephone lines.

The production and distribution of television, as for movies, increasingly reach beyond U.S. borders. The television exports are not just entertainment programs—exports of news and sports programming have also been growing. Deregulation of the European market (where TV was formerly for the most part publicly owned) multiplied the number of television stations and created a booming demand for programs to fill the available airtime. European stations paid more than $1 billion for American program rights in 1989, triple the level of five years earlier (Greenhouse, 1989). While the United States is also importing more programs as a result of cable expansion, these consist mainly of English-language productions and represent only a small fraction of the international exchange (Carter, 1989b). The importance of foreign markets in the television industry has led to international coproductions and encouraged globalization of investment.

Unlike other sectors of the entertainment industry, broadcasting is regulated by the government, specifically the Federal Communications Commission (FCC), which was created to allocate scarce space in the broadcast frequency spectrum. The FCC regulates the number of stations a single company is allowed to own, limits cross-media and foreign ownership of stations, and on children's shows, limits the number of commercials that may be aired. The 1980s brought deregulation, removing many of the rules governing radio and loosening those directed at television, placing reliance on market forces to keep broadcasters in line. Recently regulation has reemerged, but only in relation to children's programming.

Of crucial importance to the television networks have been the financial interest and syndication rules, enacted by the FCC in 1970 and known as "fin-syn," which barred the networks from the syndication business and prevented them from taking an equity position in programs they put on the air. As the business began to change in the 1980s with competition from cable, the networks protested more and more vigorously. When the FCC decided to reconsider the rules, motion picture producers entered the fray to protect their exclusive control of the lucrative syndication business. While the issue was being debated, cable and "independent" television businesses were permitted to produce their own programs and sell them to other stations here and abroad, and the networks were gearing up for more in-house production (Fabrikant, 1989). In 1991, a bitterly divided FCC voted a compromise, allowing networks to acquire full resale rights to 40 percent of their prime time schedules and royalties for the rest of their shows, as well as rights to sell reruns in foreign markets, but continued to prevent them from distributing shows produced exclusively for syndication, including popular game and talk shows (Stevenson, 1991). After that order was struck down by the U.S. Court of Appeals, the FCC reversed itself and granted the television networks the right to own all of the prime time shows they carry (Andrews, 1993).

On another front, television broadcasters successfully pressed for congressional action to force cable companies to pay for programs they pick up by satellite and transmit as part of their service to subscribers (Goldman, 1992). So, while broadcasters may decry government regulation, they also use it as a weapon in the competitive struggle for profits.

The major costs incurred by radio and television are for programming and operating. In television, programming expenses have risen faster than operating expenses, which tend to be more predictable.

In recent years, the costs of news and sports broadcasting have come under intense scrutiny. Although television news programs cost substantially less than most entertainment programming, the expenses of maintaining worldwide news-gathering networks greatly outstrip revenues. Originally viewed as a public service, news programs were considered obligatory even when they lost money; but deregulation, which eliminated the public service obligation, and rising costs, fueled by fierce bidding for star anchors and the need for worldwide travel, led to drastic budget cuts in network news departments and opened discussion of the possibility of eliminating coverage and leaving it to the cable networks that can provide it more cheaply. Despite these problems, however, Roper polls have found that news programs are one of the two types of shows (along with full-length movies) that most viewers "really like to watch on regular TV" (Kubasik, 1987). So the networks continue news programming but seek ways to cut costs. NBC, for example, bought into Visnews, Ltd., an internationally owned news-gathering service, to share production expenses (Gerard, 1988).

Intense competition for sports broadcasting among the networks, independents, and cable networks has driven up the price of sports contracts. When CBS acquired the rights to broadcast major league baseball in 1988, it paid as much money for a four-year contract as NBC and ABC combined had paid for the previous six years. While the major networks claim to be losing millions of dollars on professional football, they continue to bid for sports as part of an overall strategy to capture the top position in Nielsen ratings. In this struggle, sports broadcasting becomes the loss leader to attract viewer attention.

In addition to their programming and operating costs, networks have paid out considerable sums to compensate affiliates that carry their programs. (This compensation constitutes about five percent of affiliates' revenues.)

Although there are thousands of radio and television stations in the United States, the business of broadcasting has been dominated by the Big Three networks—National Broadcasting (NBC), CBS, and American Broadcasting Companies, Inc. (ABC), which feed programs to local affiliated stations and compete with one another for listener and viewer ratings. In recent years, the competition has intensified, first by the entry of Fox, and more recently by other virtual networks and cable.

The trend toward cross-ownership, seen in other sectors of the entertainment industry, also characterizes television, where networks acquire cable properties. Recent takeovers have come from conglomerates with holdings in other lines of business and telephone companies are beginning to enter the bidding war. (See Les Brown, this book, for detailed discussion of these trends.)

Foreign firms have been buying U.S. media facilities at a faster rate than U.S. counterparts invest abroad, a phenomenon attributed to the decline of the dollar against foreign currencies.

Changing patterns of ownership have brought about increased concentration in all of the mass media, including newspapers and magazines as well as the electronic media (radio, recording, television, and motion pictures). While there are currently twenty-five thousand media companies in the United States alone, worldwide twenty-nine leading corporations are alleged to do most of the business. It is predicted that this number will shrink to six by the year 2000 (Bagdikian, 1983).

Despite the concentrated structure of ownership in broadcasting, technological change stimulates competition between cable and independent companies and the networks, leaving some room for smaller companies to work around the edges (Vogel, 1986).

Because operating costs (at least in the short run) are relatively stable, profitability in broadcasting is largely a function of the revenue stream from advertising. Historically, trends in broadcast company profits have tended to follow general trends in the economy, rising in prosperity and declining with recession (Vogel, 1986).

Pretax profit margins for broadcasting have historically been well above the average for other industries. However, recent challenges for home audience share by cable and videocassettes, along with debt accumulated in buying and selling broadcast holdings, raise questions about future profitability. In general, the networks have been faring less well than their affiliates and the studios from which they purchase films, both of which make about a 30 percent return on their sales. The comparable rate of return for networks is only 3 percent. Network strategies for coping with the profit squeeze, in addition to cost cutting and advertising lures, focus primarily on producing their own programs and taking advantage of the opportunities afforded by foreign sales.

Unions and Bargaining Structure

The arts and entertainment industry broadly defined employed almost one million people in 1992, including 380,700 in motion picture production and distribution; 244,900 in radio and television broadcasting; and 134,000 in cable television (U.S. Department of Labor, 1992). Average weekly earnings for this industry are relatively low: $326.70 for motion picture and $472.93 for radio and television broadcast employees (U.S. Department of Labor, 1992). These averages mask a wide range of salaries from "stars," who are extremely highly paid, to intermittently employed performers and technicians with minimal annual earnings. The average employee in the industry is attached to his or her craft more in spirit than in measurable employment. For the many who seek work in the industry and are unable to find it, earnings and hours attributable to AEEM approach zero.

The industry is highly unionized. Unfortunately, there are no accurate figures for the extent of unionization by sector. Knowledgeable observers say that almost all performers are union members and work under union contracts. For technicians and production workers, it is universally accepted that the union sector has declined. One observer has estimated that 85 percent of Hollywood productions were unionized in 1983 and that the figure had declined to 60 percent by the end of the decade (Cooper, 1988). The broadcast, recording, and live entertainment sectors are highly organized but the cable sector is not.

According to union and industrial officials interviewed for this study, talent unions (with the exception of those for musicians) have registered explosive growth in recent years, while membership in craft unions has remained stable. Raw union membership figures support the above generalizations.

Table 1.1 provides a list of the major labor organizations representing employees in the AEEM industry, with areas of jurisdiction and most recent membership figures. Each of the four AEEM sectors involves two types of unions: above-the-line unions representing creative employees (actors, musicians, writers, etc.) and below-the-line unions representing craft and technical workers.

Membership in above- and below-the-line unions in entertain-

Table 1.1. Membership in Major Labor Organizations in the Arts, Entertainment, and Electronic Media Industry.

Union	Year Formed	Jurisdiction	Membership 1988	Membership Change 1979–88	Membership 1994	Membership Change 1988–94
1. Performers Unions						
		Above the Line				
Actors Equity Association (AEA)	1913	Actors, singers, dancers, and stage managers in theatrical live performances	40,000	+82%	36,000	−10%
American Federation of Musicians (AFM)	1896	Musicians in all forms of entertainment, except concerts	207,000	−38%	150,000	−27%
American Federation of Television and Radio Artists (AFTRA)	1937	Actors and announcers in live and taped performances for radio and television; performers in recordings; and technicians in local television	63,000	+63%	75,000	+19%
American Guild of Musical Artists (AGMA)	1936	Singers and dancers in opera and dance; and all solo artists	5,700	+14%	5,287	−7%
American Guild of Variety Artists (AGVA)	1936	Performers in night clubs, circuses and variety shows	5,000	+6%	N.A.	N.A.

(continued)

Table 1.1. (Continued)

Union	Year Formed	Jurisdiction	Membership 1988	Membership Change 1979–88	Membership 1994	Membership Change 1988–94
Screen Actors Guild (SAG)	1922	Actors, singers, and dancers in motion pictures and filmed television productions	70,000	+80%	78,000	+11%
Screen Extras Guild (SEG)	1946	Nonspeaking performers in motion pictures and television (recently merged with SAG)	5,000	+28%	5,000[b]	N.A.
2. Nonperforming Unions						
Directors Guild (DGA)	1936	Directors in motion pictures, radio, and television	8,600	+72%	10,098	+14%
Writers Guild (WGA) (divided into Writers Guild East and West in 1979)	1954	Writers for motion pictures, radio, and television	9,900	+38%	11,154	+13%
Society of Stage Directors and Choreographers	N.A.	Live performances	N.A.	N.A.	N.A.	N.A.
Below the Line						
1. Craft Unions Exclusively in AEEM						
International Alliance of Theatrical and Stage Employees (IATSE)	1893	Skilled production and technical workers in stage, motion pictures and television production; operators in movie theaters	60,000	–3%	50,000	–17%

		Jurisdiction in AEEM	AEEM Membership 1988	AEEM Membership Change 1979–88	AEEM Membership 1994	AEEM Membership Change 1988–94
National Association of Broadcast Engineers and Technicians (NABET)	1933	Technicians in radio and television	12,000	+64%	18,500	+54%
2. Other Unions						
International Brotherhood of Teamsters (IBT)		Drivers and production workers in motion pictures and television productions	12,000[a]	N.A.	N.A.	N.A.
International Brotherhood of Electrical Workers (IBEW)		Electricians in motion pictures and technicians in radio and television	14,000[a]	N.A.	N.A.	N.A.
Other Basic Crafts (AFL-CIO Building Trades Union)		Construction crafts in motion picture production	Unknown	Unknown	N.A.	N.A.

Source: All figures are from Gifford, 1994, except where noted.
[a]These estimates are from phone interviews with union officials.
[b]Prior to merger with SAG in 1992.
N.A. = Not available.

ment is, with few exceptions, based on narrowly defined occupations. It is worth noting that many of the AEEM craft unions owe their existence to a new technology or art form that was neglected by an existing union. For example, in the early days of motion pictures, Actors Equity (AEA) considered film acting to be outside its primary craft jurisdiction; and, after a preliminary try at organizing, allowed the formation of the Screen Actors Guild (SAG) rather than seeking to represent actors on film (O'Neal interview). Likewise, the American Federation of Television and Radio Artists (AFTRA) was born out of the desire of SAG members to separate themselves from the new communication form of radio, which formed the basis for later organizing in television. While these early distinctions have grown less and less important over time, particularly between SAG and AFTRA, they still describe significant distinctions between the unions. SAG and AFTRA have entered into merger discussions more than once, and currently they jointly negotiate contracts for television commercials. Also, many performers hold multiple memberships in AEA, SAG, and AFTRA and work under their contracts. Thus, while there are multiple performing unions, those distinctions have blurred in practice within the performing community.

Such a trend is not the case with the below-the-line unions. They are also craft-dominated, with the exceptions of the Teamsters (IBT) and the National Association of Broadcast Engineers and Technicians (NABET), but multiple membership is not an important force and the distinctions between unions, and even locals, are critically important. NABET is the most significant of the industrial-type unions, representing employees in many kinds of craft or technical occupations within the television industry. In recent years, NABET had begun to make forays into the film industry, where it was applying the same basic principles of industrial-based union organization. In October, 1990, the NABET film local (15) affiliated with the International Association of Theatrical and Stage Employees (IATSE), which represents the majority of skilled employees in motion pictures and all skilled craftspeople in live production, thus ending a small movement toward industrial unionism in film production, at least for the time being.

Perhaps in part as a result of multiple union memberships in above-the-line organizations, potential combinations and mergers of unions in the industry have been hinted at for some time. Longtime discussions between SAG and AFTRA have yet to result in a merger but have led to significant cooperation between the two organizations. A major impediment to merger is the difference in structure between these organizations. The SAG is a national union with no local affiliates, while AFTRA is decentralized with locals holding major decision-making power. Also, because AFTRA's membership is increasingly influenced by television, sports, and news personalities, and behind-the-camera employees rather than actors who hold dual SAG/AFTRA memberships, it may be that interest in a merger will decline rather than increase. Meanwhile, the Screen Extras Guild has merged with the Screen Actors Guild, ending a long debate about the desirability of this union.

Below-the-line unions have also entertained notions of merger in recent years. Cooperative arrangements among IATSE, IBEW, and NABET, the dominant below-the-line craft unions, have fueled speculation about mergers. Informal discussions and proposals for merger have been floated without yielding tangible results. In 1993 NABET worked out an affiliation agreement with the Communications Workers of America (CWA).

Table 1.2 graphically defines the bargaining structure in the industry by sector and gives more of a sense of the representational scope of each of the unions. Above-the-line unions in the live performing arts sector include Actors Equity (AEA), the American Federation of Musicians (AFM), the American Guild of Musical Artists (AGMA), and the American Guild of Variety Artists (AGVA). Announcers in live performances may belong to the American Federation of Television and Radio Artists (AFTRA). Below-the-line workers are represented by the International Alliance of Theatrical and Stage Employees (IATSE).

Bargaining in the live entertainment portion of AEEM is the most decentralized. While employer associations exist in some major metropolitan areas and regions with significant theater and ballet activity (particularly New York City, where the League of New York Theaters negotiates contracts with all the unions), live entertainment bargaining is largely characterized as single-employer, single-union.

Table 1.2. Bargaining Structure in the Arts, Entertainment, and Electronic Media Industry.

Employer Group(s)	Scope of Agreements	Unions
Live Entertainment		
Theater		
League of New York Theaters (LNYT) League of Regional Theaters (LRT) and other associations Individual Theaters	Local or regional, often multi-employer	AEA, IATSE, AFM
Opera		
Individual Companies	Local, single-employer	AGMA, AFM, IATSE
Symphony		
Individual Orchestras	Local, single-employer	AFM, IATSE
Ballet		
Individual Companies	Local, single-employer	AGMA, AFM, IATSE
Solo Concerts	Local, single employer	AGMA
Night Clubs/Variety/ Arena Concerts	Local, single employer	AGVA, AFM, IATSE
Motion Pictures		
Production		
Alliance of Motion Pictures and Television Producers (represents studios, independents, suppliers, payroll, and post-production houses) (AMPTP)	National, multi-employer	SAG, SEG, AFM DGA, WGA, IATSE, IBEW, AFL-CIO, Basic Crafts, IBT
Independents[a]		Same
Distribution		
Theatrical Exhibitors	Single employer, multi-site	IATSE
Recorded Music		
Recording Industry of America (RIA)	National, multi-employer	AFM, IBEW, AFTRA
Television and Radio		
AMPTP	National, multi-employer	SAG, SEG, AFM, DGA, WGA, IATSE, IBEW, AFL-CIO, Basic Crafts, IBT
Networks		
ABC	National, single employer	NABET, AFTRA, IATSE, WGA, DGA
CBS	National, single employer	IBEW, IATSE, WGA, DGA, AFTRA

(*continued*)

Table 1.2. (continued)

Employer Group(s)	Scope of Agreements	Unions
NBC	National, single-employer	NABET, AFTRA, DGA, IATSE
Local Radio/Television	Local, single-employer	AFM, AFTRA, NABET, IBEW
Commercial Television	National	AFTRA, SAG

Note: Full union names are given in Table 1.1.
ᵃAll production companies not affiliated with AMPTP.

This should not be interpreted in the same way one might look at a single-factory, single-union structure, however. Spheres of influence on bargaining emanate from the most important contracts in New York. Thus, conditions in Chicago or Atlanta are at least loosely connected to bargaining outcomes in New York. In symphony orchestras and ballet, moreover, the AFM seeks more formally to coordinate activities nationally, as does IATSE with its locals; therefore, while salaries and working conditions around the country are not uniform, patterns are replicated to some extent.

Unions in the recording sector include the AFM, AFTRA, and the International Brotherhood of Electrical Workers (IBEW). An employer association, the Recording Industry of America (RIA), negotiates primarily with the AFM for recorded music contracts. Live music contracts in cities with significant activity in this area (Las Vegas, for example) are negotiated locally with local employers' associations and the AFM.

In filmmaking, above-the-line workers are represented by the Screen Actors Guild (SAG), Writers Guild (WGA), Directors Guild (DGA), Producers Guild (PGA), and AFM. Below-the-line workers are represented primarily by IATSE. Other below-the-line unions include the IBEW; the IBT, representing drivers; and Basic Crafts, which consist of the AFL-CIO Building Trades Unions representing construction workers.

One set of collective bargaining contracts dominates the entire motion picture industry. The Alliance of Motion Picture and Television Producers (AMPTP) negotiates contracts with actors, directors, writers, and musicians above the line as well as the major below-the-line unions in Hollywood and New York. With film now dominated by seven or eight major studios, collective bargaining in motion pictures is the most centralized in the AEEM industry. However, it should be noted that the employers, while representing divergent interests, bargain jointly through AMPTP while the unions currently negotiate separately with this association.

In the broadcast sector, each of the major networks negotiates individual contracts with unions representing their employees on a national basis. These contracts are supplemented by local agreements for individual local stations and cable networks. Actors are represented by AFTRA and SAG. Other above-the-line broadcasting unions involved in the television sector are the DGA, WGA, PGA, and AFM. Below-the-line radio and television unions include NABET, IATSE, and IBEW. Negotiations in this segment have been particularly difficult as a result of rapid technological change and the explosive growth of competing cable television.

The Impact of Technology on Employment and Labor Relations

Business and labor leaders agree that technology has been the single most important influence on employment and labor relations in the AEEM industry. Changes in technology have an impact on the number and types of jobs available as well as on the compensation and working conditions of employees. Also affected are union jurisdictions and the relative bargaining strength of unions and employers.

Employment

Explosive technology has been responsible for long-term growth in all sectors of the industry except the live performing arts. Although millions of jobs have been created, employment growth has been selective, generally creating jobs for performers and other above-the-line personnel while eliminating jobs for technicians and skilled craft workers. In a special category among performers are musicians, whose employment opportunities have dwindled over the past century, first as a result of sound movies that eliminated jobs in movie theaters and then by recordings that were used to replace live musicians in night clubs, radio, and other media. Today the synthesizers that simulate all musical sounds threaten to eliminate musicians from most forms of paid employment (Seltzer, 1989).

Early in the history of moviemaking, many performers lost work in the switch from silent to sound movies. While performers in recent years have largely been exempt from technological replacement, a synthetic nonhuman voice is in development (one called Dectalk has already been introduced). Digital voice sampling is being used as a substitute for live choruses in recorded commercials and could spread to other forms of entertainment, and computer graphics, which are already substituting for performers in special effects, have the potential of displacing middle-level performers.

Many below-the-line occupations have become obsolete through the introduction of new equipment. For example, handheld cameras created a revolution in television employment by sharply reducing the number of workers needed on a camera crew from three to one. Some news operations are suggesting that reporters carry their own cameras, which would completely eliminate the need for camera operators. The proliferation of lighter and more mobile equipment has caused full-time traveling crews in television and movie productions to be replaced by part-time local contractors.

Because the pace of innovation in broadcasting is so rapid, equipment is replaced rather than repaired when it breaks down, thereby reducing the need for repair technicians. Movie theater projectionists have been hard-hit by shrinking employment opportunities since the invention of equipment that makes it possible for a single operator to deliver several movies simultaneously in different locations. Projectionists who previously worked in race tracks and airplanes have also lost jobs through the introduction of videotape.

In radio broadcasting both FM and AM radio stations have been proliferating. The number of translators (short-range boosters) has multiplied tenfold in the last decade, and new FCC regulations and technological innovations, such as the vastly improved walk-around personal stereos, could lead to a thousand new FM and five hundred new AM stations in the mid-1990s. Nevertheless, employment opportunities at local broadcasting stations are threatened by innovative technologies such as satellite transmission, which makes it possible for stations to broadcast network programming instead of employing local announcers and disc jockeys. The Satellite Music Network already makes such programming available to stations around the country.

Job Content and Working Conditions

Technicians in the AEEM sector complain that technological innovation has "deskilled" their jobs. As traditional functions are increasingly performed by computers that make it possible for employers to hire more part-time and temporary workers, technicians no longer consider themselves indispensable and see their jobs becoming less and less secure.

Technology is also being used to shift work previously covered by collective bargaining agreements into the domain of management. For example, after the introduction of computers at NBC, NABET insisted on maintaining control over the new jobs that were created, since they involved the use of technical equipment and replaced work formerly done by NABET members. NBC management maintained that computer operators perform managerial functions that cannot be separated from technical work and therefore should not be included in the bargaining unit. According to a NABET representative, "the promise of no layoffs plus high salaries for the existing workers suggests that the introduction of computers is not in the traditional mode of cost-saving, but rather an attempt to take away the workers' control which workers exercise over the workplace through their jurisdiction over the technological equipment" (Moffett interview).

For above-the-line unions, technological changes—notably the introduction of new media—have also led to the renegotiation of rules governing working conditions. Moreover, technology has created new occupational safety and health hazards, particularly for employees involved in special effects. With each technological innovation, these issues of employment and work rules resurface.

Compensation

Because technology affects productivity, it influences rates of payment in all categories of work. Of special concern to above-the-line personnel—writers, producers, directors, and performers—is the dilemma posed by the proliferation of media outlets created by new technology. For example, old movies are being rereleased as videos and shown on cable television, sometimes after "colorization." Old music performances are being cleaned up electronically and reissued as compact disks, a process that can be five to twenty times cheaper than recording new performances. Ironically, some performers today are finding their current performances in direct competition with their own previous work.

The distribution of profits realized from reissuing old works has created immense problems in the past and has sharpened concern by unions over how residuals (payments to artists for works reissued) will be handled in the future. In 1960, for example, SAG and WGA struck over the issue of artists' residuals for films shown on television. A 1973 writers' strike was precipitated by the introduction of pay TV and the anticipated proliferation of videocassettes. SAG in 1980 and WGA in 1981 struck again over pay TV residuals. When innovations in film editing technology made it possible to introduce fifteen-second-commercials with smooth transitions (the previous minimum was thirty seconds), SAG narrowly averted another strike by negotiating a new formula for performer residuals in 1985. In 1988 the WGA struck again, this time over syndication residuals related to the network programming and its eventual foreign sales.

When video disks were introduced, the major issues in union-management negotiations were the amount of the initial payments, the time before extra compensation would be due, and the rate and calculation of the extra pay. Six different unions were involved in the discussions, and there were three strikes before they ended.

Union Power and Jurisdiction

Because employees in the AEEM industry have traditionally been organized along carefully drawn craft lines, changes in production have a profound effect on union jurisdiction. In recent times, technological changes have led to turf wars among existing unions which jealously guard traditional jurisdictions.

The switch from live television to taped or filmed programming, for example, stimulated intense interunion competition both above the line (between SAG and AFTRA) and below the line (among IATSE, IBEW, and NABET). The introduction of the minicam resulted in a transfer of work from IATSE, which represents film crews, to NABET and IBEW, which represent engineers (see Goldstein, 1978 for a detailed description of the ensuing litigation). Video editing and computer graphics are also affecting union jurisdictions in film production. As graphic artists are replaced by technician/artists, who will represent them—WGA, NABET, or IBEW? Of great concern to film unions has been the long-awaited introduction of high-resolution video, which threatens to end celluloid production and could cause "the greatest transfer of bargaining unit work ever seen in the history of the industry" (Tajgman interview).

Technological change can also influence, positively or negatively, the bargaining strength of unions and employers. For example, the automation of broadcasting may make strikes obsolete for certain below-the-line units (Moffett interview), as illustrated by the disastrous NBC strike in 1986, in which striking technicians were quickly and easily replaced by supervisors and vendor representatives. On the other hand, competition among media created by new technology may strengthen the strike threat for above-the-line unions, as illustrated by the 1988 writers' strike, during which many viewers and advertisers switched from network to cable television.

Labor-Management Conflict

Technology has been the source of conflict both between unions and between unions and employers. An official of SAG contends that all of the major strikes of the talent unions have been "technology driven." While the introduction of new media, from movies to television to cable, VCRs, and satellites, has expanded the demand for talent, each of these innovations has also created conflict over compensation and working conditions (Chassman interview).

As previously noted, strikes by above-the-line unions have focused primarily on the issue of compensation, or residual payments, but below-the-line unions have also had their share of conflict generated by changes in technology. IBEW workers at CBS struck in 1971 over the introduction of the handheld camera, and the NABET strike of

1986 revolved around the issue of crew size for filming of television broadcasts.

On the other hand, common interest in resolving problems created by technological change gave rise to labor-management cooperation efforts between IBEW and CBS, and more recently stimulated periodic joint consultations among AMPTP and IATSE, the Writers Guild, SAG, and AFTRA.

Union Responses to Technological Change

Given the diversity of unions and employers in the AEEM industry, it is not surprising to find a broad spectrum of reactions—ranging from confrontation to cooperation—when new technology is introduced.

The AFM, the first union to experience the threat of wholesale job displacement, fought back against the use of recorded music by urging its members to boycott the innovation. When a labor boycott failed, the union appealed to the public to join a consumer boycott. Most recently, the AFM has used labor boycotts and public appeals in its campaign against the use of taped music in Atlantic City and Las Vegas night clubs and the use of synthesizers on Broadway.

Perhaps because of the limited effectiveness of strikes and boycotts, the AFM has initiated other strategies to curtail the loss of jobs. Particularly innovative was its attempt to secure compensation for the loss of musicians' jobs through the creation of a Performance Trust Fund. The fund, supported by employer contributions, is used to provide free concerts that create new jobs for unemployed musicians. (See Seltzer, 1989 for a detailed description of AFM strategies in the 1930s and 1940s.)

The AFM has also negotiated increased rates of pay for performers who utilize new forms of technology. To discourage the use of synthesizers that replace groups of musicians with a single player, for example, the AFM has negotiated a much higher rate of pay for the musicians who operate the synthesizers. This tactic, like the Performance Trust Fund, is a form of sharing in the increased revenue created by introduction of new technology while at the same time raising the price of innovation to discourage its use.

In recent years, IATSE has attempted to create jobs by persuading manufacturers to train its members in the use of newly designed lighting systems. In response to cutbacks in employment of theater projectionists, IATSE has also pursued the idea of job enlargement, that is, adding other duties to the projectionists' jobs to protect incumbents faced with job loss.

The tools most widely used by unions to save the jobs of technicians and skilled workers in the AEEM industry are work rules and minimum crew size. For example, AFM and IATSE contracts with the League of New York Theatres specify the number of persons to be employed in each function. Similar specifications of minimum crew size are written into contracts with filmmakers and broadcasters. Union officials contend that minimum crew size provisions also benefit employers by providing a flexible pool of labor to meet changing job requirements. Work rules that prohibit employees from performing work other than that specified in the contract are another form of protection from displacement when new labor-saving technology is introduced. Unions have also negotiated employment guarantees and employee buyouts (i.e., early retirement) for members facing job loss, as was the case when NABET and IBEW confronted the introduction of the minicam.

While below-the-line unions have concentrated on protecting jobs, above-the-line unions have focused on sharing in the gains, a difference in collective bargaining goals which reflects the differential employment impacts of technology on performers and technicians; as indicated, job openings for performers have increased as a result of the proliferation of media outlets for entertainment while employment of technicians has declined. Residuals, introduced in the late 1950s in contracts negotiated by AFTRA and SAG and later adopted by other unions, compensate performers for past work that is reissued in another medium or outlet. This is a form of gain sharing that enables the employer to delay payment until costs have been recovered, thereby reducing risks. Direct profit sharing, a practice that is spreading in other industries, is rare in entertainment, however. The only current example is the Metropolitan Opera Company, whose contract provides its performers with a share of the proceeds from the sale of opera reproduction rights to the electronic media.

All of the strategies discussed thus far have evolved from the collective bargaining process. Unions have also turned to the political arena to achieve their objectives. For example, the talent unions have lobbied extensively for changes in copyright laws to protect "intellectual property" from invasion by new forms of technology. They have also been active in campaigns for increased funding for the National Endowment for the Arts.

Technological threats and other challenges to union bargaining power have encouraged interunion cooperation, including joint bargaining committees and merger talks between SAG and AFTRA. Below-the-line unions, traditionally competitive, are beginning to exchange information and cooperate in both organizing and bargaining. AEEM unions in the United States also look to their counterparts abroad for cooperation in resisting threats to their bargaining power. A decisive factor in settling SAG's thirty-day strike in 1988, for example, was an understanding with unions in Canada, Britain, and Australia that prevented producers from substituting commercials produced overseas for domestic ads (Greenspan interview).

Labor-management cooperation, a strategy that has found increasing acceptance in other industries coping with change (see Kochan, Katz, and McKersie, 1986, for examples and analysis), is also being tried in the broadcast and film sectors. Since 1971, for instance, CBS and the IBEW have been meeting on a quarterly basis to discuss trends and long-range solutions. SAG and AFTRA have developed a similar relationship with the council representing the advertising industry, and for the first time, the AMPTP has entered into periodic consultations with IATSE, Writers Guild, SAG, and AFTRA. Going beyond consultation, employees in some symphony orchestras participate on the board of directors.

Whether labor-management cooperation continues to spread depends, of course, on results. While the examples cited above are suggestive, it is too early to tell whether such cooperation will become the rule in the industry.

This survey of the major forces affecting labor relations in the AEEM industry will serve as background for the chapters to follow. Contributions by Brown, Christopherson, Amman, and Paul and Kleingartner each focus on a specific issue or area of the industry and present primary research findings to illustrate central points about that segment.

CHAPTER TWO

Technology Transforms

Les Brown

Convenient, efficient, time-saving, liberating, affording more choice—these are some of the passwords for new technologies. On these they gain their entree to modern living, a mode that is by definition readily disposed to new devices and services, whatever their implications for social or cultural change.

Products of new technologies are so easily assimilated in our time, and proliferate so swiftly, that many that seemed fancifully futuristic a decade ago are commonplace today. Indeed, the difference between living in the 1970s and living in the 1990s may well be told technologically. In the 1970s American consumers could scarcely imagine on-the-street banking, personal computers, cellular phones, compact disks, the Sony Walkman, the fax machine, electronic mail, voice mail, videocassette recorders, video games, backyard satellite dishes, pay-per-view television, and TV sets capable of receiving upwards of thirty channels of programming. Yet all these helped shape the culture of the 1980s, and at the rate of things they will be old hat by the end of the 1990s.

The other passwords for new technologies have to do, in a paradoxical way, with employment: *creating jobs* and *eliminating jobs*. Governments welcome new technologies for the former and industries welcome them for the latter. The 1980s served both imperatives, and doubtless the 1990s will as well because the technological revolution, at least as concerns communications, has only just begun.

This revolution results from a confluence of technologies that previously had seemed discrete and headed in separate directions—television, computers, satellites, telephone, cable, and lasers. In the 1980s the convergence produced a variety of new video delivery systems to compete with conventional terrestrial television; and since the possibilities from the merging technologies are far from exhausted, more products and refinements can be expected in the next decade and beyond. As an industry, television may not experience the equilibrium it enjoyed for the first forty years until well into the twenty-first century.

But while technology is credited with creating the turbulence in television, the revolution is actually being powered by business and public policy. The 1980s demonstrated that technological developments that do not turn into successful businesses or that fail to serve the needs of business might as well not exist. Such technological marvels of the 1980s as teletext, videotex, two-way interactive cable, over-the-air subscription television, RCA's mechanical video disk, and ABC's home-taping pay TV service known as TeleFirst—having lost huge amounts of money for their promoters—are now in purgatory along with 3-D movies and Picturephone.

Significantly, the surge in new electronic products coincided with the start of the Reagan presidency. With so many new video systems on hand, the new administration, intent as it was on liberating business from government interference and trusting regulation to market forces, had no difficulty discarding longstanding regulations for the television and cable industries. Ownership restrictions were substantially eased for broadcasting and municipal control over subscriber rates was jettisoned for cable.

Efforts at revising regulation had begun during the Carter Administration; the objective was to create what was termed "a level playing field" for television and cable, while preserving the essential public-interest standard that had stood from the very beginnings of broadcasting. Democratic Congressman Lionel Van Deerlin of California, then chairman of the House Subcommittee on Communications, had in the late 1970s proposed a top-to-bottom rewriting of the Communications Act of 1934 to allow for the new video technologies that were on the horizon. He was widely hooted for his efforts by both the industry and public-interest groups, and his preoccupation with the rewrite proposal caused him to lose his office. But soon after Reagan's election, many of Van Deerlin's recommendations were adopted by the Republican-led Federal Communications Commission with hardly a stir. Deregulation began in 1980, Reagan's first year in the White House, and proceeded during his two terms.

Under the free market policies of his administration, radio and television broadcasters were no longer regarded as public trustees. The theory held that those who served the public best in a competitive marketplace would make the most money; thus, those who made the most money were presumed to have served the public best. It was argued that consumers held the ultimate power because they controlled the dial. There was also a First Amendment rationale for deregulating broadcasting when the viewer had a range of other options: a government that did not have rules for newspapers, magazines, or videocassettes should not impose standards or restrictions on television programming. Moreover, the old restrictions for TV could not be administered equally for cable, since cable systems are essentially regulated by municipalities and not by the FCC. The kinds of sanctions applied by the federal agency to TV stations for egregious violations of the fairness doctrine, for example, could not be applied as easily to local cable systems.

With broadcasting essentially freed of its historic mandate to serve "the public interest, convenience and necessity," with TV and radio licenses made reasonably secure, and with both media given the government's tacit blessing to concentrate on profit taking, the broadcasting industry became intensely interesting to acquisitive corporations and speculators in business.

Coincidentally, this occurred somewhere near the fortieth anniversary of television as a mass-audience medium, a time when many of the commercial TV pioneers who built the networks and the local stations after World War II had reached advanced age and were, in the vernacular, "cashing out," putting their properties up for sale.

All in a wave in 1986, the three networks—which had been rock-solid institutions, each with a distinct corporate culture—were dealt to new owners, and only ABC to a company with true broadcasting credentials, Capital Cities Communications. NBC and its parent,

RCA, went to General Electric, and CBS to Laurence A. Tisch, a speculator whose other interests included the Loews hotel chain, the Lorillard Tobacco Company, and the Bulova Watch Company. Tisch's stock holdings in CBS fell just a trace short of constituting a legal buyout; if they had reached twenty-five percent, he would have been required by law to dispose of the CBS radio stations in markets where the company also had a television property.

Many of the broadcast groups that had local stations were traded to new owners who were steeped in business but not in the traditions of broadcasting. Moreover, a large number of the purchases were leveraged buyouts, which meant the investors were immediately faced with servicing debt. Like the new stewards of the networks, they were determined to operate in a more businesslike fashion than had their predecessors. And in an extraordinary quirk of timing, they arrived on the scene just when the cracks in the old television structure were becoming apparent.

They responded by slashing costs, principally by cutting staff, executive perquisites, and the nonessentials, which in many cases meant eliminating certain departments and scaling back others. There was also rising interest in automation and other new production technologies that reduced the payroll. At the networks, the news divisions were the hardest hit by the personnel cuts, in part because they represented the only form of programming in which the networks could control costs. But the new owners also reasoned that since newspapers make money with news, and local TV stations do as well, they should not be straddled with a loss leader budgeted at nearly $300 million a year—especially since Ted Turner was profitably running two twenty-four-hour news networks, CNN and CNN Headline News, on half the investment.

Shortly after acquiring NBC, General Electric sold off the entire radio division, including the network that had started national broadcasting in the United States in 1926. Tisch trimmed down CBS, Inc. to its TV and radio properties, getting $2 billion from Japan's Sony Corporation for CBS Records, the largest recording company in the world and the original sibling of CBS, known through most of its history as Columbia Records. (The network began its existence in 1927 as the Columbia Phonograph Broadcasting System.)

By the late 1980s, the television industry bore scant resemblance to that of the past. ABC, CBS, and NBC were not the companies they had been in the 1970s; nor were Warner, Time, Lorimar, Group W, Columbia, 20th Century–Fox, Disney, Viacom, MGM, or MTM. Venerable broadcast groups like Metromedia, Storer, Taft, Field, RKO, and Golden West had vanished. The new managements were a different breed, in the main, hard-edged traders in media properties with no sentimental attachment to the history of the companies they acquired. With repeal of the regulation that required new owners to keep a station a minimum of three years before putting it up for sale, TV stations began to be traded like commodities.

Broadcast culture had changed, and so had the business mentality and moral code of the industry. Under the old code, the broadcaster's first responsibility was to the public; under the new, the primacy of the citizen had yielded to the primacy of the stockholder. That was perhaps the most revolutionary change in a revolutionary era.

The End of Television as We Knew It

Time Inc.'s bold decision in 1975 to transmit Home Box Office (HBO) by satellite was the shot heard around the world. It signaled in the U.S. television industry tumultuous change that by the end of the 1980s would spread to Europe and other parts of the globe.

Time's move was a large gamble. HBO was then a struggling regional pay cable service beaming out of New York City by microwave to a number of eastern cable systems. The leasing of a single transponder on RCA Satcom I was a $7.5 million commitment, and at the time only two cable systems in the country were equipped with earth stations, or receiving dishes, to pull down the signal. A satellite signal that spanned the country was meaningless in the absence of receiving equipment. But by May 1977, a scant two years later, the hundredth cable system had installed its dish and become an HBO affiliate; and by October of that year, with subscribers at the one million mark, the enterprise had edged into the black.

That fateful business decision not only reversed the fortunes of both HBO and the cable industry, it forged an irrevocable link between cable and satellite technologies. There was yet greater significance to the HBO success: it demonstrated that instant networks could be created by satellite, obviating the need for land lines and prohibitively costly local loops, and proved that Americans were willing to pay for television, something they had been accustomed to receiving free. Those two developments—people paying monthly fees for a special channel and national networks made possible overnight—spurred the television revolution of the 1980s.

New television technologies became a gathering storm when HBO began making money. If people were subscribing to cable on a monthly basis and paying additionally for its premium channels, would they also buy the information retrieval systems known as teletext and videotex, or video disk players, video games, home videocassette recorders (VCRs), or backyard receiving dishes? Would they choose the technological alternatives to cable—STV (over-the-air pay television), DBS (direct-to-home broadcasts by satellite), or MDS (multipoint distribution systems, known today as MMDS and for marketing purposes as "wireless cable")? All these technologies were poised to enter the marketplace in the 1980s.

With HBO as a national pay channel, cable finally had the hot new product it needed to carry it beyond those areas of the country where reception of terrestrial signals was poor. Up to that time, cable's chief original offering was the distant signal—one or more independent TV stations from nearby cities brought in by microwave. Very soon, HBO was joined on the satellite by a number of new cable networks, including Ted Turner's ingenious invention, the superstation. The marriage of cable and satellite allowed Turner to turn his obscure and essentially frail Atlanta UHF station, WTBS, into one that could be seen from coast to coast. As cable began to spread from rural communities to the suburban areas of the great population centers, all manner of new satellite cable networks came into being. ESPN, devoted entirely to sports, was one of several to launch in 1979. It has since become far and away the most profitable of the so-termed basic (not for pay) cable services, more consistently profitable, in fact, than its older broadcast sibling, ABC-TV. Both are owned today by Capital Cities/ABC.

An SRI study in the late 1970s concluded that over-the-air subscription television (STV) would beat out cable in the next decade, because it could satisfy swiftly the public demand for a pay channel specializing in movies, especially in the big cities, where cable franchising was stalled. STV did not involve tearing up the streets, bringing another wire into the home, or asking the consumer to pay a monthly fee first for a flock of basic cable channels that were not especially wanted. On the strength of the SRI study, STV stations sprang up on the UHF band in a number of the major cities. Dallas alone had three.

Meanwhile, Warner cable had developed a dazzling new kind of cable system, one that was two-way interactive, involving two parallel cable lines hitched to a bank of polling computers that swept each home every few seconds. Warner called it Qube. (It was given that name because the system was four-faceted, but when Warner was advised that a cube had six facets the marketing had already begun; the misnomer proved of no matter.) Qube was so amazing that the national press feasted on its marvels during its test run on the Warner system in Columbus, Ohio. The system even received extensive coverage on broadcast television, the medium it was threatening to displace.

Qube's facets, on the original remote-control converter unit developed for it, were four rows of ten buttons. One row would call up the local terrestrial channels, another the satellite channels created expressly for cable, and a third offered separate channels of movies, cultural events, concerts, and sports on a pay-per-view basis. The fourth row of buttons were the fascinating, interactive ones. With these the viewer could cast votes on amateur-hour contestants, counted in less than a minute; react positively or negatively to what a politician was saying in an interview; participate in public opinion polls; or buy merchandise off the screen.

In sweeping each subscribing household every six or seven seconds, the computers also allowed the system to provide burglar- and fire-alarm protection.

Qube was so clearly the ultimate in cable that when the franchising process began in the cities during the early 1980s, almost no city would settle for anything less. Warner beat out the other contenders for Pittsburgh, Cincinnati, Houston, Dallas, and Milwaukee, but these proved dubious triumphs. Because of requiring dual cable, Qube systems cost almost twice as much to build as conventional cable systems, yet there was no assurance that they would produce revenues soon enough to justify the investment. By the mid-1980s

Warner's franchising victories were beginning to seem a curse. Gustave Hauser was replaced as chairman by Drew Lewis, the former Secretary of Transportation in the Reagan Administration. To get Warner back into profitability with cable, Lewis promptly shut down the Qube operations and managed to persuade the cities that his company had overpromised; it could not profitably provide service under the terms for which the franchises were granted. If those cities wanted cable they would have to accept what the industry called "plain vanilla," essentially what the other cable companies were offering—an array of basic, advertising-supported channels and some scrambled pay services. The terms were accepted and Qube effectively vanished in mid-decade. So, in fact, did all the higher aspirations for cable. The medium settled into being, essentially, more television.

By 1982 there were forty-seven full- and part-time cable channels on the satellites, which prior to HBO's uplinking had only carried one-time transmissions. Three of the new contenders for slots on the nation's cable systems were satellite networks backed entirely or in part by the major networks: CBS Cable, a cultural service; the Entertainment Channel, a pay service featuring TV adaptations of Broadway shows and exclusive access to BBC programming, in which NBC had an interest; and the Satellite News Channel, a competitor to Ted Turner's CNN, in which ABC was partnered with Group W. All changes were occurring in the first half of the decade. The network managements attached little meaning to them and proceeded with business as usual.

Cable not only produced a flock of new networks by satellite, which together began cutting piecemeal into the network audiences, it also served to foster the extraordinary growth of independent television in the 1980s. In the ten-year span from 1977 to 1987, independents grew in number from 88 to 337. Most of the new ones were on the UHF band, and they sprouted for the reason that cable made these stations as accessible to the consumer as those on VHF.

That there were only three TV networks prior to the cable/satellite era was a consequence of how stations were allocated by the FCC, each spaced so as not to conflict with a signal from a nearby city. The typical market area had three stations, and all logically became network affiliates, because these drew the biggest audiences and were the most economical to operate. The largest cities also were able to sup-

port one or more VHF stations that were unaffiliated, or independent. A few independents tried to make a go of it in the less desirable
UHF band, but with scant success. UHF stations have a smaller range
than those on VHF and nearly twice the noise level (static in the picture), require a special antenna, and are generally harder to tune in
than VHF channels on the older TV sets. Cable eliminated the UHF
handicap, making those channels the equal of any other. So as cable
penetration increased in the 1980s, the number of new UHF stations
grew.

Their existence enlivened the syndication business, allowing producers to create programs expressly for station-by-station sale. But
since the new independents could not afford to pay hard cash for each
program in an eighteen-hour-a-day schedule, most of the programs
came to be syndicated on a barter basis. This meant the stations could
receive a program free, in exchange for carrying its built-in national
advertising spots, which typically consumed half the available ad
breaks; the remainder of the spots the stations could sell. For national advertisers, barter syndication soon became an alternative to buying time on the major networks, and for the new stations barter was
a godsend. A chief variation on this style of delivery was to sell the
more popular syndicated shows for a combination of barter and cash.
By the mid-1980s it was possible for an advertiser to achieve national coverage virtually equal to what the networks could provide (ratings aside) on independent stations. *Wheel of Fortune* at its height
amassed a national rating in syndication that was the equivalent of a
prime time hit on the networks. *Star Trek: The Next Generation*, with
a major league production budget of around $1 million an episode,
bypassed the networks and went straight into syndication, where it
was a solid hit. Many of the affiliated stations preempted the networks to insert the program in prime time.

After buying 20th Century–Fox Film Corporation and then the
independent Metromedia station group (for which he became an
American citizen), Rupert Murdoch of Australia made the audacious
move in 1986 of starting a fourth TV network, known as Fox, on a
part-time basis. With its own stations as a base and an original line-
up of ninety affiliates—less than half the number of the major networks—Fox offered, first, a single late-night program which failed
and then three-hour prime time blocks on Saturday and Sunday

nights. Murdoch's venture defied the common wisdom and was deemed by most experts an indulgence in hubris. A network with only half the distribution capabilities of ABC, CBS, and NBC and carried, moreover, on seldom-watched independent stations could not, it seemed, afford very long to produce shows of network quality and endure the prevailing failure ratio. Such a network could not hope to compete with the networks' great promotion machines or attract the hottest producers in Hollywood. Most analysts wrote off the Fox network as a reckless undertaking destined to fail.

But the Fox strategy was to produce shows that were somewhat different from, and less expensive than, those of the big networks, programs that appealed particularly to young people. Moreover, the plan was to introduce these shows when the networks were at their weakest, in the summertime, opposite the reruns. The strategy worked. Television critics, having little to write about in the summer, gave the new programs considerable attention. Beyond that, the programs had great word of mouth among the young. Within three years, Fox was operating in the black with very few failures behind it, and often, in the height of the season, beating at least one of the major networks in the ratings. In the summer of 1989 Fox added a Monday night schedule. By then its affiliate infrastructure had grown to 126 stations.

Fox succeeded, in the main, by taking the low road—the route of Murdoch's chief successes in publishing. The new network was probably most responsible for the "trash television" trend in 1989, with such tabloid-style shows as *A Current Affair, America's Most Wanted,* and *The Reporters,* programs that often mixed reenactments with news footage, blurring the line between fact and fiction. One of its sitcoms, *Married . . . With Children,* went a step too far with suggested nudity and set off the moral backlash that caused public groups to threaten consumer boycotts of advertisers supporting programs they considered objectionable. Nevertheless, Murdoch proved that the networks, with their rigid programming formulas, did not have the patent on ways to reach the mass audience.

Murdoch's network venture was a triumph of vertical integration. The Fox schedule raised the ratings and public profile of its owned stations and, of course, boosted their ad revenues. Some of its programs were produced by 20th Century–Fox and others under the guidance of Murdoch's specialists in tabloid newspapers. Since Fox was not recognized by the FCC as a full-fledged network, and therefore was exempt from the financial interest and syndication (fin-syn) rules that had barred the Big Three from engaging in domestic syndication, the reruns of Fox's long-running hits could be recycled in sales to local stations, as well as to markets abroad, via the 20th Century–Fox syndication arm.

As no previous cable or terrestrial network had done before, Fox penetrated the armor of the big commercial networks. Meeting them head-on, despite a huge handicap in distribution and promotion, Fox proved that the networks were not invincible, and that they did not have the undisputed corner on mass-appeal programming. By the end of the turbulent decade, Fox had firmly established a niche of its own on the new television landscape.

This is a landscape in which the new TV owners must not only compete with one another and Fox but also, on some level, with more than threescore advertising-supported cable networks, five superstations, eight national pay-cable services (in addition to regional ones), five shopping channels, seven pay-per-view companies, scores of barter syndication distributors, and 40,000 video rental shops.

Cable is now in 65 percent of American households (compared with only 20 percent in 1980), and pay cable in more than 30 percent. About 60 percent of homes receive 30 or more TV channels, many have more than 50, and a few 100 or more. VCRs are in 71 percent of households and remote-control tuning in 75 percent. Pay-per-view is available to more than 12 million households. More than a dozen regional sports networks have sprung up on cable, and some 3 million homes are equipped with backyard satellite dishes. In addition, low-power television, laser video disks and MMDS ("wireless cable") are all gaining ground in the marketplace.

All, moreover, continue to proliferate, making steady claims on the audience and advertisers the networks once considered secure.

Meanwhile, in the United Kingdom, DBS is the local new technology, with Murdoch's British Sky Broadcasting (BSkyB), a multichannel service, having the field to itself after buying out its competitor in 1990. BSkyB's success in the U.K. has revived interest in DBS here, with three services—Primestar Partners, Hughes Communications' DirectTV, and Hubbard Broadcasting's USSB—all launching auspiciously in 1994 and, by means of digital compression, prepared to provide as many as 150 channels.

The use of video compression in satellite-to-home broadcasting signaled the start of the digital revolution in the television media. Broadcast TV, cable, MMDS, and home video all are expected to convert from analog to digital technology by the end of the decade. The compression of signals allows each existing channel to multiply at least fivefold, so that a thirty-channel cable system can upgrade to 150 without replacing existing lines. Still, such cable giants as Time Warner and TCI, and virtually every regional Bell phone company, are replacing existing plant with fiber-optic lines to give their installations a capacity of five hundred or more video channels.

Digitization, moreover, allows for sophisticated interactivity when the systems add switching capability. Cable and telephone thus become technologically identical, differentiated only by their definitions under federal regulation. Cable can provide local phone service and telephone companies a television service to compete with cable. The cable industry refers to its state-of-the-art installations as "full service" systems, while the phone companies' new service is called Video Dial Tone. Both are major components of the so-called information superhighway.

Driving the construction of megachannel systems are the prospective billions in revenues to be derived from the transactional services they can provide, ranging from shopping to gambling. But the principal service is to be video on demand, permitting consumers to order up programs from an enormous catalog and to rent current movies electronically rather than from a local video shop. The programming is stored in computer memory banks known as file servers and is organized horizontally, by category or genre, rather than vertically in the manner of television channels. Advertisers on the interactive networks will know exactly how many households they are reaching and the demography of those households. They may even elect to send different commercials simultaneously over the vertical TV channels to different demographic groups.

An important byproduct of digitization is high-definition television (HDTV), important less for improving picture quality, perhaps, than for resolving a sticky global issue. For years the United States, Japan, and western Europe were in a race to establish an HDTV system that would be adopted worldwide, making for a universal transmission standard so that programming could be exchanged among countries without the need for technical conversion. Long considered the television of the future, HDTV can beam a television picture nearly equal in definition to one on 35-millimeter film.

Japan's public broadcaster, NHK, developed the first version of HDTV in the late 1970s in attempting to improve a transmission system that is markedly inferior to that of European countries. Japan and the countries of North and South America continue to broadcast under a standard known as NTSC that dates to the 1930s and produces a picture on the screen in 525 horizontal lines. Later technology permitted a much sharper picture using 625 lines, and when color telecasting began in the late 1950s, Britain and other European countries switched to the 625-line standard, although it made their original black and white TV sets obsolete.

Television had spread so quickly in the United States that to change the technical standard to 625 lines was deemed unfair to consumers who had bought black and white sets, so the United States adopted a color system that was compatible with existing monochrome sets. That, of course, made it incompatible with either of Europe's two transmission standards, the German-developed PAL system or France's SECAM, which are themselves incompatible.

Japan's superb HDTV increases the number of horizontal scan lines to 1,125, more than twice those of NTSC, but it has some serious drawbacks. One is that it would make all existing TV sets and transmission equipment obsolete, because it requires a new receiver with a rectangular screen the shape of widescreen movies. Another is that it requires greater bandwidth than present TV transmissions, equivalent to one full channel and part of another. In the United States, that would necessitate a reapportioning of frequencies and the sacrificing of some existing stations, which is highly improbable. Moreover, no network would give up its present ability to reach 98 percent of the population for a superior transmission that would require building an audience universe all over again.

Even more troublesome to the countries of Europe and North America is that Japan, whose industry would own all the patents and do most of the manufacturing, would realize a bonanza such as no country has ever known if its HDTV system were adopted worldwide.

Estimates are that the sales for the new TV sets and VCRs alone would come to around $40 billion a year around the globe. But in order to go forward, Japan needed the acceptance of the United States and western European markets, and both began playing for time while developing their own versions of HDTV.

How to proceed with HDTV became an issue in the highest reaches of the United States government because of the economic tilt to Japan and the implications for a number of American industries, including computer chip manufacture. In 1988 the FCC tentatively ruled that any system adopted in the United States had to be compatible with existing TV sets. And a consortium of American companies with financial assistance from the Pentagon began working at developing a form of HDTV to rival Japan's and give the United States some claim to the mammoth new industry.

That quest has effectively been ended by rapid advances in digital technology. Clearly the perfect television picture will be developed digitally. But it is not clear that the American networks and stations are eager for it, since the conversion of equipment will entail a large investment without a foreseeable increase in profits. The technology thus far has been driven by politics rather than business.

The FCC attempted to deal with that problem with a radical proposal: it would give every existing TV station a second station on the UHF band so that the same programs could be broadcast simultaneously in analog and digital HDTV. After a reasonable period of years, when the consumer conversion to high definition was virtually complete, the FCC would take back the original analog stations, and all broadcasting would be in HDTV. Few broadcasters expressed enthusiasm for the proposal, but some were intrigued by the possibilities a digitized station afforded. Through compression, each station could be multiplied by five or more, inviting new terrestrial networks for each.

The TV revolution will rage on in the 1990s. The 1970s may be remembered as the last decade of television under the absolute dominance of three networks, when each jockeyed for Nielsen numbers by playing to some mystical common denominator, when audiences and ad revenues grew in spite of what was broadcast, and when no price was too high for a program or personality that virtually assured the delivery of the requisite rating points.

As Laurence Tisch, then the new chief executive of CBS, observed in one of his early speeches in 1987: "A once unified and coherent industry seems to be splitting down further and further into separate components, as though some unstoppable biological process were at work."

The New Television Economy

In 1988 the three TV networks had combined advertising revenues of $9 billion, a record high, and those for the entire cable industry were just over $800 million. Yet CBS reported a small profit and ABC a "slight loss" for the year, while at least a dozen cable networks claimed to be operating in the black. Nothing better illustrates the radical transformation of the television economy.

Most, if not all, of those cable revenues, which grew to more than $1 billion in 1989, would have gone straight to the networks' bottom line. ABC alone would have shown at least $200 million in profits, not counting the additional millions if the Fox network had not existed.

The cable networks are able to thrive on much smaller ratings and ad dollars than the broadcast networks can because they have a second revenue stream. Each receives fees from the local cable systems at rates ranging from one cent to fifty cents per subscriber, depending on the program service. The most important ones receive the highest fees, and as the fees go up the difference is passed on to the consumer through periodic rate hikes by the local operator. These leading cable networks, in addition, receive more than half of their revenues from advertising.

The combination of subscriber fees and advertising sales has made ESPN, the all-sports network, far and away the most successful of the cable program services and often more profitable than some broadcast networks. This is a huge comfort to Capital Cities/ABC since it owns 80 percent of ESPN. The other cable networks in which ABC has a major stake, Lifetime and Arts & Entertainment, are also profitable, although more modestly than ESPN. Such national cable services as USA, CNN, MTV, the Family Channel, Nickelodeon, Superstation WTBS, the Nashville Network, Discovery, and Black Entertainment Television (BET) reportedly are making money, along with such pay services as HBO, Cinemax, Disney, and Showtime. Ted Turner's network, TNT, which began in October 1988, established itself quickly and within two years was in the black.

Yet only rarely do the combined ratings of all the cable networks in prime time come close to equaling the rating for CBS, NBC, or ABC. More nearly they approach that of Murdoch's Fox network, which like the cable services is a lean operation.

Two other terrestrial networks gained prominence in the late 1980s, Telemundo (owned by Saul Steinberg's Reliance Capital Group) and Univision (owned by Hallmark Cards, which purchased and renamed the Spanish International Network). Both have targeted the same niche in the U.S. market, the twenty million Spanish-speaking Americans, and both have substantial coverage of the main Hispanic population centers through their owned stations and affiliates. Together, out of the $300 million spent in Hispanic television by advertisers, the two networks realize about $175 million in annual revenues—a mere flea bite to the major networks. But the two contend that the Hispanic market is poorly measured by the ratings services, and in 1989 both invested heavily in audience research from the conviction that proper measurement will expand their portion of the TV advertising pool to $1 billion a year. Even half that would be significant.

While public television has never been much of a competitive factor to the networks in its twenty years of existence, its share of the audience becomes fairly sizeable in a continually fragmenting market. To its credit, it has withstood the changes in the television environment—including the competition from such cable networks as Arts & Entertainment, Discovery, and Bravo, both for acquired foreign programming and for viewers—and still maintains the flat 3 percent to 4 percent share of audience in prime time it has held since the 1970s.

All these contenders for the national audience—along with barter syndication, now a $1 billion a year business—have succeeded in breaking down the viewing patterns that were formed when the networks had a virtual monopoly on television. After some forty years as a table d'hôte medium, whose menus were prepared by ABC, CBS, and NBC for a captive audience ranging on a typical evening from seventy million to one hundred million viewers, television has become an à la carte medium. All the carefully mastered techniques of scheduling to maximize viewing in a three-network competition—the concentration on audience-flow, counterprogramming, and hammocking—have been undone by the fragmentation of audience and advertising, and by the liberating technology of the remote-control tuner. The more complex structure of the market makes it difficult now for any network to reach the mass audience, and it has produced a new, stratified television economy.

Television has split into two families, which may be described for convenience as wholesale and retail. Wholesale is the form that is sent out widely, distributed over the air or by wire or satellites to homes equipped to receive the signals. Retail is the kind that has to be purchased or rented specially and that is sold to one home at a time. The various pay cable networks, pay-per-view, hotel movies, and cassettes gotten at video stores, whether rented or bought, typify retail television. Broadcasting and basic cable, along with advertising-supported DBS, belong to the wholesale family. Both families are expanding.

The wholesale sphere is coming to resemble the magazine field, in which specialized publications with ten thousand readers can coexist profitably with mass-interest publications reaching ten million consumers. In the top stratum are the TV networks whose success level in prime time is defined by Nielsen ratings of at least 15.0, or around twenty-five to thirty million viewers. Programs scoring at 12s and 13s may be retained in hopes that they will build over time, but any falling below that must be canceled as a drain on revenues. The Fox network and major syndicated shows like *Star Trek: The Next Generation* are in the second stratum, where ratings of 8.0 to 10.0 more than suffice for success. At the next tier are the more typical syndicated shows and local programs, for which expectations are ratings of 3.0 to 6.0. And lastly come the cable networks, which generally range from ratings of 0.5 to 1.5, although ESPN has been known to hit 10s with its part of the National Football League package. This is an important development, because it means that programs which may be lacking in mass-audience appeal can find a niche in United States television that never existed before.

As with magazines, the cable network ratings—while minuscule by broadcast standards—hit well-targeted audiences: young men, in the case of ESPN; young women with Lifetime; teenagers and young adults with MTV; children with Nickelodeon, and the better-educated viewers with Arts & Entertainment. For this they are valued by advertisers.

ABC, CBS, and NBC still have the best access to the mass audience and remain the most efficient way for advertisers to reach consumers across the country. Any network in prime time will still reach at least 20 percent of the households viewing in any hour. But they are like large department stores on the main streets coping with growing numbers of boutiques sprouting up around them and bidding for their trade. Around 60 percent of U.S. homes can receive thirty or more TV channels today and another 25 percent have between eleven and twenty-nine channels. As the new channels proliferate, profits for the networks become ever harder to achieve. They are caught in an upward spiral of costs and a downward spiral of diminishing audiences. There seems no end to either.

When it was the leading broadcast network in the ratings in 1989, NBC had operating margins of 9.3 percent, according to Wall Street analyst Jessica Reif of CL Global Partners, while those of ABC and CBS were both below 6 percent, a considerable decline from times past. The networks' huge investment for the relatively modest return is justified, however, by the profits flowing from the TV stations they own—all of which gain high visibility in their markets from identification with the networks, as well as high ratings and leverage in buying the top syndicated fare. The owned stations have excellent profit margins, ranging from 40 percent for the CBS group to 55 percent for those of Capital Cities/ABC with its vaunted "lean and mean" style of operating. Other affiliates not owned by the networks have 30–40 percent operating margins, but these margins are becoming harder to maintain in the changing environment. Affiliates typically receive 60 percent of their programming from the networks; and as the networks continue to lose audience, affiliates of course lose as well.

The three-network share of prime time audience has declined steadily from 93 percent in 1977 to around 65 percent in 1991. Moreover, in homes with cable and pay cable, these shares have been known to drop almost to 50 percent. In the same period, the network share of national television advertising declined by 9 percent, from 60.1 percent to 51.2 percent. A study by Veronis, Suhler & Associates, an investment banking firm specializing in media, found that in 1987 the average household watched the network channels an average of 30.2 hours a week, independent stations 11 hours, basic cable 5.2 hours, and pay cable 2.8 hours. Of the $17.3 billion spent that year on national TV advertising, the networks received 51.2 percent, national spot 39.6 percent, national cable 5.0 percent, and barter syndication 4.2 percent. Significantly, the cable and barter share had tripled in size from five years earlier, while the network share declined by six percentage points.

Cable's growth as a competitor is likely to continue, paradoxically with considerable help from the broadcast industry. When TV stations developed an aversion in the late 1980s to the off-network reruns of hour-long action-adventure series because they did not perform as well in syndication as sitcoms, they were sold in droves to the cable networks. That gave cable recognizable shows of network quality to compete with, shows with attractive track records that advertisers could appreciate, among them *Cagney & Lacey* and *L.A. Law*. When the networks decided there would be no lavishing of money on sports rights just for the prestige of having the event, ESPN and USA picked up much of what the networks passed over and added to their audience appeal. Broadcast television is a hit-driven business; cable is not. That difference allows cable to become a safe haven for distributors, independent producers, and promoters of events whose properties are turned down by the networks or station syndication.

New networks continue to be created for cable, although government reregulation of the industry may have closed the window on channels offered as part of the basic package. In response to consumer complaints about the steady rise in cable rates, the FCC has put a cap on what systems may charge for additional monthly fees.

By mid-1994 there were seventy-two national and regional cable networks, with more than one hundred aspiring niche program services in the wings, all waiting for the explosion in channel capacity expected to come from digital compression and new fiber-optic installations. As a rule of thumb, a basic cable network needs to be available in thirty million households to be considered a national advertising medium, and many of the newer ones fall well short. Only around twoscore of the long-established networks have reached or exceeded that number, and the few that have reached fifty million have become very profitable.

Cable is a medium that is still inventing itself and probably will continue to change for decades to come as it evolves into an interactive five-hundred-channel cornucopia. But for nearly twenty years, since the mid-1970s, the cable networks steadily drew audience away from broadcast television until collectively they claimed nearly one quarter of the viewing. Though each cable channel typically drew minuscule ratings by broadcasting standards—usually less than a single ratings point—they flourished because they maintained small staffs, minimized overhead, and derived revenues from two sources, advertising and subscriber fees.

While cable seems assured of continued growth and prosperity, the broadcast networks have been having difficulty adapting to the changing environment largely because they have been, in several ways, locked in to the old system. There is the matter of affiliate payments, for example. In contrast to the cable networks, which receive monies from their local affiliates, the big networks must pay affiliates for the use of the air time, a convention dating back to the earliest years of network radio. Among them the three annually pay $350 million in affiliate compensation. Any reduction in that amount would go straight to the bottom line, but it is a revenue source the stations depend on and is crucial to network-affiliate relations. Nor can the networks increase revenues by adding commercial positions in their programs at will; this too has to be negotiated with the affiliate body. The networks' greatest strength is their ability to reach nearly all of U.S. households, and this is achieved only through their affiliations in every TV market. Tampering with affiliate agreements could be difficult, as CBS has discovered in its attempt to reduce substantially its payments to stations.

The networks are also bound to an arrangement with their advertisers under which they guarantee, in effect, the ratings for shows. When programs fall short of the numbers and audience profiles projected for them, advertisers are given "make-good" spots in other programs to compensate. This reduces inventory and revenues, sometimes significantly. An attempt made by CBS in the early 1980s to eliminate the guarantee met stiff resistance in the advertising community. Plummeting sales caused the arrangement to be quickly reinstated.

Because of regulations that were adopted in the 1970s to curb the networks' great power in the TV marketplace, ABC, CBS, and NBC were barred from owning cable systems, from engaging in domestic syndication, or from having equity positions in programs they put on the air. As a result, while other entertainment companies were expanding to achieve vertical integration, the networks could not.

They are faced besides with program economics that made perfect sense for thirty-five years but now are growing unfeasible. The networks pay around 80 to 90 percent of a program's production costs for the right to show each episode twice, once during the season and repeats during the summer. Their whole profit structure is based on the scheduling of reruns. But the rerun season, as was discovered in the summers of 1988 and 1989, is when the networks are most vulnerable to assaults by the competing media—Fox, for example, has been introducing its new programming in the warm months, a clever and successful ploy. The networks' summer ratings have dropped so severely (much of audience lost to cable and home video) that the networks have been scheduling original series and reducing the number of reruns. That has the effect of hiking program costs just when the networks are struggling to contain them.

Wall Street analysts confirm the networks' claim that programming represents some 70 percent of their overhead. When barred from owning programs or negotiating an equity stake in those they put on the air, the networks have no direct control over production expenses in Hollywood, except to order more or fewer car crashes. Costs continue to rise in part because of the heated four-network competition and the mania for hits. Demand for the proven writers, directors, and actors builds up their fees, and increased emphasis on high production values and location shooting adds heavily to the technical expense. Multiple millions are spent in program development—the ordering of treatments, scripts, and pilots. Typically some eighty to one hundred pilots are produced each year, with perhaps one-quarter of them graduating to series. Yet, statistically, four-fifths of those will not last the season. In their cost-cutting efforts, which began in the mid-1980s, the networks put caps on what they will pay for episodes and have taken to ordering only five or six episodes of untried programs that might have to be canceled quickly.

Their most successful ploy, however, was to give over prime time slots to magazine and other news-based series that could be produced in-house because news programming is exempt from fin-syn. These series, all descended in some way from *60 Minutes* and *20/20,* are not only less expensive than entertainment shows but also help amortize a network's large investment in news. As the programs proliferated, the Hollywood studios found themselves with a shrinking program market—a strong reason for seeking a network merger.

But even as the networks may reduce costs somewhat in these ways, their promotion costs grow greater each year from the ever more urgent need to have the new programs "sampled," or examined, by the dedicated TV viewers.

Stations and Automation

Interest in electronic media ownership was so intense in the 1980s that, despite cable's advance and the excitement over other new forms of video delivery, applications for TV and radio licenses increased. Cable, of course, provided much of the impetus for the expansion of UHF independents, but sixteen new stations came on as network affiliates, a number of others as home-shopping stations, and dozens more as public TV stations. The radio census also grew, and local entrepreneurs clamored for the new low-power TV station licenses when they became available.

The National Association of Broadcasters reported 10,505 radio stations on the air in 1989 and 1,400 TV stations, compared with 8,101 radio and 1,045 TV stations operating in 1982. In addition there were 470 low-power stations in 1989, against none in the comparative year, with the number expected to exceed 1,000 in the 1990s.

The rise in broadcasting employment during that period was not exactly in proportion. With 2,404 radio stations added in that six-year span, radio employment increased by only 6,000—from 107,000 employees to 113,000—according to the U.S. Department of Labor's Bureau of Labor Statistics. In television, with 355 additional stations, the number of employees grew by 20,600—from 107,000 in 1982 to

128,000 in 1988. What had happened during that period was that stations found ways to operate with less personnel.

The typical radio station in 1982 had a staff of thirteen; six years later the typical station had a staff of eleven. With television the staffing at the typical station declined from 103 in 1982 to ninety-five in 1989. One television broadcaster, Tim McDonald, who headed the TVX station group, made up entirely of new UHF independents, devised a minimalist plan for staffing; under his table of organization each station would have only thirty-five employees. His plan apparently failed; TVX experienced serious financial difficulties in the late 1980s and had to reorganize.

The need to reduce staff as part of the overall cost cutting in the industry was an effect of rising local competition, which naturally tends to drive up program costs while driving down advertising rates. At the same time, the TV networks' struggles were being felt at the affiliate level in declining audience shares. With cable networks, regional sports networks, the Hispanic networks, and the Fox network all making claims on national advertising budgets, national spot revenues began to shrink, a serious concern to stations. In 1987, local advertising for the first time exceeded spot advertising in dollar volume—another sign of how radically the TV business is changing—and local dollars remain today the dominant revenue source for stations. Local billings grew from $3.4 billion in 1981 to $6.9 billion in 1987; spot from $3.8 billion to $6.8 billion. The growing importance of local sales in the 1980s suggests that TV stations were building up that part of the staff—with sales, marketing, and sales service personnel—while cutting back in other areas. This means that reductions in the more traditional station jobs, especially those on the technical side, were more severe than the general industrywide employment figures would indicate.

Stations were aided in their staff-cutting pursuits by automation technology—robotics and computers. Beta-cart, an automated playback system for commercials, replaced similar equipment requiring more maintenance and full-time operators. Other automated carts are used to load story segments for the newscasts, displacing videotape operators; and newsroom computers feed scripts directly to the TelePrompTer, eliminating another technician. Robotic cameras that can be operated from the control room by the technical director have served to eliminate two and sometimes three camera operators, plus a lighting technician, from newscasts and other kinds of programs that involve basic, everyday shots. Many stations also have automated master control and monitor their transmitters by remote control. The NBC network was able to eliminate 186 broadcast engineer jobs in a year's time, between 1988 and 1989, by means of robotic cameras, cart machines, computers, and new diagnostic equipment. That does not include the personnel trimmed at the company's owned stations by similar technology. When there are temporary staff shortages, the networks and major stations hire the needed technical staff on a per diem basis, usually at 130 percent of union scale. Many of the larger cities now have a community of unionized freelance technicians for daily hire. News staffs are similarly kept lean and are augmented by freelance journalists for special projects. While the per diem fees may exceed union scales, they allow the stations the flexibility to spend as needed while saving additionally on employee benefits.

Under the old rules for radio, the FCC required a full-time chief operator for each station. Developments in technology brought about a rule change that today allows radio stations to use contract chief engineers instead of resident staffers. In some cities, three or four stations may use the same radio engineer on a freelance basis, usually for emergencies.

Automation became an industry obsession in the 1980s, not just in the United States but in countries such as Japan and Australia, as well. Most managers praise the systems for both their cost efficiencies and their operating efficiencies, speed, reliability, and accuracy of performance. Those who swear by automation say it allows fewer people to perform more jobs in less time than ever before.

WTMJ, Milwaukee, has achieved such a high level of automation that the on-air operations essentially are handled by a single engineer. Outlet Communications had an independent UHF station in Atlanta that operated with just one person on the premises from 5 P.M. Fridays until 9 A.M. Mondays. Mel Olinksy, the operations manager of WFSB-TV, Hartford, Connecticut, says that computers make it theoretically possible to have a newscast with just the talent and one person in the control room.

TV newsrooms use computers today to generate closed captions for the hearing impaired, to retrieve old news footage through electronic searches, and to coordinate story assignments with other stations in the region to avoid duplicative camera crews. Computers are also used for field communications with reporters using laptop models. Ultimately, some managers believe, all studio equipment will be run by remote control from a computer.

Robotics, however, seem suited only for the larger TV stations best able to afford the huge investment. The NBC network spent around $1 million for its robotic camera system, and according to Tom Wolzien, vice president of editorial and production services, the cameras paid for themselves in wage savings in less than eighteen months. But Wolzien said that robotic cameras only make sense at stations with exceptionally high labor costs, such as the network-owned stations in the major cities. In markets where labor costs are substantially lower, the investment might not be feasible.

The blue-collar ranks in the TV industry are shrinking, giving way to so-called "super techies" who can operate a range of sophisticated computerized equipment, from character generators to beta-carts. The new station technologies require a new set of skills and, moreover, the ability to keep up with and master the newer computerized products and systems that continue to come. Not all the single-skilled technicians who mastered the old technologies are suited to the new. Many who were displaced have gone into corporate TV or have found work in cable or such developing technologies as MMDS. Others have had to switch fields. The new breed of technician, being highly skilled and versatile, is also more highly paid than his or her predecessor.

Television is not only a new business today; it is also, like newspaper publishing a decade ago, a new technical process. And more than anything else, the computer—a white-collar instrument—is what has been making the difference.

International Developments

Communications satellites posed no new territorial problems in North America, which is why they have been in commercial use here well before in much of the rest of the world. Footprints of U.S. satellites come down over much of Canada, but this kind of invasion across frontiers is not a new issue between the two countries, which have had their struggles for decades over the terrestrial broadcasting signals crossing the border. Besides, Canada's own Anik satellites cover much of the United States and indeed were used by American entrepreneurs in the first attempt at DBS in this country.

In Europe, however, where countries with distinct cultures, laws, and mores are bunched together geographically like the American states, satellites were a delicate issue for a number of years. There was a reluctance to be the country making the first move, because satellites have no respect for the sovereignty of borders; one launched in France or Luxembourg, for example, will cover virtually the entire western part of the continent. But the realization that satellite technology cannot be held back and that cultural invasions from the sky are inevitable in Europe may well have triggered the television revolution that began sweeping the continent in the late 1980s. Every one of the western European countries has opened its airwaves to privately owned commercial television, more or less after the American model.

For three or four decades, most European countries had only state-run networks—typically operating on two channels—which produced virtually all the domestic programs in-house. There was no independent production industry to speak of. Advertising policies varied greatly from country to country: Sweden accepted none, Germany allowed twenty minutes of TV advertising a day, and others permitted more, but none in amounts to compare with the United States, except for Italy. For political reasons, Italy deregulated television in 1975 and let commercial operators compete with its state-run RAI networks. Today it has three private networks owned by the same media tycoon, Silvio Berlusconi; two other private networks; three state networks; and hundreds of local independent stations.

Europe's most powerful publishers of newspapers and magazines, whose lobbying efforts were chiefly responsible for the severe limits on TV advertising in the past, are today the most vigorous proponents of liberalized commercial policies for the medium, because nearly all of them are involved in the ownership of private channels. Governments have also been under pressure from the advertising industry and from influential corporations desirous of more airtime to promote their products. With technology the catalyst, all these agendas jelled in the spirit of 1992, the year when the twelve member nations of the European Community expected to inaugurate their Common Market, harmonizing their economic policies and permitting the free movement of programming and advertising across borders, the better to compete with the United States and Japan. Together, as a sort of United States of Europe, they will comprise a market of 352 million potential viewers, almost one-third larger than the U.S. market. That makes the Common Market formidable, but it would be even more so if the countries spoke the same language and if their separate histories were not laced with bitter disputes and wars with one another.

The switch to private television in western Europe represents nothing less than a cultural revolution. France took the first step by privatizing its main state network, TF1, and letting in three other commercial networks—including the pay channel, Canal Plus—while maintaining two public TV channels. Germany followed France and in the closing months of the decade Spain awarded licenses for three national commercial channels (including one partially owned by Italy's Berlusconi and another by France's Canal Plus), after having fostered in the 1980s the establishment of half a dozen regional channels. Holland, Denmark, Norway, and Greece have also weighed in with new private stations.

Two attempts at pan-European satellite networks, Sky Channel and Super Channel, both broadcasting in English, failed commercially. But Sky, owned by Rupert Murdoch, immediately repositioned itself as a British DBS channel and faced down prospective competition in that sphere from BSB, a government-sanctified channel whose principal investors were the regional companies that hold the franchises to the private ITV channel. After both invested huge amounts in programming, mostly from the major American film studios, Sky bought out BSB. The existence of program-saturated satellites has given new impetus to the expansion of cable in the U.K. Long-term policies for Britain are still being debated, but a fifth terrestrial network is contemplated for the mid-1990s.

The new European channels have created a boom in the international program market, with the United States, of course, the chief beneficiary. American movies, action-adventure series, and serials such as *Dallas* and *Dynasty* have always done well abroad, if for no other reason than that they are offered at relatively low rates, since most have recouped their investments at home with runs on the networks and then domestic syndication. Before the boom, international sales were considered a minor contributor to profits for most American distributors. Today, with the American domestic market having gone flat, the world market has been sustaining a number of smaller distribution companies that might not otherwise have been able to survive, while becoming a major profit center for many of the larger companies. Europe's new stations have created competition not only for advertising but for desirable programming, and the effect has been to drive up prices for certain American shows.

Michael Jay Solomon, president of Warner Television International, cites the case of the serial *Knot's Landing* as an example. In the old European economy, the series, with a library of 250 episodes, might have done well in receiving between $5,000 and $10,000 an episode in a country like France. Instead, the bidding among the various French private channels drove the price up to $50,000 an episode, or $11 million for the entire package, paid by the leading network in ratings, TF1.

Solomon notes that typical production costs for programs like *Knot's Landing* are $850,000 to $1 million an hour, of which the American networks pay approximately 80 percent. The profits ultimately come from domestic syndication, where stations buy the reruns to "strip" them—that is, play them every night in the same time period. But the minimum library for stripping is one hundred episodes, which means that a program has to play on a network for four years, and sometimes five, to qualify. Most programs fail to run the course. As Solomon points out, 80 percent of network programs end up losing money for the studios. The average deficit for an American network program is in the range of $200,000 to $400,000 per hour, which could add up to $4 million or more a year. "The only way to make it up, if there is no domestic syndication," says Solomon, "is to sell it to the world's six major markets—Canada, the U.K., Germany, France, Italy and Australia."

Foreign broadcasters do not require a large library for stripping; many are content with acquiring twelve to twenty episodes, or whatever number is being broadcast by a network that year. Republic Television claimed that the deficit for *Beauty and the Beast*, when it was a weekly series on CBS, had been covered season by season from sales abroad. Companies like New World Pictures, which went into a tailspin in the American market after a period of phenomenal success, was kept alive for years by the foreign markets. A number of small independent distributors owed their survival in the 1980s to the safety net of cable and the international market.

In industry parlance, the networks and domestic syndication are the "front end" of the program market, and everything else—cable, home video, school and library sales, and foreign distribution—the "back end." By the close of the 1980s, however, the back end was expanding as rapidly as the front end was shrinking, causing companies to become more cognizant and respectful of the after-markets. Because the American networks are still effectively barred from owning programs or engaging in domestic syndication, they select programs without regard for the subsequent sales abroad; that burden is on the producer. Each network has an international sales division which chiefly sells its news, sports, and documentary programs abroad. But these divisions have taken to acquiring independent foreign programming to sell in international markets, so as not to be left out of the flourishing new field.

The introduction of private channels has given birth to a community of independent producers in the United Kingdom and on the continent, where none had existed before, many of them tying in with the independents in Canada and Australia in coproductions. Unlike American producers, who have a native market large enough to justify ambitious projects, these producers have to arrange for multicountry partnerships to cover basic costs and to create programs that are capable of competing with American works in the international market. Canadian producers are especially adept at making these collaborative deals because they have survived on them for years. With a population one-tenth the size of that in the United States, and with virtually every American program also distributed north of the border, Canada has had to develop mechanisms to support native production if it is not simply to yield up to the U.S. onslaught. Through a combination of government grants and a Canadian network commitment, most Canadian producers can raise two-thirds of their financing at home—but for the remainder they have to look abroad, and that has made them pioneers of coproductions.

The boom in France has given an enormous lift to the French-Canadian industry with its universe of six million viewers in the province of Quebec. Indeed, it has worked both ways; most French producers can count on Quebec as a market. The entire French-speaking world, including various countries in Africa, has been drawn more closely together, oddly, by the economics of television productions. But while the francophone nations stubbornly insist on producing programs for global distribution in their own language, most other major coproductions make strong concessions to the English-speaking countries, which represent around three-fourths of the television world. They do this by casting American and English actors in conspicuous roles and often by shooting the entire program in English and then dubbing it for their native market. Because of the size of the anglophone component, English has become the lingua franca of world television.

The United States, once the most insular television market in the free world, is today not only availing itself of foreign programming, mainly through cable and public television, but also has begun behaving like a member of the international television community. American producers have been teaming up with foreign companies in coproductions and some are getting serious about the idea of inventing some kind of mid-Atlantic program, one involving a partnership on both sides of the Atlantic and meeting creatively halfway, blending the U.S. and U.K. styles of drama.

The internationalizing of television has profound implications for the future development of the American industry. Production is bound to become widely dispersed, with the entire world becoming Hollywood's extended backlot. Meanwhile Hollywood itself has become internationalized through the acquisition of its companies by foreign operators. Not long after Murdoch's purchase of 20th Century–Fox, England's TVS bought MTM Productions and Thames Television acquired Reeves Communications. Coincidentally, both British companies later lost their broadcast licenses in the 1991 auction of the franchises. Australia's Qintex Productions bought United Artists and Hal Roach Studios before going bankrupt. But then came the bombshells. In swift order Japan's Sony Corporation purchased Columbia Pictures for $3.4 billion and Matsushita Electrical Industrial Company snatched up MCA Inc. for $6.13 billion. Pathe Communications, owned by Italian financier Giancarlo Parretti, bought MGM for $1.3 billion but lost it soon after to Parretti's European bankers. Finally, Time Warner, acting to reduce the huge debt created by the merger, sold a 12.5 percent interest in its entertainment units—Warner Brothers, Time Warner Cable, and HBO—to two Japanese companies, Toshiba and C. Itoh and Company, for $1 billion. These transactions left Paramount and Disney as the only major studios wholly under American ownership.

As foreign media and entertainment conglomerates positioned themselves for direct access to the lucrative American market, several U.S. companies in turn—notably ABC Video Enterprises, Disney, and Group W—made investments in networks and production companies abroad, each to obtain a strategic foothold in the burgeoning European commercial television market.

The frenzy of consolidation that took place among American media companies during the 1980s was in part a strategy to fend off takeovers but was also intended to enable companies to keep pace with the world's media titans—Berlusconi of Italy, Roberto Marinho of Brazil, Leo Kirch of West Germany, and such publishing powers as Hachette and Bertelsmann—all of whom are building global empires. The celebrated merger of Time Inc. and Warner Communications into the world's largest media conglomerate received the U.S. government's blessing chiefly because it promised to preserve America's dominance in communications/entertainment—its second largest export, after aeronautics—against the threats posed by the stirrings abroad. So it is ironic that not long after the merger, Time Warner Entertainment took in two Japanese partners.

The Nineties and Beyond

The eras of television are marked by technology. Each technical advance, with all that it made possible, served to put the medium on a new programming course. And each altered, in some way, the broadcaster's employment needs.

First was the era of live, local broadcasting, built on the radio model, with most of the programming produced in-house. This was before the networks had achieved coast-to-coast interconnection, when national programs originating in New York or Chicago aired in the western part of the country by kinescope, and when syndication barely existed. The stations buzzed with activity, as the programming switched from one studio to another—children's shows, musicales, personality programs, game shows, public affairs programs, and newscasts. Most of the commercials were produced live.

This kind of programming called for a house band and a staff of writers, directors, producers, singers, talent coordinators, announcers, and makeup artists, as well as a raft of engineers and studio technicians. It was an era, too, when in addition to an operator the studio camera required a technician with a screwdriver to keep the camera in register.

When the networks finally crossed the country and started making larger claims on the stations' airtime, local production began to evaporate. Syndication sped the process along, offering low-budget filmed series and libraries of vintage movies, which usually drew better ratings than the local, live shows while costing a good deal less. The personnel rosters were quickly reduced, and stations have not had studio orchestras or staff writers since. The networks, however, originating most of their programs from New York, produced a great deal of live studio drama, drawing from the Broadway talent pool, and even more in the way of comedy and variety shows. Employees who were skilled in the TV crafts flourished in New York.

Videotape created a sensation when it was introduced at the 1956 National Association of Broadcasters convention in Chicago, and it produced the third era of television—one that obviated the need for most live presentations and that allowed studio productions to be preserved and repeated. Videotape made TV operations more efficient and economical, and it created new categories of jobs on the technical side at every station. Ironically, the technology arrived just when most prime time programming was shifting to the West Coast, drawing from the Hollywood talent pool and produced predominantly on film. The shift sharply reduced the need for video technicians and directors of studio productions, while expanding job opportunities in the film crafts.

Color TV actually predated videotape but was broadcast on a regular basis only by NBC for almost a decade (to help sell sets manufactured by its parent, RCA). In 1965, the proliferation of color TV receivers was sufficient to cause the other two networks and all the local stations to join in. Again there was a creation of new technical job categories, since color transmissions are somewhat more complex than are those in monochrome. And during the period in which the studio equipment was converted, there was substantial below-the-line expansion in the industry.

Cable TV represented the fifth era, and the miniaturization of equipment the sixth. The latter revolutionized television news, liberating it from the studio and the film processing laboratory and allowing live broadcasts from scenes of breaking news without the need for cumbersome mobile units. Satellites opened the next era, permitting live broadcasts from abroad and rapid news exchanges among stations in the United States. This was in the 1980s, also the era of MMDS, DBS, home video, pay-per-view, and the various automation technologies, all of which are transforming the industry as never before.

High-definition TV promises to key the next technological era, which could amount to nothing less than the reinvention of television, but no one can be certain if HDTV will make itself felt in the 1990s or after the year 2000. The significant industry changes in the 1990s are as likely to come from policy decisions by the federal government as from developments in technology.

Dramatic changes in the economics of television are meanwhile taking place in the 1990s, with the major networks proving the beneficiaries. Most cable program services are really *faux* networks, twenty-four-hour channels of automated videos prepared a week in advance. Unlike broadcast stations and regular networks, which can interrupt their programming for news bulletins, the cable networks play on mindlessly in times of crisis (except of course for CNN and others that are live at least part time). This undoubtedly has limited cable's claim on broadcasting's audience.

That became apparent in 1994, the year the terrestrial networks rebounded. As new cable networks entered the market, they tended to draw their audiences from other cable services rather than from broadcast TV. With cable feeding off itself, the steady audience erosion that had plagued the major networks since the early 1980s appeared to have leveled off, and national advertisers spent record amounts at ABC, CBS, NBC, and Fox, presaging a year of record profits. Despite their loss of audience to rival media, the TV networks remain a national advertiser's surest means to a nationwide audience.

The networks, moreover, had won two victories in Washington that allowed them to play a larger role in the changing marketplace: first, a ruling that they were as entitled as cable networks to be compensated by cable systems for carriage, and then the decision to free them from the highly restrictive financial interest and syndication rules, which had arrested their growth for more than twenty years.

Rather than try to extract cash from cable operators after the first ruling, three of the networks instead negotiated a deal with the MSOs to carry a new cable channel each proposed to create: ABC a second sports network, ESPN2; NBC an all-talk-show network, America's Talking; and Fox a channel of general entertainment, FX. CBS alone was shut out, the result of having pursued the fruitless quest of cash payments from cable. When that strategy failed, CBS proposed a news-oriented network—another mistake, since the largest MSOs were protective of CNN, in which they held equity stakes. So CBS came up empty.

Under fin-syn, which had gone into effect in 1971 to break the networks' dominance over the program market, ABC, CBS, and NBC were prohibited from taking an ownership position in the programs they commissioned from Hollywood studios and from engaging in domestic program syndication. This meant that they could license a program for two airings but could not participate in the after-market sales. *Dallas, Dynasty, M*A*S*H, Cheers,* and *Cosby* all made many millions of dollars in syndication and foreign sales for their studios, but the networks that ran the initial investment risks and promoted the shows into gigantic hits received not a penny from the windfall. A companion rule had barred the networks from owning cable systems.

Thus restricted, the networks found themselves at a severe disadvantage in a rapidly changing marketplace; while other companies were free to expand through acquisitions for vertical integration, the networks were chained to a previous era. Fin-syn ruled out any possibility of their merging with Hollywood studios, because the studios owned programs and were very active in the lucrative syndication field.

The FCC during the Reagan Administration had flirted with lifting the rule but then left it to the Hollywood and network industries to work out their own compromise. Years of futile negotiation served only to strengthen the polarity, and the issue became something of a holy war in which each side—the networks on one, the Hollywood production community on the other—believed its very survival to be at stake. Oddly, it was the presence of the fourth network, the interloper Fox, that brought fin-syn down. Rupert Murdoch created the network after buying the 20th Century–Fox studios, but while that was clearly a violation, the FCC exempted Fox because in the beginning it operated only a few hours a week. Besides, the FCC wanted to encourage a fourth network. Later, as Fox began to add more evenings to its schedule, the FCC created a definition of a network: one that broadcast more than fifteen hours a week in prime time. Then in the spring of 1991, at the instigation of Fox Broadcasting, which was concerned that fin-syn might prevent it from expanding into a full-blown network, the FCC reexamined the rule and attempted to modify it. What resulted was a complex scheme that became a whole new tangle of regulation. Ultimately, with the courts supporting repeal of the rule, the FCC set November 1995 as the official date of fin-syn's abolition.

The unshackling of the networks from the financial interest and syndication rule is sure to transform the industry. Having some participation in the back end will prompt the networks to think in larger terms when selecting programs for their schedules. Rather than playing strictly to American viewers, they will likely consider also the potential appeal of shows to foreign audiences and the resale prospects in the home video field. The series *Twin Peaks*, for example, was still a colossal hit in Europe the season it petered out on ABC and was canceled. Had ABC owned a piece of the show, it might have kept the series on the network to reap the profits from abroad.

The combination of fin-syn's imminent repeal and the networks' economic resurgence immediately sparked merger talks, principally involving CBS and NBC and such suitors as Viacom (new owner of Paramount Pictures), Time Warner (Warner Bros.), Disney, Ted Turner, and former Hollywood mogul Barry Diller. Meanwhile, both Paramount and Warner had started enlisting unaffiliated stations for new networks of their own, hoping to fill the distribution gaps with cable channels. Few in the industry doubted that one way or another several of the Hollywood majors would, like 20th Century–Fox, become network operators if only to ensure distribution for what they produce.

A network-studio marriage could serve to improve the economic system that dates to earlier and easier times, and help bring program costs under control. Programming represents some 70 percent of a network's overhead, and costs rise year by year because of the heated four-network competition and the mania for hits. Perhaps the networks need to be able to contend with new technologies such as DBS, wireless cable, five-hundred-channel cable systems, Multimedia, CD-ROM, and ultimately the telecomputer. Momentous changes in television could result from the FCC's decision in 1992 to allow local telephone companies to offer video series on their fiber-optic installations with virtually limitless capacity for voice, data, and video signals. The phone companies stand to become fearsome competitors to cable because they have already wired virtually every household in the nation. Clearly, their entry will be felt by broadcast television as well.

The daunting task for the federal government is once again to create a level playing field on which all the new technologies may compete for the consumer's favor. There is hardly a doubt that the changes to come, whether brought on by technology or policy, will be more rapid and convulsive than at any time since the invention of television. Employment is bound to follow the ebb and flow of each of the emerging industries and probably will not be stabilized until there is a shakeout, if indeed there can ever be one, given that the reinvention of television has only just begun.

CHAPTER THREE

Flexibility and Adaptation in Industrial Relations: The Exceptional Case of the U.S. Media Entertainment Industries

Susan Christopherson

Since the 1950s, there has been a gradual but decisive orientation of labor institutions in the U.S. media industries to the external labor market and to individual contract bargaining. This evolving orientation has had complex consequences for industrial relations in these industries. On the one hand, it reflects an exceptional case of adaptation and flexibility in an industrial relations system. In contrast with other industries faced with the challenges of internationalization of production and markets, labor and management in the media industries have been able to negotiate their way to a system that responds to the ways products and profits are produced in an international industry.

On the other hand, adaptation has had its costs, particularly a lack of cohesion among segments of the labor force and bargaining organizations. The ability to take positions requiring cross-occupational solidarity has become problematic, in part, because internationalization led to different labor market conditions for various segments of the workforce. At the same time, with changes in the way media products are produced, both the functional roles and substantive identities of important segments of the workforce have been altered, blurring the boundaries between occupations and between labor and management. This has complicated the negotiation process but has also created opportunities for coordination that do not exist in other industries.

In conjunction with the redefinition of interest and collective identity, distinctly different objectives have emerged both among and within unions and between the organized and unorganized workforce. In the contemporary media entertainment industries, labor strife is as likely to involve internecine battles among segments of labor as actions against management. This differentiation of interests has not meant that union influence has lessened. Unions remain central to industry functioning, maintaining a skilled labor force in an industry characterized by a high level of uncertainty and providing critical services to both management and labor.

To illuminate how the industrial relations system in the media industries has evolved, I examine some critical points at which the organization of production changed and how labor institutions responded. Context is very important to this story. The paths of firms and the associated adaptations of industrial relations institutions must be understood in the context of U.S. regulation of capital markets and employment contracts. The effects of this regulatory context are manifested in the relationships among finance, production, and distribution in these industries, in the way in which continued oligopoly has been combined with different forms of production organization.

Continued Oligopoly and Changing Production Organization

Although the motion picture and television industries have been characterized by different production regimes over time, we can trace a development path showing both continuity and change in the ways in which financing, production, and distribution are carried out. Continuity is manifested in the continuous oligopolistic control of distribution by the seven major film studios and the three major television networks. For example, the seven majors (Paramount, MGM/UA, Warner Brothers, 20th Century–Fox, Universal Studios, and Columbia Pictures and, more recently, Disney) who dominate film distribution in the United States control 85 percent of the domestic box office and account for two-thirds of the $7 billion market for videocassette purchase and rental.

The entertainment media industries have combined continued oligopolistic control of distribution with production organization that has varied between almost complete vertical integration in the classic era of the "studio system" to one in which a substantial portion of production was carried out "on the market" (Gomery, 1986; Christopherson and Storper, 1986; Storper and Christopherson, 1987). The contemporary situation lies somewhere between a vertically integrated and vertically disintegrated structure, combining tight control by the distribution firms over what is produced and how it is produced with substantial subcontracted production.

The reasons behind continued oligopoly in these industries have been well documented. They can be traced to the situation of the industry in the U.S. political economy and the history of industry finance (Wasko, 1981). The contemporary media entertainment industries are global but the United States (and within it Los Angeles and New York) retains the central functions of financing and innovation. The very character of the industry is a function of its development within the United States. This is widely recognized with respect to the nature of the product, a mass entertainment product, but U.S. dominance has also shaped firm financing and investment patterns. From its beginning in the 1920s, the oligopolistic structure of the industry has been reinforced by the nature and sources of investment capital. Banks, the major source of continuous financing, initially invested in the major studios because of their assets, particularly in real estate. Bank financing supported internationalization and diversification by the major studios and technical innovations, such as sound in the 1920s which increased the studios' competitive advantages. Bank financing also helped the major studios weather unpredictable markets in the 1950s by enabling diversification across product and geographic markets (Wasko, 1981). Although the power of banks waned in the 1970s as the industry became further internationalized and alternative sources of capital became available, the oligopolistic structure was largely fixed.

The continuous financial relationship between big banks and major firms allowed the firms to achieve economies of scale in distribution by financing the expansion and organization of their markets. Major motion picture firms maintained control of markets, even as they diversified, through discriminatory pricing—charging patrons different prices to see the same film depending on where (in which distribution media) and when it is seen. Since the major studios control the first-run market, they create a barrier to entry in the other media through differential pricing of films in these ancillary markets (Gomery, 1984). One of the strongest examples of the effect of this system is the limited foreign film distribution in the U.S. market. Although they appeal to a substantial segment of the market, films produced outside the United States rarely enter the market through the major distribution networks. So, for example, less than three percent of the films shown in the United States each year are from foreign producers. And, in the *potentially* more open video market, only eight percent of the thirty-five thousand video rental outlets carry foreign films. There is simply not enough profit for the majors in distributing foreign films and since the major firms overwhelmingly dominate national distribution networks, foreign films have little access to the U.S. market.[1]

At the level of product financing, entertainment media production is a risky business with a long-term profit cycle. In addition to controlling markets, the major studios function as stable risk-absorbing institutions to protect capital investments in a highly competitive U.S. capital market (Wasko, 1981). The "sunk capital" in both distribution and finance in major distributors is one of the reasons why potential investors have been more interested in acquiring existing firms than in trying to establish new distribution firms.

In addition to highly competitive capital markets, regulation responsive to firm interests has played a role in the continued oligopolistic character of the industry in the United States. Regulation that would prohibit "collusion" among firms domestically allows collusion when it is aimed at foreign markets. In the motion picture industry, a legal cartel, the American Motion Picture Export Association, regulates the flow of product exports and limits competition among the major distributors, effectively shaping the international market along domestic lines.[2] The tacit approval of collusion to reg-

---

[1] These films are locally distributed in media entertainment production centers such as New York and Los Angeles as much for their value as creative production inputs as for their entertainment value.

[2] The separation of the two major forms of media production, television and motion pictures, was a consequence of regulation not economics. This is beginning to change under new financial syndication rules and there is an expectation of mergers between the two industries.

ulate prices and control the flow of product in the international market works to reinforce the market power of the existing distribution organizations. The practices of the AMPEA are not unlike the practices of Japanese "combines" in other sectors.

Within a clearly oligopolistic structure, different forms of production organization have arisen over time, ranging from the vertically integrated structure of the "golden age" of Hollywood motion picture production in the 1930s to the disintegrated production organization of film production in the late 1970s. Throughout the history of production, however, the large oligopolistic firm has been the pivotal feature of the industrial structure. In addition to the financial and regulatory conditions favoring oligopoly, the dominance of a few large firms is a consequence of two other interrelated factors: (1) the continuous need for innovation in these industries; and (2) the absence of other innovation-sheltering institutions, such as state-supported broadcasting, in the United States. Innovation may not occur in the networks and major studios but they provide a conduit for capital and a continuous and stable market for innovative producers.[3]

The organizational form of the relationship between distribution and production functions has changed over time in conjunction with the distributors' control of end markets and the relative profits to be made from distribution and production. To the extent that the major studios and networks owned and controlled end markets, whether station affiliates or exhibition houses, they have tended to integrate production functions. To the extent that end markets were not owned and controlled by distributors, they have tended to turn to the market to organize the production process, redistributing risk to the producers.

In the television industry, a vertically integrated structure (distribution companies carrying out production in-house) has persisted over time because of the need to supply affiliate stations with programming. This arrangement began to break down slowly in the 1970s with an increase in the number of independent broadcasting

---

[3] Other types of institutions, such as state broadcasting, that could support the continuous innovation required in these industries and absorb the risks inherent in media production have never existed in the United States. It is possible to speculate that they never developed here because of the early success of the mass market-oriented entertainment industry.

stations and with cable television. In the motion picture industry, on the other hand, there have been major fluctuations over time in how production is organized. A vertically integrated structure prevailed after the industry was fully established in the 1930s because the major distribution companies owned exhibition houses and needed to provide a flow of product. With the Paramount decision in 1948 (*U.S. v. Paramount*, 334 U.S. 131), prohibiting ownership of exhibition houses by the major studios, and with the advent of television, motion picture industry production began to disintegrate. Major functions moved to the market. Directors and stars, for example, were released from long-term contracts and hired project by project or on a "package" series basis. With the dismantling of studio production facilities and the subsequent development of a subcontracted production system organized by independent producers, risk was redistributed downward to production companies. Given the fluidity and unpredictability of the market for films, the major studios were able to benefit from the continuous innovation in the system without paying up front for product development or even, in many cases, for production costs.

The return to a more integrated distribution-production system or "virtual integration" in the late 1980s reflects firm strategies in response to changes in the ownership of end markets and also to the proliferation of end markets, which has made production more profitable relative to distribution. Despite the reemergence of market conditions which broadly resemble those of the 1930s (in the sense that distribution firms can own end markets), however, production organization is not returning to its 1930s form, predominantly in-house production. Instead, reintegration begins with and uses the flexible subcontracted network system of the 1970s.

What this story suggests is that rather than being evidenced by distinct divides between one form of production and another, changes in production patterns are more effectively described in terms of a production path (Dosi et al., 1988; Nelson and Winter, 1982; Storper, 1991). Although there are periods that can clearly be distinguished from one another—such as the golden age of the studio system and the disintegrated production organization that appears to have reached an apex in the late 1970s—there is also continuity and development. For example, the major firms that control distribution in the 1990s rely on subcontracted production, albeit under contracts or with equity investment, rather than on in-house production. This reliance can be traced to the vertical disintegration of the industry from the 1950s onward and the institutional and organizational adaptations spawned by that disintegrative process, including those in industrial relations.

Changing Firm Strategies and Production Organization

In the 1950s, when an assured film entertainment market was lost because of antitrust decisions and with the advent of television, production was shifted gradually outside the studios to independent production companies. The studios maintained the roles of production finance and distribution but the actual making of films was carried out largely by networks composed of production companies and their subcontractors (Christopherson and Storper, 1986; Storper and Christopherson, 1987). A similar trend occurred in television production with the financial syndication rules and consent decrees restricting the amount of network-produced television in the 1970s. More production was opened to independent production companies, which increased in number and profitability during this period. These two processes overlapped in the 1970s with independent production companies moving across industry boundaries and producing for both media.

This synergistic vertically disintegrated production organization produced a high level of innovation in television and motion pictures. The distributors, both networks and motion picture distributors, could pick and choose among a range of projects proposed to them without making financial commitments for product development. The relationship between distributor and producer during that period was typified by the "negative pick-up" or postproduction purchase of a film by a major distributor. In the motion picture industry, the major studios had the power of the purse but because of the number and variety of production organizations, they had to bid for talent along with independent producers.

In television, independent producers, such as Desilu, Lorimar, and

MTM Entertainment, profited from the regulatory restrictions on network production. The risks associated with innovation in television were shared among producers and distributors. Because regulations prohibited them from producing their own programming, the networks were forced into cooperative ventures with independent producers in order to fill prime time television slots. Although distributors had immense power because of their control of the market in both the motion picture and television industries, they also were dependent on independent producers to produce a continuous flow of ideas and to organize the production process. Producers, in turn, reduced their own risks in this highly competitive product market by organizing production around a network of subcontracting production companies which became increasingly specialized and provided services to both television and motion picture producers, to independent producers as well as to the majors and networks.

The vertically disintegrated, flexibly specialized production organization which dominated the 1970s had some major drawbacks for the distributors. First, television networks could not realize the extensive profits from the burgeoning alternative end markets although they were competing with these markets for advertising revenues. Second, vertically disintegrated production contributed to escalating production costs and, thus, to the price distributors had to pay for films or television programs. Over the 1970s television production costs rose 14.4 percent per year, tripling over the decade (Vogel, 1986). Spiraling costs were the consequence of the bargaining power of the independents and also resulted from the extensive transactions required to put productions together using production inputs with competing demands and contractual commitments. Finally, vertically disintegrated production also contributed to uncertain production schedules and distribution schedules since distributors had only indirect and limited control over the production process.

The vertically disintegrated network system of production prevailed despite its costs because it maximized innovation and minimized risk under highly uncertain market conditions. Both the multiplication of end markets and the changing regulatory environment have altered the risk factors associated with investment in production. These two developments are reshaping the motion picture and television industries.

Forces for Change: Market Proliferation and Regulation

Although it is difficult to sort out the exact course of events that has led to new corporate strategies and altered the way today's media products are produced and distributed, two changes in the competitive environment appear to be particularly significant. The first is the multiplication of end markets. The second is a dramatic change in the regulatory environment in western Europe and in the United States.

New Distribution Technology and Market Multiplication

With the reorganization of the world market for consumer products in the late 1960s and 1970s, new ways of marketing and distributing goods and services emerged. What might be considered a series of experiments took place through which management strategies and new technology were applied to distribution with the aim of improving quality (marketability) and creating, redefining, and capturing new markets. While technology has changed the production process (for example, combining video and film equipment), the most significant technological innovations are those altering the modes and range of distribution. The consumer has a broader range of choices in purchasing entertainment products (theater, videocassettes, cable, pay-per-view television, commercial television). At the same time there has been little diversification in the types of products available. As has already been noted, this is because the costs of distributing a product worldwide are so high and because mass entertainment products garner higher profits than products aimed at specialized market segments. Despite the proliferation of types of end markets, the major distributors of mass entertainment products have been in an almost unassailable position because they finance and distribute the products that enter these end markets.

So, while the proliferation of end markets in cable, video, and independent television stations presents a potential for increased competition, that potential is not realized. A case in point is the cable industry. What has driven the development of the cable industry in the United States is a dual revenue stream from advertising and subscriber fees. Although there are many proposed cable channels for specialized audiences (such as Celticvision, a channel aimed at Irish Americans), the channel company cannot obtain sufficient investment capital to get off the ground. The successful channels, such as ESPN and MTV, are supported by advertising or, in the case of HBO and Showtime, by subscriber revenues. New networks find it difficult to get local cable systems to carry them because they might compete with the major revenue producers for the cable companies. The result in most media markets (not New York or Los Angeles) is a selection of similar programming aimed at very broadly defined niche markets (Lippman, 1991).

The second major force for change, the deepening of the international market, is demonstrated by the size of U.S. exports in film and television, which increased dramatically in the 1980s. Sales of television programming to foreign broadcasters in 1988 were $1.3 billion, an increase of 30 percent from 1987. Almost all this increase is attributable to expansion of the European market. The export revenues of American film distribution companies increased from $800 million in 1985 to $1.05 billion in 1987 (Stevenson, 1989b; Economist, 1989). And the number of television stations in western Europe increased from 38 in 1980 to 125 in 1990.

The current drive to expand the trade for commercial entertainment products in foreign markets has been stimulated at least in part by a weakening and fragmentation in the U.S. mass market. The major American television networks have been affected by a decline in viewership, weak demand for reruns of old programs, and a downscaling of the viewing audience. Rather than modifying what they produce, however, the major distributing firms have chosen to expand the market for the mass entertainment product that is their stock-in-trade. They fully expect the U.S. market to become a secondary source of revenue in the mass entertainment market (Stevenson, 1989b).

Regulatory revisions have also significantly altered the media market within the United States. The two most important of these are: (1) a federal decision not to enforce the antitrust provisions (the Paramount decision, 1948) which have prevented production and distribution firms from owning distribution outlets (video chains, television stations, and movie theaters); and (2) relaxation of Federal

Communications Commission rules governing financial interest and syndication.

One premise behind the lack of enforcement of the Paramount decision is the proliferation of end markets. In the 1930s and 1940s, the major studios inhibited competition through ownership of the only end market—theaters. They were sued under antitrust provisions by independent theater owners who did not have the same access to product as did the studio-owned chains. Although the independent theater owners won their suit, the subsequent decline in production by the studios was even more damaging to their economic interests. In the recent situation, there has been an expansion in the number and type of end markets, appearing to increase competition (and certainly undermining the premise of the Paramount decision, which was restricted to theater ownership). The studio-distributors can once again assure a market for their products through ownership of one or more of these end markets.

In effect, the entertainment industries are being allowed to own the means of distribution for the first time in forty years. Since 1985, about 10 percent of the 22,500 exhibition screens in the United States have been bought directly or are controlled by the corporate parents of Warner, Universal, and Columbia (Farhi, 1989). And, in 1990, four of the seven major film studios owned independent television stations. These outlets provide the distributors with an assured market for any product they produce.

The financial syndication rules, adopted in 1970 by the Federal Communications Commission, restricted the ability of television networks to produce and syndicate programming. The new rules, adopted in April 1993 by the Federal Communications Commission (after a court battle) allow the networks to produce up to 40 percent of their prime time schedules, to buy a financial interest in outside programming, and to engage in foreign syndication without any restrictions (Kolbert, 1993).[4]

Both the decision not to enforce *Paramount* and the potential relaxation of financial syndication rules are encouraging horizontal and vertical integration in the television and motion picture industries.

[4] As of 1993, the ability of the networks to operate under these new rules is still restricted by a consent decree arising from a Justice Department suit in 1980 accusing the networks of monopolistic practices.

Even before the fin-syn rules were relaxed in April 1993, independent producers (not dependent on the major studios or television networks for financing) increasingly found themselves squeezed out as suppliers of prime time television programs to the major networks. In 1990 only about 14 percent of prime time television programming on the major networks was produced by independent production companies, as compared with 57 percent in 1988. The major motion picture production studios, in contrast, accounted for 70 percent of prime time programming. Analysts compare the situation in the 1990s with that in the 1950s when the major studios made their first big move into television production, bidding up production costs and buying out smaller program suppliers, such as Desilu. This period of integration ended because of FCC regulatory restrictions which gave networks more control over programming and gave independent producers the right to syndicate their own programs. This led to expansion in the number of independent producers in the 1970s and to extensive subcontracting networks to put together productions.

The new period of integration was initiated by the refusal of the networks to pay production costs because of declining advertising revenues flowing to television in the 1980s. More recently, deregulation has encouraged more in-house production by television networks and closer integration with the Hollywood major studio production facilities. Interestingly, critics of this integration process are less concerned about the loss of competition in the industry than they are about the loss of innovative capacity (Kolbert, 1993).

According to a major media analyst, "What entertainment companies want today is to have maximum domination over their end markets. If they produce films, they want to own the TV stations, theaters and pay TV services that carry them." Media experts predict that four or five program distributors will dominate the international market for broadcasting entertainment products by the end of the 1990s.

Internationalization

In response to the opportunities presented by the expanded market, there has been a deepening of the international character of U.S. motion picture and television production and distribution firms through mergers, acquisitions, and joint ventures. The major media distributing firms, especially in film, have always been dependent on international exports but now they have become international in their ownership as well as in their trade patterns. And international investment provides even more capital to the largest firms.

The major firms have the capital and management capabilities to test large numbers of entertainment products in the world's biggest single market, the United States. And, because these firms are located in the largest market, they have been able to recoup production costs domestically and then sell copies of films and television programs outside that market at prices one-tenth of original production cost. Foreign revenue for U.S.-headquartered distribution firms rose 34 percent to $2,344 billion between 1985 and 1987. Television exports are the fastest-growing portion of this trade, growing 53 percent and $480 million during this two-year period (Delugach, 1988). An example of the scale of profit increase is that by MCA Inc., parent company for Universal Pictures and a distributor of both films and television programs, some of which it also produces. MCA's television revenue from distribution outside the United States increased by 50 percent from 1986 to 1987 to $135 million.

The multiplication of end markets, particularly in television and cable, and the ability to own the means of distribution and to profit from syndication have had two effects. First, the complexity of distribution and the risks associated with deriving profits from placing products in multiple end markets have increased. Second, the profits to be derived from production have increased while the risks have decreased. As a consequence, the television networks and major studios are making major investments in production capacity either directly or through acquisitions. At the same time, the way that production is being carried out is also changing with significant implications for industrial relations in these industries.

The Effects of Increased Concentration on Production Organization

As the motion picture and television industries become more financially concentrated, a new production system is emerging. The vertically disintegrated production systems organized around indepen-

dent producers as well as the majors and studios are being dismantled. The middle range of independent production organizations is
either being acquired by the distributing firms or failing.[5] And the
highly complex set of subcontracting firms that could exist in the
high-production-cost environment is also being rationalized.

Despite the ownership of end markets by the distributors and their
need for production capacity, these industries are not moving back
to a classically organized vertically integrated production system such
as that which characterized the film industry in the 1930s. Instead, as
the evolutionary models of industrial development would suggest,
the new production system has developed out of the flexibly specialized production organization that characterized the industry until
the early to mid-1980s. For example, many of the input suppliers in
the vertically disintegrated production systems served both television
and motion picture industries. This integration at the bottom of the
production hierarchy broke down barriers between the two industries, allowing production firms to draw on a large and various pool
of talent and subcontractors. The historical development of industry
integration at the level of production as well as finance has contributed to the ability of the major distributors in film and television
to merge into mega–media entertainment firms.

A new set of relationships is developing between the remaining
producers, who often operate as individuals rather than through their
own firms, and the major production and distribution firms in television and motion pictures. The close contractural relationship
between producers and distributors can be contrasted with the
"arms-length" relationship between distributor/financer and producer in the vertically disintegrated system, where the producer
assumed more of the risks associated with production but also
retained more control over the production process, and the producer redistributed risk and maintained the flexibility to produce different products by utilizing a set of subcontracting firms and individuals to produce the motion picture or television program. The
necessity for this flexibility remains but is now balanced by greater
incentives to control production cost and "quality" (as defined in

[5] Examples include De Laurentis Entertainment Group, Cannon Films, and Lorimar Telepictures. As has already been described, this acquisition process is international.

media industry terms, that is, marketability). This is being achieved through the introduction of mechanisms to reduce the distance between producer and distributor and between the producer and the firms that provide production inputs. Among these mechanisms are longer term contracts with subcontractors. This is a more integrated production-distribution system but one which remains flexible with respect to the need to produce differentiated entertainment products.

A model for the emerging corporate structure and production organization is the Disney Corporation, which owns its own cable network, the Disney Channel, and has begun to acquire independent stations, including one in Los Angeles. Disney has two production subsidiaries, Touchstone and Hollywood Pictures, each of which is expected to produce about twelve films per year. These two units have their own production, legal, business affairs, and story departments but share Disney's marketing and distribution. In addition, Disney will continue to make animated or action pictures for children under its own label.

In contrast with past practices, however, films produced by these companies will be completely financed by Disney through a limited partnership that raised $400 million and is expected to raise another $200 million. In some cases a letter from Disney agreeing to distribute will allow producers developing projects for the production units to obtain additional financing. Disney, through its production units, will participate in every aspect of the production process from financing to distribution. The production units will remain legally separate entities, distanced from the Disney Corporation and the Disney name. This distance is physically represented by their separate office locations within the Los Angeles region.

Another example of the emerging integrated distribution and production structure is the relationship between Imagine, an "independent" production company, and MCA's Universal Pictures and Television Distribution Unit. Whereas the producer-owners of Imagine once presented motion picture ideas to studios in return for assurances of future distribution, Imagine now has direct MCA investment. Nineteen percent of Imagine's stock is owned by MCA. MCA also pays all the costs for Imagine's productions. Within this new "captured" production house, the role of the producer-owners has changed. During the era of the negative pick-up, they hired themselves out as directors and producers to make money to finance their own film projects. Now they are executive intermediaries between MCA and the directors and subcontractors with whom they subcontract.

In television, the complexities of the new corporate arrangements are exemplified by NBC's decision to distribute a program produced by a company owned and operated by its rival distributor, ABC. In this case we see the networks experimenting with new ways of increasing production capacity through strategic alliances. The demand for programming and the profits to be obtained through syndication are driving the broadcasting firms to increase production capabilities to produce more programs than they can distribute through their own network. This new structure is being dubbed a "network studio system."

As profits from broadcast revenues have decreased and profits to be made via program syndication have grown, broadcast functions have become increasingly distanced from program production units and have diminished in importance.[6] A marginally successful situation comedy can make as much as $80 million in syndication (Carter, 1989a). Television networks want to maintain control of their existing markets but also want to increase their ability to produce programming for other markets. And the mission of the production company is quite different from that of the broadcast network. This privileging of production over distribution will presumably lead to different managerial strategies among the units and increase the likelihood of mergers with motion picture studios which have substantial production capacities.

The form of vertical integration now emerging in media industries might be dubbed "virtual integration" to distinguish it from the classic models of integration, which imply ownership of production functions, and from the more disintegrated firm network production systems of the 1970s. Rather than owning the facilities and employing the personnel to produce entertainment products, the major film distributors are integrating largely by contract and investment. Although distributors such as Disney or Universal pay production costs and control personnel, budgets, and shooting schedules as well as distributing the film, their productions are carried out by a legally but not economically separate firm. This firm, in turn, may sub-

---

[6] An example of the changing orientation of the broadcast networks is their decreasing interest in news broadcasts even when, as was the case during the Gulf War in 1991, they attract substantial audiences.

contract with other firms to produce film or television products or provide production inputs.

In television, the networks have retained in-house production capabilities which, until quite recently, have served their own broadcast market. This too is changing as production for other markets becomes more important. Production units are being transformed into a managerially separate source of profits. As the market for entertainment media products has broadened beyond the major networks, they are positioning themselves to produce for markets other than their own. In this instance, too, much of the new production will be carried out by contract with separate firms rather than taking place within the firm that owns the broadcasting network. The major media firms are thus moving toward contractual integration from two vastly different points—the television networks from a conventional vertically integrated corporate structure and the major studios from the more vertically disintegrated structure that has characterized the industry since the 1960s.

The present day character of vertical integration has some quite distinctive features but is, in many respects, a hybrid form emerging out of more control of end markets on the one hand and, on the other, the potential for profit expansion related to production for multiple end markets. It is also built on the previous era's decisions to externalize functions and utilize the market to organize production. These adaptations included the restructuring of labor institutions and industrial relations. The labor institutions that exist today are not the same ones that existed in the 1930s. Unions serve a membership with different individual and collective interests. And, in the interim, some functions critical to labor-management bargaining have been moved out of the firm and to the external market, enabling more flexibility in the use of the workforce and, over time, creating different roles for unions. It is these flexibly adapted industrial relations institutions that are affected by emerging corporate strategies in response to new market conditions.

Adaptations to the Loosening of Employment Ties

From the 1950s onward, vertical disintegration of the motion picture industry and the organization of production on the market produced a set of concommittant changes in the relationship between workers and firms. The loosening of ties between the workforce and the major firms also occurred in television but more slowly and less evenly than in motion pictures. The networks continued to make a large portion of their programs in-house and to use cost-efficient series formats. Consequently, they needed a stable workforce under long-term employment contracts. In some types of programming, subcontracting to independent producers did increase the use of flexible labor inputs but in many cases, labor contracts tended to be long term because of the series nature of television programming.[7] In the motion picture industry, the transformation was much more complete with, by the 1970s, the majority of production activities being organized through the subcontracting market rather than within the firm.

As the major studios shed labor and subcontracted production, the institutionalized mechanisms that maintained a skilled workforce were jeopardized. These included access to health and pension benefits, skill acquisition tied to apprenticeships in firms, and certification of experience and skill. In response, unions created and negotiated new institutions which made it possible for these critical functions to be carried on outside the firm and which indirectly enabled the flexible use of labor inputs. These institutional adaptations included the development of a roster system to maintain seniority lines and to certify skill and experience; a health and pension benefit system independent of any particular employer; and a system of supplementary payments, connected to the profit life of the product. These "residual" payments not only established claims to compensation for profits made in ancillary markets but also, very significantly, established a connection between the work to make an entertainment product and the property rights in that product.

The roster system, established in the 1950s, was of critical importance to the development of a form of production organization which used labor inputs flexibly but still required signaling devices to ensure skill and experience. Under the roster system, the major studios and independent producers sign contracts with the craft unions, whose members are placed on rosters according the amount of

---

[7] One could speculate that the fixed costs associated with network programming tended to encourage the development and persistence of the series format.

seniority they have obtained in the industry rather than in a single firm. The major studios supported the development of the roster system in the 1950s because it served as a certification and screening device, thus reducing labor market uncertainty while allowing firms to shed overhead. The craft unions supported the roster system because it allowed them to maintain control of the labor supply and of seniority rights. Another flexibility-driven institution, the Motion Picture Health and Welfare Fund, was also set up in the 1950s by the unions in response to a need to provide benefits to workers hired on limited-duration contracts. The system requires employers to pay an amount equal to 12.5 percent of total wages into a health and pension benefits fund admininstered by the unions for each worker under union contract. This system provided the unions with a new raison d'être in the increasingly contractualized industry. It also made individualized employment contracts easier to accomplish. These two successful adaptations to the labor-shedding practices of the large firms worked because they served the interests of the membership of existing labor organizations as well as being in the interest of management. They also shaped the long-term paths of these industries—the choices available to firms as market conditions changed—by making it possible to maintain and reproduce a skilled and specialized labor force without long-term employment contracts. In the tradition of American industrial relations, these adaptations were local and industry specific. They represented the first phase of the contemporary fragmentation of industrial relations that is emerging from sectoral strategies.

This first period of fragmentation, however disruptive, took place against the background of relative stability in occupational identities and union identities. The ability of the unions to respond collectively to the challenges posed by vertical disintegration was assisted by their representation of still clearly definable occupational groups. There was little confusion about who was labor and who was management (Prindle, 1988).

As the motion picture and eventually television industries carried out more production on the market, however, a set of broader developments occurred which changed the rules of the game for both labor and management and affected the viability of the flexible yet cohesive institutions that had evolved in response to vertical disintegration. These developments gradually transformed the nature of the work process and, as will be described, the culture of these industries. Among these developments were technological changes which made the production processes in television and film more similar to each other, and which allowed much production to take place outside the studio facility. In Los Angeles, this meant that the city became, in effect, the "backlot" for productions of all kinds (Christopherson and Storper, 1986). A second important change grew out of the entrepreneurial character of production in a vertically disintegrated industry. Possibly the most important of the developments to occur in conjunction with the vertical disintegration of production, however, was a dramatic expansion in the size of the labor force. This expansion in labor supply was related to the ability to obtain necessary production skills outside the union apprenticeship system or the firm and to the relative ease of entry into the production side of these industries.

The Transformation of Labor Force Size, Skills, and Boundaries

By the mid-1970s, what had been a relatively small labor force in motion pictures and allied services began to expand dramatically. While output in 1982 was 63.9 percent of total output in 1958, employment was 237.5 percent of the 1958 total. As Gray and Seeber point out earlier in this volume, there was differential growth in union membership during this period, with the talent guilds showing explosive growth while the membership in below-the-line craft unions remained stable or even showed a decline. Between the early 1970s and the mid-1980s, the Writers Guild grew from 800 to 6,000 members and the Screen Actors Guild from 13,000 to 54,000 members (Christopherson and Storper, 1989; Writer's Guild of America, 1989). The membership ranks of talent guilds continued to grow in the late 1980s as exemplified by the Writers Guild membership which grew about 7 percent per year (Writers Guild, 1989).

The composition of the workforce and union membership also altered beginning in the mid-1970s. Since talent guilds are inclusive (allowing anyone practicing the occupation to join), their membership statistics are quite good indicators of employment trends in these occupations. Screen and television writing, as is the case with all but a few occupations in the entertainment media, is dominated by white men. Beginning in the late 1970s, however, the gender composition of the occupation began to change. Women accounted for approximately a fourth of the newly admitted members to the Writers Guild each year. In addition there was a small but perceptible increase in the percentage of minority members of this guild. Although minorities constituted only between 2 percent and 3 percent of total membership between 1982 and 1988, and women members increased from 18.8 percent to 21.5 percent from 1982 to 1988, a relatively higher percentage of minority and women members were admitted to guild membership during this period of rapid expansion in total membership. The spurt in minority and female representation began in the early 1970s, coincident with the vertical disintegration of the media entertainment industries, and leveled off in the late 1980s (Writers Guild of America, 1989, page 96, table 1). Although more female writers were employed at the end of the 1980s, the earnings gap between female and male writers had considerably widened. In 1982, women writers earned 73 cents for each dollar earned by white males; by 1987, women were earning just 63 cents for each dollar earned by white males (Writers Guild of America, 1989).

These figures from a Writers Guild study are suggestive of trends in the industry toward labor force expansion and the changing composition of the talent workforce beginning in the 1970s. The talent workforce became more heterogeneous with respect to gender and (to a much lesser extent) race and access to work and property rights. For example, a split emerged between "writer-producers"—with entrepreneurial skills and property rights in the film or tape product—and a vastly increased pool of writers with dramatically varying access to work. This heterogeneity is contained within the talent guilds, leading to serious differences between segments of the workforce whose primary interest is access to work and those whose interests focus on property rights in the form of residual payments.

In contrast with the talent workforce, the below-the-line workforce remained overwhelmingly dominated by white males. While the labor force expanded, union membership remained static. The workforce became more heterogeneous but the major differentiation was between the organized and unorganized segments of the workforce. The density of craft union membership fell dramatically in the

1970s—during a period when profits in these industries were rising—and the number of nonunion productions rose.

Despite the apparent decline in collective bargaining power for all people employed in craft occupations, there were increases in individual bargaining power within the craft union membership. A small but significant portion of the unionized craft workforce, particularly in high prestige occupations, such as cinematography, was able to use individual contract bargaining to obtain property rights and more lucrative employment contracts. Thus, two different patterns of increasing heterogeneity emerged, one of heterogeneity within the occupational unions, and the other between an organized and unorganized workforce.

One of the keys to this differential development was a significant change in the way that skills were acquired in the industry and in the nature of skills required. In the studio system skills were acquired through apprenticeships and in the firm. In the classic vertically integrated firm, whether a movie studio in the 1940s or television network in the 1960s, "craft" and "talent" were hired under long-term contracts and learned occupational skills on the job. This included a form of apprenticeship for stars—the "starlet."

For craft workers, there was a deep division of labor with individuals apprenticed to occupations with particular tasks and using designated equipment with fixed technology, such as lighting equipment. The association of skill with equipment or materials was very significant since original jurisdictional disputes among the craft unions were settled by assigning workers to unions according to the equipment and materials they used.

The vertical disintegration of the film industry altered the skill acquisition process in a variety of ways. Because workers were hired on fixed time or project contracts rather than employed continuously, the craft apprenticeship process was extended dramatically. To accumulate sufficient hours for certification as a grip or script superviser, union apprentices had to spend years working on intermittant productions. Although the continued control of skill acquisition imposed hardships and frustration on apprentices, it worked to the advantage of the craft unions, which were able to control the labor supply and bargaining power. Eventually, however, the frustrations of potential industry entrants, the disgruntlement of employers over labor supply conditions, and the introduction of new production technology all encouraged the development of initial training programs outside the union apprenticeship. Film and television schools have now become the primary providers of skills in these industries in both craft and talent fields (writing, directing). Anyone with the proper educational credentials and willing to invest in the fees could apply to receive training at the University of California at Los Angeles or at the University of Southern California.

As portions of the workforce became more heterogeneous and skill acquisition occurred outside the context of union apprenticeships and outside firms with a deep division of labor and clear hierarchies, the culture of production in the industry began to change. Three features of this new culture are especially noteworthy: (1) the breakdown of clear occupational identities and of the boundaries between management and labor; (2) the emergence of collaborative, entrepreneurial production processes; and (3) increasing proprietary attachment to skills and to the entertainment products (Kleingartner and Paul, 1992). The new culture also broke down older forms of solidarity and produced contradictory interests within the workforce and even within occupations.

Entrepreneurial Culture and Bargaining

With the movement of initial skill acquisition outside the large firm and union setting, the process of becoming a filmmaker was constructed in new ways. The historical social division of labor, between craft and talent, manager and worker, was undermined and new divisions, such as those between entrepreneur–property holders and wage workers, were constructed. This transformation created new tensions between individual skills and collective identities.

To the extent, for example, that much learning took place in a series of projects with different crews and production conditions, the sense of owning skills that were individual rather than social, the expression of a particular craft, was heightened. Recognition for the use of skills came in owning "a piece of the action" or property rights in the product being developed rather than only in the form of wages.

At the same time that craft solidarity (in terms of identity) was being broken down, new ways of working were creating different work alliances and identities. Collaborative work among groups of students (the typical mode in film schools) emphasized ensemble production methods over a division of labor and increased interest in the success of the product rather than solely in individual craft inputs (makeup, set design, costume). This sense was heightened by access to new technology which crossed traditional craft boundaries and by increasingly sophisticated training in the economics of entertainment production. Out of these experiences came collaborative, entrepreneurial tape- and filmmakers rather than craft or talent workers.[8]

In industries increasingly made up of "owners" of skills and "properties" (films, tapes, and books), craft work in some fields, such as cinematography, began to resemble above-the-line work. Exemplifying this trend, highly skilled craft workers began to hire agents to manage their careers. In addition, more filmmakers began to exercise supervisory or managerial skills, thus further blurring the lines between management and labor.

The blurring of labor, supervisory, and management roles raised serious problems for the kind of traditional unionism that characterizes the media craft unions. According to Kochan, Katz, and McKersie, "One of the basic principles of the New Deal collective bargaining model was that management manages and workers and their unions grieve or negotiate the impacts of management decisions through collective bargaining" (Kochan, Katz, and McKersie (1986:179). This particular division was implausible in an industry in which a person is a crew member one day and a supervisor the next.

The fragile balance that characterized industrial relations in these industries—between individual contract and individual recognition and a work process that creates collective identity and common interests—was essentially broken in the era of flexible specialization from the mid-1970s through the mid-1980s. What has emerged is a configuration in which the interests of segments of the labor force are as distinct from one another as is that of labor from its employers.

---

[8] In some interesting ways—ensemble production, small production firms, greater opportunities for women directors and producers—the film industry of the 1970s resembled that in the 1920s before production was concentrated and rationalized in the major studios.

These conflicting interests have been manifested in the origins and outcomes of recent industrial relations disputes. In the 1985 Writers Guild strike the new arrivals to the labor force forced an end to the strike because they could not sustain a long work stoppage, particularly when the primary benefits would accrue to the established membership. And there is continuous conflict between segments of the workforce with varying bargaining power. In 1986, this erupted into a dispute between the Screen Actors Guild and the Screen Extras Guild because the Screen Actors would not support the Screen Extras' strike against producer demands for major contract concessions. In recent years, however, these differences in interest have been put to tactical use. The Teamsters, whose interests are the conventional ones of wages and work rules, have taken the lead in adversarial tactics, disrupting unorganized sets by noise making. The interests of talent workers in seeing that the product (in which they may have a financial interest) gets made and comes in under budget has caused them to encourage the producer to sign a contract quickly (Bernstein, 1991). One of the ironies of contemporary industrial relations in the film and television industries may be that although there has been a loss of solidarity, there is still room for collective action.

In response to vertical disintegration, unions and employers negotiated the development of new labor institutions and ways of working which provided flexibility to employers and protected union bargaining power. These institutions created on the external market a parallel to the institutions that had been embedded in the relationship between labor organizations and large firms. This resolution of the problems of industrial relations in vertically disintegrated industries came out of the experience and expectations of labor and management as they developed in the studio system and in network television. The solutions reached reflected the historical balance in these industries between respect for craft and property rights and the need to produce products for a mass audience. The craft tradition in media industries, with its nonproletarian attachment to the product and more equal bargaining power between labor and management, made it possible to negotiate changes in the work process and labor institutions that were difficult to achieve in more conventional mass production industries. There are still instances of such cooperation as in the negotiated agreement between selected unions and the Alliance of Motion Picture and Television Producers (AMPTP) to establish a continuous bargaining process to deal with issues as they arise and to avoid work stoppages (Counter, 1992). In this respect industrial relations in the media industries is closer to the best models of flexible adaptation in European countries with a craft tradition than to classic U.S. models (Katz, 1992).

Changes in production organization and industrial relations institutions also took shape in response to the particular regulatory environment in the United States. Adaptations in the media industries were local and industry specific. They were little influenced by nor did they influence strategies in other industries. Their relative idiosyncrasy can be compared with situations in which a national labor movement or national labor laws constrain the prerogatives of firms, and impose a measure of consistency on the responses of industries, firms, and places. From this perspective, the lack of cross-sectoral industrial relations organizations is a primary basis for fragmentation in U.S. industrial relations.

A second level of fragmentation is attributable to heterogeneity of opportunity and interest within the workforce. The flexible institutional innovations designed by the unions of the 1950s worked in an industry in which production was carried out primarily by large firms and occupational identities remained stable—that is, until the early 1970s. They began to come apart with increased vertical disintegration of production in the motion picture industry and television production in the 1970s and into the 1980s. The industrial relations system that had emerged in response to vertical disintegration was undermined by the inability of unions to control the labor supply. This failure was a consequence of: (1) the demand for new skills, both technical and entrepreneurial, outside traditional occupational definitions; (2) the development of alternative training programs outside union control and jurisdiction; and (3) labor market pressure created by large numbers of labor force entrants with skills obtained outside the union context.

Finally, there has been a continual fragmentation of interests among differently positioned segments of the workforce because of the diversification of working conditions; arising from types of employment contracts (union and nonunion); and along the lines of race, gender, and age. The homogeneity that underlay the solidarity of the pre-1970s workforce has been broken and, along with it, particular definitions of collective interest.

The flexible industrial relations institutions that emerged in response to vertical disintegration in film and partially and later in television were corporatist in spirit. They were intended to maintain the bargaining power of union members but not at the expense of employer flexibility. Although they were successful in this endeavor, they were less successful in constructively responding to challenges that emerged in the wake of vertical disintegration. Unions representing particular segments of the workforce developed strategies to protect the interests of their membership, whether residuals from a product's profit stream or security of employment. They dealt only selectively with issues affecting the industry as a whole and requiring more collective thinking and action. These include changes in labor demand, the advent of technology that crosses traditional craft boundaries, and the emergence of an industry "culture" that alters relations between labor and management. If the industrial relations system in the media industries is to remain vital and at the heart of flexible adaptation to changing production conditions, new forms of collaboration must emerge to deal with industrywide problems.

CHAPTER FOUR

The Transformation of Industrial Relations in the Motion Picture and Television Industries: Craft and Production

John Amman

This chapter examines the state of collective bargaining for below-the-line unions in the motion picture and television industries. It gives an overview of the challenges facing these unions through changes in production practices, distribution, technology, corporate management, and the rise of nonunion competition. As with other U.S. industries, labor relations in the motion picture and television industries has been directly influenced by networks (CBS, NBC, and ABC) that once dominated their respective industries but now face competitive pressures from independent producers, cable television, syndicated television, and other forces. Unions which held considerable bargaining power through their members' technical skills and work experience have seen this power erode as nonunion companies have replaced unionized companies in the marketplace and as the major studios and the networks gained greater power at the bargaining table and a willingness to demand concessions.

Of the three major motion picture and broadcast below-the-line unions, the International Alliance of Theatrical and Stage Employees (IATSE) is the largest, representing employees in the motion picture, broadcast, and theater industries. An early AFL affiliate, IATSE has maintained a strong craft orientation with each of its locals representing a separate craft or skill. The National Association of Broadcast Employees and Technicians (NABET) is primarily a broadcast union, although at one time it had two locals (15 and 531) representing film technicians. A CIO affiliate since the early 1950s, NABET has always followed an industrial organizing approach; each of its locals represent a wide spectrum of broadcast employees. The International Brotherhood of Electrical Workers (IBEW), traditionally a craft union and an AFL affiliate, was the first union to represent broadcast engineers and technicians. Although these unions have collective bargaining agreements with a variety of producers, local radio and television stations, cable television, and independent stations, the focus here is on their relations with the major motion picture studios and broadcast networks. A brief description of the historical factors behind current labor relations practices in motion pictures and television leads to an overview of the nature of industrial changes in motion pictures and television, with emphasis on how management and below-the-line unions have responded to these changes, and to discussion of the decline of union bargaining power and the consequences of this new era of collective bargaining for both union and nonunion workers in these industries.

Production and Union Structures in the Motion Picture Industry

In order to understand the relationship between IATSE and the major motion picture studios, it is important to take into consideration the way in which the union itself is structured. IATSE film locals represent members based on both craft and regional jurisdictions. For example, there are three IATSE locals representing camera operators: Local 644 covering the East Coast, Local 666 covering the Midwest and parts of the South, and Local 659 covering the West Coast. Like other film locals, each of the camera locals maintains collective bargaining agreements with employers for work in their specific regional jurisdictions. Depending on the nature of their charter with the IATSE international, many IATSE locals, particularly film locals based on the East Coast, have considerable autonomy and behave, at times, almost like individual unions; many negotiate and maintain separate contracts for their particular crafts and members. Consequently, there is no nationwide contract between IATSE and any film producer.

The origins of these bargaining relationships go back to the studio system of the 1930s and 1940s. At that time five major motion picture studios (Paramount, Metro-Goldwyn-Mayer, Twentieth Century, Warner Brothers, and RKO) dominated film production, distribution, and exhibition in the United States. The same corporations produced the films, distributed them, and owned the theaters where they were exhibited (Gomery, 1986). By controlling the three major segments of the film industry, the studios reduced the risk of films losing money at the box office and minimized competition. Certainly independent film studios existed, but anyone making motion pictures had to deal with the big studios at some point to be financially successful in the industry.

In order to feed their distribution and exhibition entities, the studios required almost uninterrupted production. Film production in Hollywood was based on a manufacturing model with each phase of the filmmaking process—from script writing to editing—taking place within the studio walls. The major studios employed full-time writers, directors, and performers in addition to film crews, technicians, and editors.

Union organizing of the below-the-line crews began in Hollywood in the 1920s. By 1926 the Association of Motion Picture Producers (AMPP), which represented the five major studios, entered into collective bargaining agreements with IATSE and with unions representing the Basic Crafts—carpenters, painters, electrical workers, and musicians (Lovell and Carter, 1955). Union representation was based along craft lines with electricians, carpenters, and camera operators, for example, being represented by separate unions. Still, interunion struggles occurred since jurisdictional lines often overlapped, were not clear, or were simply in dispute. These conflicts continued through the 1930s and 1940s, often leading to problems at the bargaining table and resulting in work slowdowns and strikes.

Through a series of union mergers, interunion battles, and organizing campaigns, IATSE emerged as the dominant below-the-line union in Hollywood and the United States. By 1946 the union's Hollywood locals, led by its international, negotiated the "Basic Agreement" with the AMPP, a collective bargaining agreement setting wages, benefits, and working conditions for employees represented by those locals. One contract set the basis of employment for all

IATSE-represented employees, and replaced the multitude of individual local agreements that had existed before.

Since film production outside Hollywood was not based on the studio system model, the Hollywood Basic structure was not replicated anywhere else. For the most part, locals elsewhere negotiated their own contracts with employers based upon specific regional jurisdictions. This is why, even today, separate camera, script, hair/makeup, and studio mechanic locals exist on the West Coast, the East Coast, and in the middle of the country. Certainly, locals within a region like the East Coast could choose to cooperate with one another in negotiations, and individual studios could choose to negotiate together with these locals, but nothing compels them to do so. Short of denying locals strike authorization, the IATSE international could only indirectly influence negotiations in regions outside Hollywood where IATSE film locals are allowed to deal with the individual concerns of their members and their own labor markets. Nonetheless, since the vast majority of film production takes place in Hollywood, the Basic Agreement had a great deal of influence on bargaining in those other regions. In addition, IATSE members dominate the below-the-line workforce. No matter where in the United States or Canada a film studio shoots all or part of a film project, it would likely have to deal with either the IATSE international or its locals.

By 1948 the U.S. Supreme Court forced the major studios out of the exhibition business in what would become known as "the Paramount decision" (334 U.S. 131). The court ruled that the major studio's ownership of movie theaters violated the Sherman Antitrust Act. Around this same period television emerged as the new mass entertainment medium directly competing with movie theaters for audiences and revenues. As a consequence, the major studios replaced the continuous model of production in Hollywood with one geared toward individual projects. Full-time employment decreased as many technicians and craftspersons were hired on a project-by-project basis. Nonetheless, the Hollywood Basic Agreement and bargaining structure stayed intact. Even as new film companies (Disney, Universal) joined the ranks of the major studios, they also became part of the Hollywood Basic and adhered to or signed IATSE agreements in other regions.

By the mid-1950s major studios themselves began to produce entertainment projects for television or rented facilities to other production companies. Consequently, aspects of the Basic Agreement and other IATSE agreements were adapted to meet the needs of television production. Other companies producing film projects for television also entered into contracts with IATSE since the union represented so many skilled film craftspersons and technicians. The ranks of employers signed to IATSE agreements continued to swell. By the mid-1960s the AMPP became the AMPTP (Alliance of Motion Picture and Television Producers), all of whose members were signed to the Basic Agreement.

IATSE's ability to control the below-the-line labor market directly was the source of its ability to get and maintain agreements with these employers. Like craft unions in other industries (i.e., construction and maritime), the IATSE locals took on the enormous task of regulating the flow of workers for productions. During the 1950s the Hollywood IATSE locals and the AMPP established the "Industry Experience Roster." Initially divided into three groups based on seniority, the roster compiled a list of eligible craftspersons and technicians according to skills and crafts. Film producers looking for electricians, for example, would first go through those listed in group 1 (experienced IATSE members) before they could be allowed to go to group 2 (less experienced), and finally group 3 members (new to IATSE). It was possible for nonunion technicians to be hired on productions and thus gain the experience to be admitted eventually to an IATSE local, but only if the employer, signed to the Basic Agreement, had exhausted the roster (Lovell and Carter, 1955). Although none of the IATSE locals outside Hollywood developed a roster, for many years they did act as hiring halls for members. Naturally, these systems and the roster itself came under attack as nonunion technicians, who often found it difficult to get into IATSE, claimed that these were mechanisms to keep work opportunities only for existing union members. In due course, the seniority lists on the Hollywood roster were eliminated and nonunion technicians with enough experience were allowed to become part of the roster.

The reluctance of IATSE locals to admit new members or even to enforce union security clauses was a source of criticism for many years. While the practice, as we will see, did lead to the growth of nonunion film technicians and craftspersons throughout the country, it was based on a belief that work opportunities were finite and that the union's role was to provide work for existing members. Given the fact that for many years a handful of employers directly controlled production, it is understandable that the IATSE locals believed that it was possible to confine work opportunities to existing members by carefully controlling the number of members in their organizations. However, this notion literally backfired on the union as the number of producers in the industry increased during the 1970s, 1980s, and 1990s.

Production and Union Practices in Broadcast Television

Broadcast television originated from radio. During the 1920s, 1930s, and 1940s, radio went from a struggling industry with a few firms and limited broadcast range to an established industry with large networks broadcasting from coast to coast. Music, variety programs, radio dramas, news, weather, and sports were all brought into the home via network and local radio broadcasts. In many respects radio combined elements of newspapers and magazines, vaudeville, concert halls, and the theater. Broadcasting was not and is not simply entertainment but acts as a continual source of information.

Like the major film studios, three major networks (CBS, NBC, and ABC) dominated the radio and television airwaves until the mid-1980s. Just as Hollywood was the center of motion picture production, New York City was the center of radio and early television production. In the early 1950s live television programs were produced and broadcast in New York City–based network studios. Although most television film production eventually moved to Hollywood (Burbank), the corporate headquarters of all three major networks remain in New York City.

Unlike film's project-to-project style of production, broadcast production has always been ongoing. Radio and television programming is done on a daily basis and so requires full-time employees. Early FCC regulations demanded that radio stations have technical engineers present at all times. Consequently, most radio and television broadcast engineers, technicians, and even unskilled workers are employed in full-time permanent positions. IBEW and NABET locals which represent broadcast engineers and technicians are not divided by individual craft, as in IATSE, but encompass a wide range of technical skills within one station or network.

The IBEW was the first union to represent technicians in the broadcast industry when, in the 1930s, it organized radio technicians in St. Louis, Missouri. As the union's organizing campaigns increased, it acquired jurisdiction over a number of CBS affiliates. By 1941 the IBEW signed its first industrywide contract with the CBS network, then the largest network in the industry. As CBS moved into television programming, IBEW technicians took up positions as television broadcast engineers and video camera operators.

In 1933, in an attempt to avoid IBEW organizing drives, NBC established the Association of Technical Engineers (ATE), a company union outlawed by the passage of the National Labor Relations Act (NLRA) in 1935. In 1940 the ATE changed its name to NABET (National Association of Broadcast Engineers and Technicians). The following year, when the FCC broke up NBC's Red and Blue networks, thus creating ABC out of the Blue network, NABET found itself with union jurisdiction in two broadcast networks (Tajgman, 1984).

In the late 1940s and 1950s, the IBEW and NABET organized network and local radio and television stations throughout the United States. Although their efforts to expand union coverage were successful, they led to jurisdictional battles. In these conflicts NABET often found itself bested by the older and better established IBEW: NABET remained an independent union, unaffiliated with a national federation, while the IBEW broadcast locals were part of a much larger electrical union affiliated with the AFL. The support of a powerful international union and AFL membership gave the IBEW locals advantages in contract negotiations and in interunion conflicts. NABET, painfully aware of these advantages, sought membership in the CIO in 1951.

NABET's choice to join the CIO was a conscious one. From the 1930s through the 1940s, NABET evolved from a company union into a broadcast union. As it expanded its jurisdiction into television, NABET also expanded its jurisdiction into areas outside the immediate realm of broadcast engineering. The industrial-based organization of CIO unions attracted NABET. When it joined the CIO, it changed the *E* in NABET from engineers to employees, signaling its intent to represent inclusively all members of the broadcast industry.[1]

IATSE is also a broadcast union, representing workers in film productions for television, videotape, and live broadcasts. IATSE contracts with the three major television networks cover stagehands, makeup artists, wardrobe attendants, graphic artists, film technicians, and lighting crews.[2] Unlike the IBEW or NABET, IATSE has had a tradition of freelance employment in the broadcast industry. Although a core workforce is employed full-time, freelance union members are hired when the work load exceeds the capacity of regular crews. As in the western film locals, East Coast IATSE members find employment through their local unions, which traditionally have had strict entrance requirements for new members.

In the early days of television, the skills of broadcast technicians were extremely rare and difficult to acquire; the industry required highly trained and educated individuals. Since much of the equipment used in television production was new and experimental, the networks relied a great deal on the expertise of its broadcast technicians. Video camera operators, for example, often became so intimate with the idiosyncrasies of their equipment that they were more adept at repairing them than were the manufacturers. The skills of production personnel and the relative spontaneity of live television broadcasts gave these unions considerable strength. In the early 1950s, quality production crews were difficult to replace in case of a work stoppage, so the networks attempted to minimize labor conflict.

Throughout the 1960s and 1970s both NABET and the IBEW made strong gains for their members in wages, benefits, and union security. Members' technical skills helped to contribute to these unions' bargaining strength. Since both NABET and the IBEW had union shop agreements with the networks, their membership grew as

---

[1] NABET even adopted CIO terminology. The more genteel term *chapter,* used to describe a section of the union, was replaced with local. The term *chapter chairman* was replaced with local president.

[2] IATSE film camera operators covered news stories for the networks until the early 1970s when news coverage was done with videotape.

the networks and their owned stations across the country expanded; this too contributed to the unions' collective bargaining power. Although these unions generally represent the same type of employee, divergence in their organizing and bargaining techniques stems from differing union orientation.

Especially during the 1960s and 1970s, NABET had, perhaps, the most confrontational reputation in collective bargaining of the three unions. Described by some Network executives as a grievance-happy, strike-happy union, NABET regularly utilized the threat of strikes and job actions during negotiations. The IBEW, although a strong union, has generally taken a less militant, more conciliatory approach to bargaining with CBS. Since 1972, after a failed strike over control of electronic journalism, the IBEW and CBS have met four times yearly to discuss matters of common concern and to resolve problems that might otherwise go to arbitration. The IBEW maintains that this approach avoids undue work stoppages without diminishing its negotiating strength. Whatever the approach, both unions have made relatively equal gains in wages and benefits for their members over the years.

Transformation of the Motion Picture and Television Industries

The relationship between management and below-the-line labor in these two industries during the 1950s, 1960s, and 1970s was very similar to labor-management relations in other U.S. industries. Initially, unions made gains in negotiations based upon the skills they brought to production and management's desire for uninterrupted production. Throughout much of this period, the networks and studios were relatively successful, dominating their markets through their command over both audiences and profits. Not until the early 1970s in the motion picture industry, and the 1980s in television, did leading firms experience any serious challenge to this dominance. During this era of prosperity, studios and networks ensured continued profits simply by getting their products out. In order to keep production uninterrupted, firms in both industries sought to minimize labor turnover and maximize labor peace. Strong unionized firms and stable product markets, combined with powerful unions, helped produce the relative labor relations stability both sides desired.

Three factors tilted the balance of collective bargaining in both industries: new technology, rising competition, and new corporate leadership. New technology changed the nature of work and production in both industries. Technological innovations have made some labor-intensive practices obsolete while creating new tasks requiring different technical skills. Union work rules, job categories, and interunion jurisdictions have all been altered or threatened by technological change. New competition (independent filmmakers, VCRs, cable television, and syndicated television) intensified the pressures brought about by technology. Both the studios and networks complain that the markets for their products have become more complex through the entrance of new firms. Since audiences have more choices, the economic pies have been sliced into smaller pieces; the major studios and three major broadcast networks are not the only shows in town. In some cases, these new competitors work without below-the-line union contracts and are thus not restricted by the same union work rules, jurisdictions, or job categories as are the networks and studios. Studio and network management have reevaluated old production and labor relations practices. No longer willing to assume box office success or high ratings, managements in both the major studios and the networks have sought greater control over the production process. Flexibility and efficiency in production are recent catchwords in both industries. The result of these efforts, in contract negotiations, has been management demands for concessions from labor in contract negotiations.

The Motion Picture Industry

Independent filmmakers have gone from artistic outliers to major producers of feature films and entertainment television programming in the United States. Identified by the IATSE leadership and rank and file as the single most important labor issue in the motion picture industry, independent productions have set the industry literally on its head by challenging established production practices. Between 65 percent and 70 percent of Hollywood feature films are made by independent producers,[3] including everything from small film companies established for the life of one or two films to large nonsignatory motion picture studios (e.g., Cannon, Atlantic Pictures). The exact statistics regarding independent film productions vary according to one's definition of nonunion or independent. Many independent producers are not signatory members of the AMPTP or do not have ongoing labor contracts with IATSE, although they may have contracts for individual film projects with IATSE or a NABET film local. And roughly 11 percent of crew persons employed for nonunion production in Hollywood hold union cards (KMPG Peat Marwick, 1988). This figure includes union members from IATSE, NABET, and the Screen Extras Guild. So, while the individual IATSE member's skills are still in demand, the union's influence in the industry has been threatened. In the early 1980s, roughly 85 percent of all Hollywood productions were under IATSE contracts; by 1988 that figure had dropped to 60 percent (Cooper, 1988).

These same independent producers have collective bargaining agreements with above-the-line unions: the Screen Actors Guild (SAG), the Writers Guild of America (WGA), and the Directors Guild of America (DGA). Unlike IATSE, above-the-line unions have inclusive membership which encompasses all professional performers, actors, writers, and directors. These unions have made membership an essential step toward professional recognition in their occupations. However, the absence of nonunion competition has not come without a price; these guilds often complain about high rates of membership unemployment and the stiff competition for work.

Major studios complain that independent producers are able to make feature films at a 20 percent to 30 percent lower rate than the studios because they are not bound by IATSE or Basic Craft contracts (Cooper 1988). Union agreements not only set standards for wages, benefits, and overtime; they also establish work rules, job categories, and working conditions. Hollywood producers argue that many of

---

[3] These statistics were obtained from KMPG Peat Marwick, 1988 and *Variety,* 1988. Roughly 20 percent of episodic television programs are done with nonunion crews.

these rules, such as those prohibiting crossover between job categories, were established during the 1940s and 1950s, when the majority of productions took place in the studio backlot, but are obsolete today.[4] Able to utilize the skills of nonunion film technicians throughout the United States, independent producers are able to make films with smaller crews, under relatively flexible working conditions, and at lower costs. Larger independent studios like Cannon and Atlantic Pictures have adamantly refused to enter into company-wide agreements with craft unions and, with the exception of individual film projects, have avoided massive organizing drives.[5]

While labor unions argue that through VCRs, cable, and syndicated television the studios have gained new markets and greater profits, the AMPTP contends that these new markets actually compete with box office receipts by drawing audiences away from movie theaters and network television, the studios' primary markets. The alliance maintains that profits cannot be made at the box office alone, and that studios can no longer consider profits earned through syndication or the sale of films and television programs to secondary markets as extra income ("found money"). This is especially true as returns on theatrical releases have become riskier (according to the AMPTP, four out of ten theatrical releases do not recover production costs and one out of ten makes a profit from all markets). Since the networks have had to compete with cable for audiences and advertising, they have not raised their own advertising prices. In order to make up losses due to inflation, they have lowered fees to producers selling programs to the networks. Producers claim that current fees for their programs cover only three-quarters of their production costs and that they must rely on syndication to reap real profits (Counter interview).

There may be some evidence that the VCR has actually inspired greater turnouts to the theaters (Knowlton, 1988). Nevertheless, the argument that VCRs are competing with films and television programming continues to be raised by the studios during negotiations with IATSE.

---

[4] Crossover allows individuals from one job category to perform work in another. On non-IATSE productions, a makeup artist might also help with wardrobe or a camera operator might transport camera equipment.

[5] Cannon did enter into a contract with IATSE for films over $6 million. The studio made almost all of its films under $6 million during the contract period.

The Hollywood studio system was effectively dismantled by the late 1960s and early 1970s. Backlot production had become too expensive. The production focus shifted from big-budget productions to films with leaner budgets that could be shot on location with smaller crews. During this time many of the major studios were acquired by corporations outside the film industry. For example, Coca Cola purchased Columbia Pictures, MCA purchased Universal, and Gulf Western purchased Paramount. As old studio heads gave way to younger management and many of the studios became subsidiaries of conglomerates, they were under greater pressure to keep costs down and profits up. Backlots and other studio real estate were sold off; studios found that they could rent equipment for film productions, and, if necessary, rent studio space or film on location. Some editing, mixing, dubbing, special effects, and film development could be sent out to specialized firms (Christopherson and Storper, 1986). Under new studio leadership, production became more cost conscious. Studios attempted to reduce production risks by reducing production costs.

Technological advances have made postproduction less labor intensive. For example, with the introduction of linear editing, postproduction houses now use video and computer technology to edit filmed television programs. This process is faster than the more tedious editing by hand. Sound dubbing, the process of adding sound to action in a film, has traditionally meant reenacting the shots in a sound studio to append squealing tires, screams, and shattering glass. Computerized sound dubbing now allows programmers to provide an almost infinite number of sounds at the touch of a keyboard. Combinations of video and computer graphics have changed the nature and reduced the labor intensity of special effects as well.

Below-the-line unions argue that there is no link between rising production costs and below-the-line costs, claiming that increases in production budgets are due to rising star salaries. The fact that below-the-line labor costs are relatively fixed and hence lack the variability of other costs in the motion picture industry makes them easier targets for cost reduction. According to a vice president of production for a major studio, each film project is like a small company, with a particular set of nuances and problems, making it difficult to generalize regarding the relationship between below-the-line and other costs. However, he did admit that, in some productions, a single star's salary may exceed all below-the-line costs including labor and equipment.

In any case, as the process of film production changed, as technology made postproduction less labor intensive, and as studio management became more bottom-line conscious, the outcomes of collective bargaining also changed. Throughout the 1980s, the major studios successfully obtained concessions from their below-the-line unions, particularly in work rules and jurisdiction. In the 1982 and 1985 negotiations, for example, the AMPTP got IATSE to agree to allow more crossover between work done in various job categories. In the 1988 negotiations the alliance made even more aggressive concessionary demands on IATSE and the Basic Craft unions.

During the summer of 1988, the WGA began what would become a twenty-two-week strike with the producers over residual formulas and creative control over scripts and screenplays. By July, when the AMPTP was preparing to meet with IATSE and the crafts, the strike had virtually crippled television production in Hollywood. IATSE claimed that the strike delayed individual local unions in their preparations for bargaining. IATSE and the studios agreed that many individual issues would remain unresolved during the WGA strike, and that the drop in production and unemployment resulting from the strike would only frustrate negotiations. Thus, IATSE sought an extension to the Basic Agreement and postponed negotiations for six months.

Under the Teamsters' leadership, the Basic Crafts decided to enter into negotiations and began discussions in July 1988. They hoped that the alliance's preoccupation with the Writers' strike and its desire not to slow film production further would give them bargaining leverage.

The Basic Crafts decision to negotiate separately from IATSE was unprecedented. In past negotiations with the alliance, IATSE and the Basic Craft unions had always negotiated their contracts together. Although individual IATSE and Basic Craft local agreements differ, provisions of the Basic Agreement (e.g., health and welfare benefits and pensions) negotiated by IATSE have been applicable to the Basic Craft unions.

In addition to its July 1988 demands, the AMPTP proposed to reduce or freeze wages for Teamster members during these separate craft negotiations (Robb, 1988a). By late September negotiations had reached a stalemate largely because of the studios' demands for wage reductions, interchangeability of drivers from all crafts, and no pay for the seventh day on location at an out-of-town set if no work is performed (Robb, 1988b). A federal mediator was unsuccessful in his attempts to bring about an agreement and avoid an impasse. By October 3, the Teamsters, the Laborers, and IBEW Local 40 were on strike, although the unions insisted the job action was precipitated by a lockout of their members by the studios (Robb, 1988b). The unions later filed unfair labor practice charges through the NLRB against the AMPTP, claiming that the studios forced the stoppage through a lockout. The board held that the studios' actions were legal.

Since during the strike-lockout studios successfully hired replacement workers, the Teamsters and other craft union supporters were unable to slow down production measurably. By October 31, the strike-lockout ended. The following are some major contract changes that resulted from the negotiations. Teamster raises in the contract were forty-five cents an hour per year.[6] Mealtime penalties were reduced. On-production employees lost night premiums, and off-production employees' night premiums were reduced 20 to 50 percent. The Teamsters also agreed to a limited class of "hyphenate drivers" represented by other unions but obtained a guarantee of 50 percent of all such work for its members. The union was not able to block the studios' proposal to eliminate automatic Saturday and Sunday double time, a longstanding Hollywood tradition. Under the new contract, double time now begins after forty hours regardless of the day of the week (called a five out of seven work week).

Although seen as a major setback for the Teamsters and other crafts, the settlement was ratified by the unions' membership by a vote of 1,039 to 190. In separate speeches to their memberships, Earl Bush, secretary-treasurer of Teamsters Local 399, and Pat Bray, busi-

---

[6] In the 1985–87 Teamster/AMPTP contract, yearly wage increases were about $1 an hour.

ness manager of Laborers Local 724, admitted that the studios were able to continue to replace striking workers, so they urged ratification of the agreement (Ulmer, 1988). Since the concessions included the elimination of longstanding provisions for which the union had fought in past negotiations, there was rank-and-file dissatisfaction over the bargaining outcomes (Ulmer, 1988). Nonetheless, a Teamster representative interviewed for this study maintained that in spite of the concessions, the union still fared better than if it had negotiated jointly with IATSE.

The IATSE negotiations which followed in January 1989 faced similar demands for concessions; however, unlike the Teamsters, IATSE did not attempt to challenge these demands with a work stoppage and agreed to the management-initiated concessions of eliminating Saturday and Sunday double time and institution of the five out of seven work week. Delegates from the IATSE Hollywood locals voted 128 to 92 in favor of the new contract.[7] IATSE members in Hollywood reported that there were grumblings over the settlement, particularly among older members and regarding the elimination of the Saturday and Sunday overtime, which was a long-established production practice. The memory of Teamster picket lines easily broken by nonunion replacement workers was still in the minds of IATSE negotiators.

Observers attributed the failure of the Teamsters strike to the availability of nonunion workers willing to cross Teamster picket lines, and to the anxiety created among union workers by the months of lost work during the WGA strike. IATSE rank and filers claimed that members lost considerable work during the WGA strike, which imposed great financial burdens and levels of debt so high that some members even lost their homes. Other unions felt that their members, anxious to get back to work, could not afford the hardships of a prolonged strike. In the end, not only did the Teamsters and crafts lack the interunion support they needed for success, but the craft unions no longer negotiated together. Now the IATSE and Basic Craft contracts expire on different dates.

IATSE went into the negotiations with a keen sense of how far or how little the studios could be pushed and focused on trying to min-

---

[7] IATSE rank and file voted against the new contract (5,046 to 4,394).

imize the number and the effects of management concession demands at the bargaining table.

Outsourcing: Motion Picture Industry

In the 1950s, 1960s, and 1970s, independent producers and nonunion
postproduction houses emerged in Hollywood and across the United States, making it possible for the studios to contract out for the
production, editing, developing, and mixing of film footage. As relations between nonunion firms and unionized studios developed,
IATSE contracts stipulated how and under what circumstances these
relationships could take place. Article 20 of the Basic Agreement
binds the major studios contractually to informing IATSE, in
advance, of subcontracting or financial relationships.

It should be remembered that distribution—the sale of feature
films and television programs to theaters, the networks, cable, and
overseas—is a basic source of profits for major studios. By concentrating their efforts on marketing films, both their own and others,
the studios have created relative economic security in what can be a
very risky industry.[8]

Major motion picture studios have two types of relationships with
independents which relate to distribution. These are "negative pick-
ups," through which the major studios can purchase and distribute
independent films; and financial or joint venture agreements,
through which the major studios collaborate with independent producers on film projects by helping them with the cost of production
and distribution (Bension, 1988). Through both relationships, major
studios have been able to fill gaps in their own production schedules
and to capitalize on the potential success of an independent film.
While the studios must inform IATSE in advance of subcontracting
or joint venture relationships, they are not bound to do so when they
purchase a film through a negative pickup, since this only involves
distribution rather than production.

The IATSE leadership complains that the major studios are blurring the lines between negative pickups and financial agreements by

[8] Exhibitors usually pay 35 percent to 55 percent of their gross box office receipts as
film rentals to distributors (Bension, 1988).

claiming to be merely distributing films in which they have invested money, thus violating article 20.

IATSE charges that the studios back "shell companies" which either finance independent productions on behalf of the studios or are themselves "false independents" supported by the studios (Cooper, 1987). Independent producers in these types of relationships are often advised by the studio on how to avoid union organizing attempts. One independent producer recounted her experiences with a unionized studio. "EMI was a signatory to the union [IATSE] contract. We set up the production through my own company, and EMI told me to shoot out of town to avoid IATSE. The money was funded to us through a company friendly to EMI, based in Liechtenstein" (Cooper, 1988). According to an industry observer, the Disney Corporation, which purchases independent films through its subsidiary Buena Vista Distribution, actually produces a number of films it calls negative pickups "under the table" outside of Hollywood. Recently the Teamsters made allegations that Paramount Pictures created a sham company (Out of Town Pictures) to avoid union contracts.

There are similar stories with other studios. A number of IATSE and former NABET 15 representatives interviewed for this study claim that major studios often make union avoidance mandatory before they fund an independent film project. By funding and distributing independent films, major studios can reduce their own production risks while being able to share in the profits when the project is successful. This allows them to concentrate their own production efforts on more calculated blockbuster hopefuls like Paramount's *Batman* or Disney's *Roger Rabbit.*

Contractual Integration

Finally, the major studios have begun to return to vertical integration to help them control markets for film products. In 1985 the Justice Department ended its enforcement of the 1948 Paramount decision, thereby allowing major studios to exhibit the feature films and television programs they produce (Cray, 1989). Currently, some of the major studios are not only buying into theater chains, they are purchasing television stations as well. For example, Paramount owns ten television stations and Time Warner holds 568 cable systems through both companies (Freeman, 1990). "The acquisitions are part of the trend toward `Vertical Integration' of the entertainment business, which has seen the studios . . . buy theater chains and cable networks in their effort to control their movies and television programs from conception to consumption" (Richter, 1989). By owning exhibition facilities, the studios can maintain steady markets for their productions. For example, Fox and Disney, which both own cable stations, not only produce programs for them but use the stations as outlets for their films.

Major studios now have the capability to produce, distribute, and exhibit their own feature films, in a manner similar in effect to but different in form from their practices in the 1940s. As Christopherson points out in her chapter, the major film studios are able to exercise their industrial control through contractual agreements with producers as well as through ownership of distribution and exhibition facilities. These series of "dotted line" relationships provide major studios with a variety of production options which allow them great flexibility and make them less reliant on their below-the-line unions. In order for the IATSE to recapture its production dominance, it would have to organize the vast number of production and postproduction companies.

The Television Industry

In the early 1970s new technology increased the number of jobs for NABET and the IBEW members when the minicam, a mobile videotape camera, replaced film equipment for remote news coverage. These two unions had jurisdiction over electronic and videotape broadcast technology, while IATSE held jurisdiction over all film-related work with the networks. As electronic journalism expanded, jurisdictional advantage shifted and the membership and influence of the IBEW and NABET grew. According to an IBEW official, new jobs and membership peaked in the mid-1980s. Today new broadcast technology (robotic cameras, automated carts, computers, and graphics) requires less maintenance, is less complicated to operate, and makes broadcasting less labor intensive. As a result, the networks have become less reliant on their technical staff. The camcorder, a lightweight, relatively easy to operate video camera, can be operated by one person as opposed to the two- or three-person crews required for its predecessor, the minicam. While it has historically been true that new technology has created as many jobs as it took away in the broadcast industry, the future is not clear. The same IBEW official feared that new technology would lead to loss of jobs for broadcast technicians. In addition, automation has allowed the FCC to relax rules demanding that radio and television stations keep a set number of full-time staff on hand. This, in turn, has encouraged the networks to use temporary, per diem, or daily hire workers on tasks formerly performed by full-time staff.

During what are referred to now as the salad days of the broadcast industry, the three major networks dominated that industry. Competition was minimal as the vast majority of local television stations were affiliated with CBS, NBC, or ABC. By the mid-1970s the networks had command over 92 percent of the American viewing audience. At that time cable or pay TV was in 17.5 percent of American homes (Zoglin, 1988). Since cable stations then earned profits by selling subscriptions and did little advertising, they were not a direct threat to the networks' main source of revenues. By the 1980s this picture changed; recent estimates indicate that cable currently reaches more than 60 percent of American homes. This trend is likely to continue and attract audiences away from the networks. Cable channels now sell advertising time just as the networks and their affiliates do. Independent television stations which are not affiliated with any major network are also on the rise. In 1976 there were seventy-six independent television stations across the United States; in 1988 that number had risen to 320. Like cable, independent stations directly compete with the networks for audiences. Stations run syndicated programs (entertainment programs which are not committed to a specific network). Like the motion picture industry, managements in the three major networks have pointed to increased competition as the major spur for their current demands to change production practices and reduce production costs.

All three networks have downsized by laying off administrative and hourly staff. Administrative staff cuts took place largely at the mid-management level. The rationale given by CBS for downsizing staff seemed to be shared by the other two networks, "to eliminate unnecessary staffing where the same work could be done with fewer people, to eliminate marginal activities, and to eliminate jobs that were duplicating work already being done within the three operating groups" (*Broadcasting,* 1986).

It was to be expected that the networks, after cutting administrative staff, would begin to make demands on their hourly unionized staff. Contract negotiations reflected efforts by management to remove what they saw as obstacles to flexibility. For the unions the negotiations focused on retaining control and jurisdiction over the production process and maintaining job security.

During the mid-1980s, a series of mergers and acquisitions took place involving all three major networks: NBC and its parent company RCA were acquired by General Electric; ABC was merged with Capital Cities; and CBS shared the same CEO, Laurence Tisch, with the Loew Corporation. Although both GE and Capital Cities had been players in the broadcast industry, this was the first time that the networks had been owned by corporations with largely nonbroadcast experience. With the change in corporate ownership of the networks came changes in management and corporate goals. Some of the measures to cut costs through reducing administrative and managerial staff were implemented after these mergers. In some cases unprofitable network divisions were either revamped or sold off. For example, for the first time network news divisions were expected to earn profits. This decision was controversial, since for years news divisions had been considered a public trust or a public service, and hence were immune to budget cuts, while entertainment and sports divisions had been expected to earn enough profits to make up for any news deficits. Downsizing took place anyway in spite of WGA protests and congressional hearings (*Broadcasting,* 1987). GE sold NBC radio, the parent of NBC television, to the Westwood Corporation, because the division was at best only marginally profitable.

While to some network executives the new leadership has brought long-needed changes to broadcast production, labor leaders argue that, in their drive toward maintaining the bottom line, new network managements have traded off quality for profits. Labor leaders contend that the original network owners would not have gone to such lengths to increase profits and they fear that the real motive behind efforts to increase profitability is to enhance the cash value of the networks and their divisions for sale in the near future. Responding to network management demands for sacrifices to ensure network stability, some labor leaders are suspicious of the new owners' commitment to their recently acquired corporations.

Network executives state that many of their current bargaining demands were made in the 1970s and early 1980s before their companies changed hands but attempts to bring about change were nearly impossible given the collective bargaining climate at the time. For example, during the 1983–84 NABET-NBC negotiations, the network management was unsuccessful in its attempts to negotiate daily hire clauses. The union effectively fought concession demands by prolonging negotiations for nineteen months and continually threatening to strike if these management proposals were not removed.

By 1987, under new corporate ownership, NBC negotiators renewed demands to hire temporary and freelance workers and allow on-the-air reporters to handle equipment (Barnes, 1987). The network claimed that production costs and risks continued to rise in television. The industry, it argued, was not the same as when the networks virtually monopolized it. With rising competition, a number one position today did not guarantee a number one position tomorrow. Since the industry was changing, becoming more fluid, production practices had to become more flexible, even in areas like the news. As an NBC spokesman at the time put it, "You've got to look at the long term position, what we're really trying to do is find ways to operate more efficiently" (Barnes, 1987).

NABET adamantly refused to accept the notion of per diem workers and refused to discuss the possibility during negotiations. However, unlike in past negotiations, the NBC management was not intimidated by NABET's strike threats and pressed ahead with its own proposals. By March, when the contract expired, negotiations went into a deadlock. Three months later, on June 29, 1987, NBC unilaterally implemented its proposed contract. Although the union went on strike, the walkout had little effect on NBC's broadcasting abilities, at least from the viewers' perspective. Regular programming went on without interruption. Six months prior to the strike, NBC trained clerical and administrative staff to operate basic equipment in order to replace striking workers. Advanced technology allowed these replacement workers to learn a number of broadcast operations in a few hours. In addition, the network brought in nonunion technicians from its RCA research center in New Jersey and employed other union and nonunion strike breakers. The company operated all of its owned stations with a crew of about 1,500 employees (total union staff was about 2,500) with no major incidents. NBC and GE referred to the work stoppage as a "living laboratory," an opportunity to see how the network operated under more efficient methods utilizing new broadcast technology.

The eighteen-week strike was not only one of the longest in the industry's history, it was an almost complete failure for the union. The prolonged strike created great financial burdens for members due to months of lost work. Strike benefits could not offset rising personal debts. The fact that the strike itself had no apparent adverse affect on NBC's ability to broadcast further demoralized the NABET rank and file. The network won almost every major concession it asked for. The most significant gain to the network was its expanded use of temporary employees in network news. A former NABET official gave the following reasons for the negotiations outcomes: the financial strength and political connections of the network under GE ownership; the disunity and lack of NABET support from other NBC unions; and changing broadcast technology. The combination of events signaled a change in the industry's labor relations practices. In the event of a work stoppage, it was possible for management to replace much of its broadcast workforce; labor's bargaining leverage was considerably weakened.

The 1987 strike affected other labor negotiations which took place the same year. CBS demanded the unlimited use of per diem workers in broadcast and news-gathering positions. The IBEW and CBS had agreed on clauses for per diem workers since 1976, but the workers involved were employed for high-skilled, high-salaried positions on remotes (news stories covered on location) and sporting events, neither of which greatly affected regular full-time staff. In the 1987 negotiations CBS wanted to use per diems "in-plant" or inside the network and owned stations. While IBEW members did not see per diem employees as a threat to their jobs, they perceived such workers as a threat to their overtime and, thus, overall earnings. According to an IBEW official, the issue may have been further aggravated by the NABET-NBC conflict and the stock market crash of 1987. Union negotiators maintain that the NABET-NBC strike made CBS tougher in pushing its demands, and made the IBEW careful to avoid a similar work stoppage. After an agreement was reached, the IBEW international and local business managers spent time presenting the final agreement, which included the per diem clause, to the rank and file and convincing them to accept it. A walkout was avoided, but some rank-and-file grumblings over the contract were reported.

ABC and NABET learned from the 1987 negotiations as well. When they sat down to negotiate in March 1989, Capital Cities/ABC advanced proposals for use of per diem or freelance workers and for other concessions. The NABET locals having contracts with the ABC network and owned stations had agreed not to enter into a work stoppage no matter how strong concession demands were from the management side. A representative from NABET Local 16, which has the ABC contract in New York City, admitted that the 1987 strike convinced the union to avoid a walkout at all costs. ABC offered its employees a settlement bonus equal to 10 percent of their salaries if the contract were signed before the March 31, 1989 deadline. However, the best laid plans of both labor and management did not proceed as smoothly as each might have hoped. One of the primary issues, per diem hiring, was settled early on; this was done deliberately because it was such a controversial issue. However, the negotiations reached an impasse in part because of a management proposal for separate seniority categories for the ABC network, owned-station, and radio divisions. Formerly seniority for ABC's/NABET employees had been companywide. When layoffs took place, high-seniority employees from one division (e.g., radio) could bump employees in another (e.g., network news). The network claimed that this system disrupted overall company efficiency; the union claimed that the separate seniority proposal threatened the entire employee seniority system. Although the company made a no-layoff promise for the life of the negotiated contract if NABET accepted separate seniority, the rank and file voted it down. Further delays in the settlement occurred because of resistance to management proposals that members pay part of their health insurance coverage. The signing bonus was extended and, by May, a federal mediator was brought in to attempt to resolve the negotiating impasse. By August of 1989, NABET and ABC reached a final agreement which was ratified by the union's membership. In it, ABC and NABET agreed to a formula for hiring per diem workers based upon the number of days worked by full-time staff. ABC radio employees were to be maintained on a separate seniority list as originally proposed. However, only television employees hired after July 20, 1989 would be placed on a separate seniority list (Lowry, 1989). NABET-represented employees began to pay for part of their own health insurance ($20 for an individual and $40 for a married employee per month). In the end, ABC paid a six to seven percent settlement bonus.

As in Hollywood, much of the struggle here was not over wages but over job control. Management claims that labor costs are high not because of wages, health insurance, and pensions per se but because of lack of flexibility (overtime, meal periods, and work rules). What the unions have referred to as job security and union security, management calls featherbedding. Network negotiators have simply stated that the networks should not employ more employees than they need, reflecting the overall drive for cost efficiency. Both NABET and IBEW negotiators counter that the networks don't know when efficiency ends and cheap productions begin. Both unions have complained of the potential threat management proposals pose to their membership and of their threat to overall production quality. They argue that management cost-cutting efforts cheapen the end product because of declining reliance on full-time staff and more dependence on part-time or per diem employees and subcontractors. Both unions contend that the networks currently have all of the flexibility they are ever going to need and that their focus should be on improving the quality of news, sports, and entertainment programming.

Outsourcing: Television Industry

There is a potential for relationships between the major television networks and cable television stations which would parallel the relationship between the major studios and independent filmmakers. The increased technical and professional sophistication of local stations has brought their production quality up to network standards. Technology in the form of satellite dish–equipped vans allows stations to send their own news teams to a breaking story and broadcast a report to viewers before the networks are on the scene. CONUS (an acronym for continental U.S.), a freelance news group based out of Minneapolis, sells news coverage to local, cable, and independent stations. "Local stations have discovered that, with the aid of resource-sharing innovations like CONUS, Group W's Newsfeed and Potomac Communications' flourishing Washington-based service, they can put together their own national and international roundups" (Waters and McKillop, 1988). CNN, the twenty-four-hour news channel, currently sells videotape and news coverage to other cable stations and the networks. International media groups similar to CONUS are able to edit news stories to meet the needs of a wide variety of clients. While the networks complain that these freelance news groups and cable news channels drain away their audiences, union representatives allege that the networks are customers as well as competitors.

Networks are already moving into cable television either by owning their own cable stations or through joint ventures with cable networks. For example, NBC owns CNBC (Cable News and Business Channel), a twenty-four-hour business and finance service; has a 38 percent stake in Visnews, a television news service distributing international news stories to eighty-four countries (Huff, 1988); and has a pact with the Australian Television Network Ltd. (Lowry, 1988).

The End of Financial Syndication Rules

For years, while the FCC was reevaluating the financial syndication rules limiting the networks' ability to earn profits from the sale of programs to other markets, the major networks have been gearing up their in-house production facilities to produce programming for themselves and anyone else willing to purchase shows.

In an industry undergoing major changes, it is becoming clear that "the people who own the product, the software, are the ones in the best position to weather the storm" (Stevenson, 1989a). The longstanding argument over financial syndication becomes understandable in light of the profits shows make in syndication to local stations and cable. However, the battle itself pits labor unions against one another depending upon where their members tend to benefit from the FCC's decisions. Unions with strong ties to the motion picture industry supported the continuance of financial syndication, while broadcast unions tended to support the network's efforts to repeal these rules.

IBEW and NABET leaders interviewed for this chapter favored increased network production, feeling it could lead to greater union security and possibly increased membership, especially if in-house production facilities are expanded. Since these broadcast unions have not agreed to subcontracting clauses like IATSE's article 20, they do not fear that the networks will engage in union avoidance tactics in video productions as studios have in film.

Labor's Concerns and Responses

In reviewing the negotiating histories of all three unions in this study it is clear that they had their greatest bargaining power when they had the greatest control over their respective labor markets. This control came when the unions represented nearly all of the skilled technicians and craftspersons and had contracts with nearly all of the employers (film producers and television networks) in their industries. The increase in nonunion film and television technicians and craftspersons who have come into the industry through film schools, as well as the rise of independent nonunion filmmakers and television producers, have greatly compromised the unions' negotiating positions. Although these unions continue to represent their members' interests and negotiate contracts with employers, they are not in a position to exert the same influence they once had in negotiations or in their industries at large. Changes in technology, especially in the television industry, have assisted in this shift in power, but they are secondary when compared to the structural changes that have occurred in the bargaining relationships.

For workers in the film and television industries, these changes have implications that go beyond contract negotiations, as will be examined below. Nonetheless, the IATSE, IBEW, and NABET are well aware of how their positions in their industries have changed and are working to regain negotiating power; some of these strategies are also reviewed in the following section.

Labor Standards

When the major studios actually produced the majority of feature films, IATSE collective bargaining agreements acted as templates for nonunion producers, giving them rough guidelines for below-the-line working conditions. While this was not an intentional outcome of the collective bargaining process, according to industry observers, it occurred because so much film production was done under union agreements. The fact that IATSE members would occasionally work on nonunion feature films or television movies during this period also helped to create an indirect union influence on nonunion productions.

Since the 1980s, independent production has increased and fewer producers have been guided by the IATSE template. In addition, the industry has seen increased violations of state and federal labor laws, longer work days (14 to 18 hours per day), employers paying "flat" wages with no overtime, and employers not fully compensating workers at the end of productions.

"[Nonunion] crew members not only make $200.00 to $300.00 a week less than they should, but often federal and state laws are broken when producers pay with cash invoices rather than on payroll, skirting social security, workmen's compensation, and unemployment insurance" (Cooper, 1988). The practice of paying nonunion film technicians on flat rates with no overtime has caught the attention of the U.S. Department of Labor (Robb, 1994). And the Internal Revenue Service has conducted investigations into the practice of treating these workers as independent contractors rather than employees. While these types of investigations have really just begun, they demonstrate the level of the problems nonunion film workers face. Anecdotal evidence shows that these practices occur primarily with producers of film projects costing under $7 or $8 million, which are typically shot nonunion.

It is important to understand that, even under the best of conditions, film production is very demanding both physically and mentally. Long work hours with short periods of time off between work days can lead to stress and fatigue resulting in workplace accidents. For example, the death and injuries that occurred in the making of the nonunion feature film, *The Crow,* were attributed, in part, to fatigue due to long work hours and inexperienced personnel. Once again, there are reports that these problems have increased as the IATSE film contracts have had less influence in the industry, or at least as nonunion productions have increased.

With the increase in independent/nonunion production it is natural that many IATSE members find employment on nonunion films, so union film technicians and craftspersons face the same problems as nonunion workers. In addition, union workers are often discriminated against in employment by companies wanting to keep the IATSE international or its locals from organizing productions. Some nonunion employers have refused to hire IATSE members or they have threatened to fire or blackball employees who engage in union organizing campaigns. In other cases, nonunion employers make IATSE technicians take financial core status with the union in order to work on their productions. Financial core allows the technicians to retain a nominal union membership by paying just enough dues to cover collective bargaining. As core members they cannot be disciplined by the IATSE for crossing union picket lines. While these practices are violations of the National Labor Relations Act, they often go unreported by both union and nonunion technicians, because employment in the film industry is freelance and workers fear that they will be considered troublemakers.

Television technicians face similar problems when working for nonunion television producers. As in film, videotape productions for television, which are then sold to one of the three major networks or to cable television, often do not adhere to the same terms and conditions found in IBEW or NABET contracts. And while a number of nonunion television networks may conform loosely to some of the conditions outlined in these agreements, they tend to drift away from them in labor markets with high levels of unemployed technicians. Naturally, the fact that any of the three major networks can purchase entertainment or news stories from nonunion producers raises major concerns among the unions. Many of the concessions the network management has demanded from the IBEW and NABET have been inspired, in part, by the production practices of nonunion producers.

The "one-man band"—one person using a television camera to gather news—a technique that was being predicted in the late 1980s as a practice for the future, is currently used by nonunion television news stations like New York 1 and by news "stringers," temporary or freelance technicians who gather and sell news stories to network and cable news programs. Here, certainly, technology has been a major factor, since the one-man band would not be possible without lightweight cameras equipped with microphones. However, it is also a product of a management practice allowing for the crossover not only of technical crafts (camera and sound) but of reporting as well. It signals a departure from longstanding practices of job classification and specialization. And it suggests major concerns, both for the IBEW and NABET, representing technicians, and for AFTRA (American Federation of Television and Radio Artists), which represents news journalists. Even where a union contract exists, there is a question which union would represent a news journalist carrying a camera.

Both the IBEW and NABET have criticized downsizing by union and nonunion employers as being dangerous and inefficient. Like film technicians, television technicians work in a variety of conditions and situations. News technicians may find themselves covering fires, floods, crime scenes, or riots. The unions claim that an individual technician covering a news story alone is vulnerable to having equipment stolen or being mugged, since the equipment is extremely valuable. They further maintain that carrying even relatively lightweight equipment can lead to severe back injuries. In short, the practice may not be effective in all news-gathering situations.

Like their counterparts in the film industry, freelance television technicians are often victim to industry whims. Employment is competitive and, while there appears to be a desire to establish and maintain wages and working conditions, individual employees are vulnerable when participating in union organizing activities or when bringing complaints against their employers. Here, as in the film industry, some nonunion employers have refused to hire technicians because of union activity. And although some practices are clear violations of federal law, the nature of freelance employment often makes it difficult for either union to get enough evidence to fight these.

IATSE Strategies for Changes

Since the mid-1980s IATSE has been reevaluating its strategies for organizing film technicians in dealing with independent film producers. The IATSE international has at various times urged, chided, and prodded its locals into admitting new members as a means to drying up the nonunion work pool across the United States. It has also attempted to establish new union locals in nonunion areas, particularly the South, in efforts to unionize local film technicians and craftspersons. The process is ongoing and the results have been mixed. The international has had to endure the criticism of IATSE locals reluctant to increase their memberships, and it has had to learn to win the "hearts and minds" of nonunion film technicians. The task has been daunting, given the ability of producers to film almost anywhere in the United States, the independent nature of IATSE locals, and the long memories of many nonunion technicians who were kept out of the union for so long.

Dealing with independent/nonunion film producers and creating a national negotiating strategy has been no less challenging. The international and many of its locals have devoted personnel and resources to organizing nonunion feature film and television productions and have experimented with alternate collective bargaining agreements for mid- or low-budget film productions. Here again, the results have been uneven because of the sectional nature of the IATSE's structure. With so many locals relatively autonomous, and regions of the United States literally competing for film production, attempts to create a national strategy for negotiations have been difficult. Nonetheless, both the IATSE international and many of its locals have engaged in creative efforts to increase the union's presence in the industry.

Organizing Film Projects

Given the nature of their film contracts, IATSE organizing projects on the West Coast and elsewhere in the United States take on somewhat different forms. Since the IATSE international controls the bargaining rights of the West Coast film locals, international representatives usually coordinate organizing campaigns. They notify IATSE locals of their intent to organize a production, directly contact crew persons on the production, and negotiate the terms and conditions with the production company. Business agents from individual film locals often assist the international representatives by ordering their members to cooperate, or, in some cases, by taking part in picketing and directing their members to cooperate in organizing campaigns. On the East Coast where IATSE film locals negotiate their own contracts, local business agents direct their own organizing campaigns. They contact their members working on nonunion productions to advise them to cooperate in organizing drives and negotiate the terms and conditions of agreements with production companies.

Certainly the fact that filmmaking is still a labor-intensive enterprise and filmmakers on location cannot easily choose to leave a location in mid-production to escape an organizing drive is to the union's advantage. Whether they are full feature films or TV movies, film projects often have tight production deadlines. Striking a project at a crucial production point (i.e., when it requires multiple cameras, when it is in a crucial location for a short period, or when it is shooting scenes with key cast members who are about to go on to other projects) can greatly increase the odds of union success. Keeping the focus of union demands relatively straightforward also simplifies negotiations and enhances the union's chance of success. For example, main topics of negotiations on organizing drives include health and pension benefits and increasing wages for members.

The IATSE international has focused attention on organizing postproduction houses as well. Since postproduction employment is often longer term than on a film production or may be permanent, longer term strategies more akin to traditional union organizing drives are needed. But editors, assistant editors, and other postproduction employees are easier to replace in the midst of a film production than are technicians, and success has been more difficult to achieve in this venue. Management resistance has been considerable and often aggressive. For example, IATSE filed an unfair labor practice against California Video Center, a postproduction house in Sherman Oaks, for alleged intimidation during an organizing drive (*Hollywood Organizer*, 1989).

Organizing Individuals

Clearly if IATSE is to regain the measure of control it once had in the film industry, it will have to admit the ever growing numbers of qualified nonunion technicians and craftspersons. For many locals this is a controversial decision, since some IATSE members feel that the level of unemployment in the industry and the number of union members are already too high. It is important to understand that in the minds of some IATSE members, the traditional role of the union has been to provide employment for existing members. Even if the local is prohibited from operating a hiring hall or preventing employers from hiring nonunion personnel, that perception still exists. Some members believe that work opportunities will simply be diluted through the addition of new members.

In spite of this, both the IATSE international and its locals have made great strides in opening the doors to new members. Many locals regularly admit qualified film technicians and the international itself has threatened sanctions on locals that have refused to admit new members or have put up artificial blocks to membership. Under the IATSE constitution and bylaws the international can put a local into trusteeship for continually refusing to admit qualified applicants.

For the film locals in Hollywood this process has been more complicated since employment with the major studios is dependent on an individual's status in the Industry Experience Roster. Union membership cannot guarantee roster status, so admittance to the roster has been used to entice nonunion technicians to join the union or to assist in organizing campaigns. For example, for much of 1989 both Local 659 (Camera) and Local 776 (Editors) not only opened the doors to union membership, they made admittance to the roster easier. This allowed both locals to take in many new members and it also allowed a large number of their existing members onto the industry roster.

During the late 1980s and early 1990s, the IATSE international actively created new studio mechanic locals in areas that had little or no union representation. The studio mechanic local incorporates a number of crafts (grip, electric, sound, props, etc.) under one structure. In Hollywood all of these crafts are represented by individual IATSE locals. The concept is not new. The first studio mechanics' local, Local 52, was established in New York City in 1924. Nonetheless, IATSE established new studio mechanic locals as a means to streamline representation of technicians and craftspersons and to organize new members. New studio mechanic locals are assigned an international representative to negotiate contracts and represent members in grievances. Especially in the early stages when membership is growing and the local is getting on its feet, the new local is subsidized by the IATSE international. A few locals have become autonomous and negotiate their own agreements; however, there appears to be a fair amount of interaction and dialogue between them. The Studio Mechanics' Caucus, which meets yearly, is an opportunity for studio mechanic locals to attempt to set industry standards for working conditions, staffing, and other matters.

Given the risks nonunion film workers in regions like the South take in joining IATSE or participating in organizing drives, the international and its locals will have to spend a great deal of time winning their respect and confidence. To do this requires patience, willingness to listen to criticism of past mistakes, an ability to inspire confidence, and an ability to point to successes, not simply in organizing but in negotiations and in day-to-day representation. In short, nonunion technicians have to feel welcome into the union, and the union has to be willing to address their specific craft and regional concerns. Heavy financial investment is needed to continue to hire organizers, to set up studio mechanic locals, and to assist existing locals in organizing drives. While these are major political issues with both the IATSE international and with its locals, admitting qualified technicians and adequately representing their interests takes the union most of the way in dealing with the independent/nonunion film producers.

Special Contracts

IATSE claims that throughout its history it has been willing to address the needs of employers signed to its contracts. However, the needs of employers who are not signed to its major studio contracts, who are independent producers working on low- or mid-budget agreements, have been more difficult to deal with. According to its own statistics for 1993, only seven of the forty-nine films with budgets below $8 million worked under IATSE contracts (Cox, 1994). Six of those seven union films shot in the report's Northeastern region (Maine, New Hampshire, Vermont, Massachusetts, Rhode Island, New York, Pennsylvania, Maryland, District of Columbia, Virginia, and West Virginia), while none of the forty-nine films in the same budget range were filmed in the report's Southwest region (California, Arizona, New Mexico, Nevada, and Hawaii) had IATSE contracts. Clearly the IATSE's East Coast film locals have developed an approach to address low-budget productions.

The East Coast Council (ECC) is a collection of East Coast IATSE film locals, most of which are based in New York City, that meet regularly to negotiate contracts for projects with budgets under $6 million. While the ECC itself has been in existence since the 1950s, it wasn't until NABET Local 15 merged with IATSE that IATSE entered into the world of low-budget feature films. In that NABET 15 had negotiated low- and mid-budget film agreements, it required IATSE to continue the practice as a condition of the merger agreement. Prior to 1990, Local 644 (East Coast Camera) also negotiated low-budget agreements, but they only cover the camera department employees. Like NABET 15's, the ECC agreements covered all craft and technical departments. In the past four years the ECC has negotiated over one hundred low-budget film and television projects.

Since the ECC agreements tend to have lower wage and benefit contribution levels than the locals' major feature agreements, producers are required to provide the locals with copies of their budgets to validate that they are below $6 million. The agreements also contain language requiring producers to pay deferred wages and benefit contributions when and if the project earns agreed-upon levels in gross earnings (usually 2.5 times the total budget). Like NABET, the ECC negotiates contracts that include all IATSE-represented crafts and departments; hence wages, benefits and other terms and conditions are uniform among the crafts. Each local is represented at the bargaining table with management and has an opportunity to address its members' particular concerns. Some elements of IATSE have criticized the ECC for negotiating agreements which would, somehow, undermine the major studios' contracts. However, this does not seem to be the case. In fact working conditions (turnaround between work days, night premiums, work week schedule, etc.) under ECC agreements are actually more favorable to the employees than in the major feature contracts. These negotiations have allowed the East Coast locals the opportunity to develop relationships with producers which had been formerly antiunion (e.g., IRS Media, Miramax Films, New Line Cinema, Republic Films). This has been important when the success of some of the low-budget projects has been followed by their producers coming back to the locals to negotiate for mid- to big-budget productions.

The success of the ECC led the East Coast locals to create a similar structure called the New York Production Locals (NYPL) to meet with independent producers with budgets over $6 million and to discuss specific concerns with major studio productions. Although

Local 644 and Local 161 do not meet with the NYPL, they actively meet and negotiate with the same independent producers, even having some of them sign their major feature film agreement. While most negotiations are on a production-by-production basis, they have allowed the locals to establish viable relationships with independent producers; to dispel myths about shooting union in New York; and to provide increased work opportunities for their members. The tendency of the locals is not to allow companies that refuse to sign three-year agreements better terms and conditions than those in the major studio contracts. Thus, while the locals are willing to meet special concerns and needs of independent producers, they often require improved work rules in return. Through these structures, the locals also negotiate television series and TV movie contracts and, thereby, helps to increase the level of production in New York City.

The fact that most of the New York IATSE locals represent a majority of technicians in their crafts has allowed the locals much of the leverage they have needed in order to conduct negotiations through either the ECC or NYPL. This relative lock on the local labor market has also allowed the locals to insist that, for the most part, concessions or special contracts be given only to companies hiring all of their film technicians and craftspersons from the locals. Besides proving to be a legal solution to the age-old dilemma of providing employment opportunities for members, this has made membership in these locals very valuable to nonunion technicians.

The Hollywood locals continue to meet together with management on a quarterly basis to discuss concerns or issues or to decide whether to grant concessions from the Basic Agreement on specific projects. However, until recently very little effort has been made to address the issue of low-budget or independent film productions. The international claims that provisions addressing low-budget productions in the 1993 Basic Agreement will allow the West Coast to enter into low-budget agreements similar to those made by the ECC. The Hollywood locals also negotiated with NBC a special TV movie agreement which was felt to address specific network concerns. NBC in return agreed to produce more TV movies in Los Angeles through its union production entity. However, the terms of this agreement have not been extended to other television movie producers.

Other IATSE locals have negotiated with independent producers based on concepts loosely modeled after the ECC or the Basic Agreement. However, the statistics in the 1994 IATSE report on total U.S. and Canadian production suggest that a unified model to address this marketplace does not exist. It is important to bear in mind that dealing with low-budget or independent projects is still controversial in some sections of IATSE. Locals outside Hollywood negotiate their own contracts, and, even if they are willing to negotiate with independent producers, do so based upon their own experiences of levels of influence in their respective jurisdictions.

National Contract

The IATSE international has stated its desire to create nationwide film contracts for all its crafts, arguing that only national agreements can eliminate regional competition within IATSE and create a powerful bargaining unit similar to SAG and the DGA. However, two main factors seem to stand in the way: (1) many IATSE locals outside Hollywood are reluctant to surrender their bargaining rights to the international, and (2) the major studios may not agree to a national negotiating structure.

Of the IATSE locals outside of Hollywood that negotiate their own agreements, many if not all currently feel better equipped than the international to address the specific issues of their members. This is not to say that, in theory, business agents and local presidents do not agree that some form of national structure would provide them with greater control of the industry; but they seem reluctant to duplicate the Hollywood Basic on a national level. Although Hollywood producers complain about the sectional nature of the IATSE structure, they seem to benefit from the ability to play one region off against another during contract negotiations. In 1992, when the two largest IATSE camera locals (644 and 659) discussed merging their negotiations with the AMPTP, the studios twice rejected their offer to negotiate a national camera contract.

Locals 644 and 659 entered into merger discussions in 1989 and as well as in 1992, but without success. Merger discussions seemed to begin to bear fruit in 1992 but broke down over questions regarding how the new local would be structured, its commitment to organizing, whether members would be allowed to work without restriction outside their old jurisdictions, and what would become of the 659 roster. While individual members in both locals have expressed the desire to have a national camera local, merging two organizations that have been in existence since the 1920s, with their own organizational philosophies and bargaining histories, has proved daunting. It may be enough for now that the attempts have been made. Clearly a success by any of the locals in merging nationally would help to create models for others to follow.

Should IATSE prove successful in creating a national structure it will probably not be based along the same lines as SAG or the DGA. Unlike above-the-line unions, IATSE does not represent a single group of employees. Any national contract or national structure would have to allow the union's various crafts a voice in the master agreements and its internal affairs. One possibility might be national locals based on craft lines with a negotiating structure similar to that of the NYPL or ECC. Such a structure could offer equal input by both the international and its locals.

NABET 15 and 531

In the early 1950s, when film was used for television news coverage, NABET incorporated film workers into its membership. Local 531 was NABET's oldest film local with contracts for episodic television and commercials and in 1965, Local 15 NABET's East Coast film local was formed shortly after a group of IATSE freelancers and nonunion film workers successfully petitioned to join the union (*NABET News,* 1965). Both locals merged into a single film unit in 1983.

The NABET film locals represented an alternative to the traditional craft union structure in the motion picture industry. Unlike IATSE on both coasts, NABET fit every category of production work into one film local in a structure that is a hybrid between industrial and craft unionism: the structure and philosophy of industrial unionism combined with the skills of craft unionism. It may be this model that has influenced the current movement within IATSE toward vertically structured film locals. Certainly it is a structure that has proven very successful outside the Hollywood studio zone.

Of the two locals, Local 15 had greater success at obtaining feature film contracts, usually in the mid-budget range. In the New York City area at least, Local 15 proved to be a formidable alternative to IATSE for independent producers. The local's membership and reputation grew during the mid-1970s and into the 1980s when it organized mid-budget independent productions. Many of the producers with NABET contracts were outside the Hollywood mainstream and posed considerable competition to the major studios. As the reputations of these independent producers grew, so did Local 15. Its leadership maintained that much of its growth was due to its vertical structure, ability to meet specialized production demands, and lower rates than the IATSE's. Local 531 concentrated on commercial advertising and episodic television work. IATSE's strong hold over feature films and its contract with the AMPTP helped to keep Local 531 from feature film contracts.

Over the years Local 15 established offices in many of the major cities in the United States, which allowed it to expand its jurisdiction in feature films beyond New York City. The local attributed much of its growth to the traditional reluctance of IATSE locals to admit new members, and to an ability to make contracts with mid-budget–range independent producers outside the studio system.

The success of these film locals based on their ability to undercut IATSE production costs put a strain on cooperative relations between the two unions. Nonetheless, by 1992 both Local 15 and Local 531 of NABET affiliated with IATSE, joining the ranks of IATSE studio mechanic locals, which they resemble.

The IBEW and NABET

Since NABET's 1987 negotiations with NBC it has been clear to the union that a strike could only be a weapon of last resort. In its 1989 negotiations with ABC, NABET agreed up front to continue negotiating no matter how difficult negotiations became and to address the most controversial topics (per diem workers, separate seniority lists, and new technology jurisdiction) in the beginning. The strategy, similar to that in the IBEW's negotiations with CBS, seems to be an effort to narrow the scope of bargaining and maintain some control over what the union gives up.

The IBEW has continued its policy of meeting with CBS management on a quarterly basis to discuss problems, concerns, or future issues. The idea of the talks has been to avoid grievances or conflicts by working problems or potential problems out in the open. All discussions are off the record, which means nothing can be used by either side during grievance arbitration. In theory this allows the participants to speak more freely. Nonetheless, the IBEW has fared little better in its negotiations with CBS than NABET has with NBC and ABC. The issue of freelance or per diem employment remains a major topic in negotiations, and management in all three networks seems bent on continuing the restructuring that began in the 1980s. Further replacement of employees with freelancers remained a focal point of contract negotiations in 1994.

The freelance issue is a particular dilemma for both unions in that the majority of television technicians are freelance, yet the network contracts have historically been based on staff employment. Certainly the IBEW and NABET have provisions in their agreements to represent freelance workers, but none of their network agreements provide freelancers with health benefits, a major issue for that group. Freelance technicians have complained that both unions spend their time trying to maintain benefits for staff workers rather than improving conditions for freelancers. This is a problem for union leaders since they fought long and hard against freelance employment taking over staff employment in the industry. While shifting the focus of negotiations toward freelancers would be in line with how the industry is changing, it might appear to signal that unions have given up the fight to maintain staff employment. Nonetheless, freelancers are the fastest growing group in the television industry and per diem employment is a pattern many employers have adopted, especially in news gathering. Currently, because the IBEW, NABET, and some IATSE locals all have television contracts, freelancers are required to have union cards in a number of unions and locals. As a consequence, many freelancers have no allegiance to any one union. They maintain union membership only as a means to secure employment, even though they might like to see a strong union presence in the television industry. As in the film industry, any union seeking below-the-line prominence in the television industry will have to attract these nonunion technicians.

In 1992 NABET merged with the Communications Workers of America (CWA), a step as significant as its affiliation with the CIO in the 1950s. As part of a much larger union, NABET/CWA may have access to resources to organize. Certainly the CWA has dealt with corporate restructuring in the communications industry and has been active in union organizing. Should the CWA agree to invest time and effort in building NABET, that union could emerge as the most powerful below-the-line union in the broadcast industry. Nonetheless, the merger was frustrating to both the IBEW and IATSE, which hoped that NABET would merge with one of them and help to eliminate some of the interunion competition in television.

International Issues

All three unions are relatively active in international union affairs, primarily through the Department for Professional Employees of the AFL-CIO and the entertainment and trade union secretariat, ISETU, which is based in Brussels. NABET, the IBEW, and IATSE are members of both organizations and through their memberships have opened and maintained dialogues with film and television industry labor unions around the world. Given the global nature of film and television and their levels of foreign investment and production, such relationships may prove crucial to these three unions in the near future. As production facilities and technical skills continue to grow outside the United States, it will be essential for all three to attempt to develop international work and professional standards. Ironically, this is also one of the areas in which the three unions are inclined to cooperate with one another. Generally speaking, there appears to be consensus among them that some level of international activity is important and that, to a certain extent, U.S. film and television unions should appear to work together in facing their foreign counterparts.

Local 644 of IATSE took some unique steps in international trade union cooperation after successfully organizing the PentAmerica feature film production *House of Cards* in Mexico in 1991. The local literally followed the production company, which had hired its members, to Mexico when the company refused to sign an agreement while shooting in the United States. A technical film union in Mexico, STIC 49, provided Local 644 with a great deal of assistance and moral support during the organizing drive. What resulted has been an agreement between the two unions to engage in further cooperation and support. Very quickly this agreement of cooperation was extended to film unions in Brazil and Argentina, creating a sort of western hemisphere labor agreement. The unions regularly keep each other informed of projects crossing one another's borders and try to assist their counterparts in negotiations with employers. This type of venture has enabled all the unions involved in this agreement to begin to meet the challenges of a highly international industry.

Some Conclusions

Given the fact that both the film and television industries are still relatively labor intensive, it is possible for below-the-line unions to continue representing workers well into the next century. To regain the prominence they once had or even to maintain their ability to represent their respective members, they must represent the majority of qualified film and television technicians and must secure collective bargaining agreements with nonunion employers. These are not simple tasks, and long-term success will require great investments of time and money. But with the right amount of commitment and a willingness to learn from some mistakes, it would be possible for any one of these unions to increase membership and bargaining strength.

The first step would be to increase commitment to organizing. This should include organizing campaigns on film productions and television facilities and—equally essential—it should include some form of outreach to nonunion technicians. Developing relationships with film and broadcast schools to give lectures and assist in internship training would give the unions opportunities to educate upcoming technicians regarding the benefits of union membership. Planting the notion that union membership should be achieved and maintained at some point in a technician's or craftsperson's career would assist the unions to communicate with these people on future organizing campaigns. NABET and the IBEW in particular must develop organizing and negotiating strategies to represent freelance employees. As we have seen, both unions vigorously fought the increased use of freelance/per diem employees in their crafts, but with no success. As a consequence they have not developed language in their agreements which offer the same protections to freelance technicians that are enjoyed by staff employees. Health insurance continues to be a major area of concern for freelance television technicians, yet neither union has developed a comprehensive strategy in collective bargaining to provide this benefit in their contracts. Failure to address freelance television technician's needs will further weaken NABET and the IBEW's hold in broadcasting and could open the door to a rival union whose focus is on freelance workers.

The unions need to do more research on changing production practices in their industries and on which organizations are hiring technicians, assembling production teams, or planning television broadcasting. It is also essential to research how productions and facilities vary with respect to employment practices and budgets. The more these unions learn about changing trends and the concerns employers face, the better unions will be able, if necessary, to create special contracts to meet employers' needs or to know how far they can be pushed in an organizing drive or negotiations. The ECC currently examines the budgets of low-budget feature film producers in order to understand where locals can give reasonable concessions and where they can make demands from management. This process also allows IATSE locals to develop a profile of producers at the various ranges of low-budget production. Similar types of research could be conducted by all of the unions with potential organizing targets. Maintaining active research departments, or at least utilizing those at the AFL-CIO, could help the unions to develop the types of long-term strategies they need to recapture their labor markets.

At present there is little hope that unions will agree to merge or integrate their organizing activities. Rival unionism will continue to hamper representation of technicians in the television industry. Nonetheless, cooperation can and should continue to exist on national issues especially in areas like legislation. And on the international level, the three unions may discuss unified policies for international trade union cooperation and work standards for film and television technicians.

CHAPTER FIVE

The Transformation of Industrial Relations in the Motion Picture and Television Industries: Talent Sector

Alan Paul and Archie Kleingartner

Kochan, Katz, and McKersie (1986) developed a hierarchical model of industrial relations systems in which (1) strategic choices by management, labor, and government, (2) the structures of collective bargaining, and (3) the technical division of labor interact to determine the pattern and performance of labor market institutions. Although there are manifold connections among the system's three elements, the authors imply that actors' top-level strategic choices have had the greatest influence in transforming industrial relations in many U.S. industries. They point to unions' participation in strategic decision-making bodies that were formerly the exclusive domain of management as evidence of this transformation.

In contrast to that analysis, we describe a profound transformation in one industry's industrial relations system that developed from standard collective bargaining practice and did not change the strategic decision-making process. Specifically, we analyze how three professional unions in the motion picture and television production industry—the Screen Actors Guild (SAG), the Writers Guild of America (WGA), and the Directors Guild of America (DGA)—developed institutions that allowed them to expand membership and bar-

Originally published as "Flexible Production and the Transformation of Industrial Relations in the Motion Picture and Television Industry," *Industrial and Labor Relations Review,* vol. 47, no. 4 (July 1994). Copyright Cornell University.

gain effectively, despite changes in production technology and the competitive environment that might easily have undermined their standing. These unions have assumed certain "managerial functions" without directly participating in decision making at either the strategic level or the workplace level. This experience demonstrates that fundamental changes in the norms and expectations underlying strategic goals may emerge from the historical and institutional contingencies of traditional collective bargaining. These changes can be described as "transformative" even though transformation was never explicitly intended.

The centerpiece of the labor relations system in motion picture and television production (MPTV) is the three-tier compensation scheme that is our focus. This scheme unfolded organically over four decades of adversarial collective bargaining, and continuing conflict between unions and employers impels its evolution even today. The three-tier pay system provides the rationale by which unions remain integral to administering the employment relationship. In this regard, MPTV's industrial relations system may be a blueprint for effective unionism in other industries that face similar types of restructuring.

A Framework for Analyzing MPTV

By the 1960s, the connection between structural and historical explanations of labor market institutions that had characterized "traditional" analyses had dissolved, and analysis tended to follow either a structural or a historical path (Brody, 1989). This situation persisted until the early 1980s, when the theoretical limitations of "disjoined" models were exposed and structural and historical theory were remarried. Such works as Gordon, Edwards, and Reich's *Segmented Work, Divided Workers* and Lipset's *Unions in Transition* were particularly important in this regard. Another seminal work was Piore and Sabel's *The Second Industrial Divide*, which is especially relevant to the present study because it also sparked a renewal of interest in MPTV.

Although Lovell and Carter (1955) could already see the effectiveness of collective bargaining as an adjustment mechanism in the earliest years of MPTV's restructuring, academic research practically ignored the industry for nearly thirty years. It was rediscovered by industrial geographers because its pattern of vertical disintegration was associated with a distinctly spatial phenomenon, the Marshallian industrial district; geographers also noted that this industry's experience confirmed Piore and Sabel's hypothesis that economic evolution is not unidirectional (Christopherson and Storper, 1986; Storper and Christopherson, 1987; Storper, 1989; also see Scott, 1984). Given the tenor of Piori and Sabel's work, it is not surprising that the restructuring of MPTV is usually delineated in the terminology of flexible production and segmented labor market theories.

Flexible production systems combine new technologies with new forms of industrial organization and labor relations to compete on the basis of time rather than marginal cost. They are predicated on continuous development of new skills by workers in unfixed job classifications. This arrangement fosters the segmentation and resegmentation of workers, and so engenders the fragmentation of their interests. Unions can survive in this environment only by accommodating an increasingly diverse membership whose goals sometimes conflict (AFL-CIO Committee on the Evolution of Work, 1985).

Christopherson and Storper (1989) considered the implications of this restructuring for MPTV's craft and technical workers. The introduction of flexible production had changed skill requirements dramatically, giving rise to new segmentations of the workforce. Christopherson and Storper predicted that MPTV's existing labor market institutions would exacerbate this trend, decreasing workforce solidarity and increasing conflict between workers and employers. Indeed, their conclusions have proven true for craft and technical workers: despite significant concessions by their unions, roughly half of Hollywood's craft and technical employment had shifted by 1988 to nonunion productions (KMPG Peat Marwick, 1988:III–18).[1]

---

[1] The relationship between union membership and employment is somewhat paradoxical for craft and technical workers: even on nonunion productions, most jobs are filled by union members. Because these workers tend to move between projects covered by union contracts and others that are not, continuous employment is predicated on union membership. Thus, although roughly half of total employment has shifted to nonunion productions and union members are a minority of the craft and technical labor force, most jobs are filled by union members. Membership thus remains important and has declined very little since 1970.

Table 5.1. Membership Growth in MPTV's Core Unions, 1970–88.

	Membership	
Guild or Union	1970	1988
Above-the-Line Unions and Guilds (Professionals/Performers)		
American Federation of Musicians (AFM)	300,000	209,088
American Federation of Television and Radio Artists (AFTRA)	24,000	63,000
Directors Guild of America (DGA)	3,650	8,680
Screen Actors Guild (SAG)	25,000	69,000
Writers Guild of America (WGA)[a]	4,346	9,230
Below-the-Line Unions and Guilds (Craft/Technical)		
International Alliance of Theatrical and Stage Employees and Motion Picture Machine Operators (IATSE)	63,000	60,000
National Association of Broadcast Employees and Technicians (NABET)	8,640	12,000

Source: Membership figures provided by unions and guilds.
[a]Totals combine WGA East and WGA West.

These events were stimulated by practices that expanded the scope of individual versus collective bargaining (described in Christopherson, 1992). Such developments are expected to diminish unions' viability, as elite workers with indispensable skills pursue their individual interests without regard to those of labor's collective body. This phenomenon ought to be especially pronounced where intraunion disparity is high, as is the case in our three unions, the membership of which includes well-known and wealthy stars alongside unknown novices. Nevertheless, table 5.1 shows that the membership of SAG, WGA, and DGA increased significantly in the 1970s and 1980s; these unions, moreover, made very few contract concessions in that period.[2] Similarly, the nonunion labor markets for actors, writers, and directors are small and remain confined to ancillary niches. How and why did SAG, WGA, and DGA avoid the fate of the craft unions?

We find our answer in the terms of the collective bargaining contracts and the particular mechanisms developed to administer them. The innovations in MPTV compensation that we consider were installed in such a way that the unions have become indispensable

---

[2] The sweeping concessions that producers planned to seek from craft and technical workers are contrasted with the "few crumbs that they wrung from the WGA last summer" by Bernstein (1989).

both to their membership and to employers. The changing norms, expectations, and assumptions associated with this development appear to be less the results of a conscious, top-down strategy of union leaders than by-products of incremental responses to successive collective bargaining agreements. To the extent that these responses had unintended consequences that alleviated problems of the flexible production system, they were preserved and enhanced.

Collective Bargaining in MPTV

MPTV has long been a highly concentrated industry. In the 1940s, its golden age (when more than 85 million tickets were sold weekly), the "big five" and "little three" Hollywood studios made 75 percent of all feature films and captured 90 percent of U.S. box office revenue (Gomery, 1986:9; Izod, 1988:113). Even the dramatic restructuring of the industry that began in the 1950s did not transform the industry's oligopolistic structure—the major studios still make 30 to 40 percent of all feature films. More important, they still define the main contours of the industry by their control over the distribution system (Aksoy and Robins, 1992) and labor relations.

Nonetheless, MPTV producers are a far more diverse group today than they were fifty years ago. Beginning in the 1940s, both technological change and antitrust litigation (see *U.S. v. Paramount*, 334 U.S. 131 [1948]) reduced the studios' control over specialized production inputs and the channels of distribution. Supported by tax codes and the expanding market for entertainment products created by the television industry, independent producers were able to emerge and compete with established studios. As a result, MPTV today is composed of a mixture of major studios (Disney, Paramount, and Sony Entertainment, for example), "mini-majors" (Carolco), and various independent producers.

The most important producers' association is the Alliance of Motion Picture and Television Producers (AMPTP), a multiemployer bargaining association. The AMPTP's main decision-making bodies, including the council that negotiates the collective bargaining contracts with the unions, are dominated by fifteen core members, who represent all the major and most mini-major studios, and finance most of the alliance's activities. The remaining mini-majors and larger independents join as signatories to the labor contracts and abide by their provisions. Smaller or less reputable producers usually try to avoid any involvement with the unions (or, failing that, seek low-budget rules waivers; Kleingartner and Paul, 1992:22).

Actors, writers, and directors are a similarly diverse group. MPTV attracts many ambitious people who will work for practically nothing to showcase their talent. They work alongside others who are household names and command large compensation packages. Despite the difficulty of organizing such disparate groups, virtually all thirty-six thousand "above-the-line" (creative/talent) workers on feature films in 1987 were union members, compared to 44 percent of the "below-the-line" (craft/technical) workers.[3]

Hollywood workers were first organized in the context of a studio system with relatively stable employment. This arrangement produced craft unions (or "guilds"), which by 1940 represented almost all Hollywood workers, including the highest-paid talent. The unions representing directors, writers, actors, and film extras operate entirely within film and television production. DGA represents all directors, whether in film or videotape production; WGA has jurisdiction over writers, including most news writers; SAG and the American Federation of Television and Radio Artists (AFTRA) represent all performers except instrumental musicians, who are represented by the American Federation of Musicians (AFM, most of whose members nationally work in live performance venues, recording, or symphony orchestras). Jurisdictional competition among above-the-line unions is now practically nonexistent (Kleingartner and Paul, 1992:4–5).[4]

Bargaining and Labor Relations

Each union in table 1 negotiates its own basic agreement with the AMPTP. This agreement, a union's most important contract, covers such issues as pay rates, work periods, and benefits provisions, for a

---

[3] KMPG Peat Marwick (1988:III-7,9). The "line" to which these employment classifications refer is found in MPTV project budgets. Creative work is accounted for above the line; below-the-line expenses include craft and technical labor, materials and supplies, and so on.

[4] The last major conflict was resolved recently when SAG took jurisdiction over film extras formerly represented by the Screen Extras Guild (SEG).

period of three years (occasionally four). Hundreds of independent producers formally empower the AMPTP to represent them, and then join as signatories to one or more basic agreements without directly participating in negotiations or in the AMPTP's contract ratification vote. Negotiations usually are staggered so that each guild faces the AMPTP in turn. Between negotiations, producers get advice and assistance from the AMPTP regarding contract implementation.

In 1991 the WGA and the AMPTP concluded their negotiations one year before the expiration of the existing agreement, and extended to 1995 the contract that was to expire in 1992. Among the new provisions of that contract was the establishment of an ongoing joint labor-management working group to bring important issues to light in the years between contract negotiations. This model (also adopted by SAG in its last contract) is indicative of a move toward a system of "continuous bargaining" that aims to avoid concentrating conflict into the short period before contracts expire (Counter, 1992).

To a large extent, this move was necessitated by the growing interdependence of unions and employers in matters of compensation, career development, and contingent employment (Kleingartner and Paul, 1992). This interdependence is nowhere more pronounced than in the administration of the pay system. That system is the centerpiece of the parties' relationship, and we now consider its main features.

MPTV's Three-Tier Compensation Scheme

All the MPTV basic agreements contain provisions that cover all workers on an egalitarian basis. Minimum pay rates, grievance procedures, work rules, seniority protection, health coverage, and retirement benefits are examples of such provisions. In this regard, MPTV basic agreements resemble union contracts in most other industrial sectors. They go beyond those provisions, however, to provide a framework for individual bargaining by higher echelons of union members. That framework is contained within a three-tier compensation scheme, the elements of which are conceptually distinct but intertwined in practice: (1) a basic minimum pay rate; (2) a framework for workers to negotiate individual personal services contracts;

and (3) an industrywide system of supplemental payments, that is, residuals.

Minimum Pay Rates

Every MPTV basic agreement contains a minimum compensation schedule. Typically, only neophyte workers are paid according to this "union scale," but the explication of those minima takes many pages of the basic agreements. The basis for the minima, which may be the time employed or the product delivered, differs somewhat among actors, directors, and writers.

For compensation purposes, actors (along with singers and stunt players) are divided into three classes—day players, weekly players, and term players—each of which has a specified dollar minimum per period of employment.[5] For directors, minimum pay is specified as a "piece rate" for completing a project, or in daily or weekly rates analogous to the actors' scheme; either way, the minima vary by the project type, length, and budget. Directors are also entitled to a minimum number of additional paid days for prefilming preparation and postfilming editing. Alone among the three unions, DGA members also receive a minimum bonus if a pilot project becomes a television series.

The minimum compensation schedule for writers resembles that for directors. There are piece rate minima for stories, treatments, screenplays, teleplays, and rewriting and polishing others' work; alternatively, writers may be employed for specified lengths of time with guaranteed weekly minima. As with directors, these rates also vary according to the project's budget or the length of the final product. But the WGA basic agreement is unique in providing for a minimum payment for an entire writing team (though it need not be evenly divided).

In all three occupations, relatively low minimum compensation rates allow neophytes to enter the labor market and establish a repu-

---

[5] Day players usually work in commercials or in bit parts in TV programs. Weekly players usually play character roles in TV programs or theatrical films. Most term players are regular characters in TV series, or have major or supporting roles in theatrical films; they are paid for a minimum number of weeks in each term (for example, 10 out of 13, or 20 out of 26).

tation. MPTV jobs that pay minimum rates are springboards from one project to another (Peters, 1971) and a relatively inexpensive means for employers to evaluate talent. High-potential individuals will attract the attention necessary to move into more lucrative work under personal services contracts. At the same time, workers who cannot make this leap can still earn a living wage because their income is augmented by residuals. This arrangement allows them to remain in the MPTV labor force until they acquire the skill to move up the job ladder.

Personal Services Contracts

MPTV basic agreements also allow individuals whose market value might exceed union scale to negotiate additional compensation through a personal services contract.[6] Such contracts are the industry's ultimate symbol of success, and negotiating their idiosyncrasies is the domain of artists' and producers' attorneys. These contracts usually call for initial compensation higher than the required minimum, and often provide for additional contingent compensation (as a percentage of net profits, gross receipts, merchandise sales, or the like). They often include a commitment to employ the worker in sequels, or to provide amenities for work on location (that is, special travel or housing provisions).

Besides serving as a compensatory mechanism, personal services contracts allow MPTV workers to use their individual bargaining power to obtain rights that their union has been unable to obtain collectively. Often, directors make part of their compensation contingent on a project's timely completion in exchange for "creative control" beyond that provided for in the basic agreement (for example, the right to control the editing of feature films for TV). Because actors' images are so important, stars' personal services contracts often specify where their names will appear on the screen or in advertisements, or allow them to hire the project's wardrobe persons or hairdressers. Writers' personal services contracts contain clauses that

---

[6] The National Labor Relations Act allows individuals to improve their terms of employment beyond those received by other members in their collective bargaining unit; see Jones (1991) on the interplay of individual and collective bargaining rights.

specify exactly what will be written (treatment, screenplay, and so on) and how the producer may use it.[7]

Personal services contracts are also a proving ground for innovative solutions to unforeseen problems. For example, star writers once negotiated clauses in their personal contracts to reserve their right to buy back and resell their work if it was not produced within a certain time. When the number of unproduced scripts rose in the 1970s and 1980s, the WGA codified the procedures contained in those individual contracts and negotiated them into the basic agreement for all writers. Similarly, personal services contracts are also used to adapt the general rules established in the collective bargaining agreement to individual circumstances (Miller, 1985). For example, many writers may contribute to a screenplay without receiving screen credit, which is needed to establish formally their entitlement to residual compensation (discussed below). In response, star writers now commonly use their personal services agreements to provide for special payments if they fail to receive screen credit.

Allowing for differences between writers, directors, and actors, all personal services contracts are similar in being a product of the individual's market power and the skill of the negotiators. In this regard, the roles of agents and attorneys have become so critical to the smooth operation of the labor market that the unions also negotiate with the agents' association to regulate who may represent their members in contract negotiations, what agents' responsibilities to their clients shall be, and what fees shall be charged.

Personal service contracts provide for the exchange of scarce, differentiable, and perishable talent.[8] Also, by deferring compensation or tying it to revenues, personal services contracts can be used to make marginal projects feasible: the willingness of star workers to gamble on windfalls and less-recognized workers to showcase them-

---

[7] General principles from the common law of copyrights were adapted for MPTV via personal services contracts during the 1930s and 1940s. They were then consolidated in the landmark 1951 Screen Writers Guild basic agreement, which held that hiring a writer conveys only the right to use the written product in a single TV or motion picture project. Other rights (to serialize or to publish in a secondary form, for example) must be formally "separated" by payment of additional consideration. See Muhl (1982).

[8] MPTV talent is perishable in the sense that trends may increase or reduce demand for workers who are specialized in a particular genre or possess a particular image.

selves for small initial salaries allows more projects to see the light of day, and so increases the number of potential jobs.[9]

Residuals

Without residuals, labor relations in the broadcasting field are complex but dull.[10] With them, labor-management affairs become exotic confrontations in the competition of high finance (Gelman, 1967:40)

Residuals, the third part of the three-tier compensation system, are additional payments to workers for the exhibition of an entertainment product in media other than the one for which it was originally created, or for its reuse within the same medium subsequent to the initial exhibition. They are sometimes called "reuse fees" or "supplemental contributions." The residual formulas call for payment of a percentage of either the minimum initial compensation or the revenue derived by the product in its new market. Payment continues as long as the product continues to be sold.

History

The principle of payment for repeat use goes back at least to 1941, when the American Federation of Radio Artists' Transcription Code required that performers be paid their original compensation each

---

[9] Although Jack Nicholson was paid a reported $50 million for his role in *Batman,* the project could move forward because the vast majority of this compensation was deferred and contingent on box office and product tie-in revenues. Similarly, the hit *Animal House* was made on a relatively low budget because many relatively unknown actors accepted contingent compensation contracts (which eventually paid much more than the actors probably could have obtained given their individual bargaining power).

[10] Information in this section was compiled by the authors from the unions' basic agreements, newsletters, and strike bulletins, and other materials archived in the Law and Theater Arts Libraries at UCLA; the DGA Archives at California State University, Northridge; Musicians Local 47; the WGA library; and the AMPTP's historical files. The interviewees listed in note 16 also provided background information. Data on the actual amounts of residual payments were obtained from the residuals departments of SAG, WGA, and DGA.

time a program they had recorded was replayed (AFRA, 1941). (Indeed, the AFM already had a payment scheme for phonograph recording in the 1920s, but payments were made to the union rather than to individual performers.) Residual provisions now appear in the basic agreements of every above-the-line union in Hollywood.

Residuals became a major bargaining issue in the 1950s, when it became possible to transfer theatrical motion pictures to commercial television. To producers, television represented a new market in which products could be resold without additional production costs. Workers, understandably, were less enthusiastic about the transfer of existing entertainment products between media. They saw it as an alternative to the production of new material, and feared a loss of employment opportunities. Individual actors, moreover, feared that the repeated exhibition of their motion picture and television images would devalue those images in the public eye and so reduce demand for their talents. These tensions were played out in a protracted series of negotiations and strikes that led to the establishment of residual payments.

Table 5.2 shows the sequence in which residuals were first negotiated for the different markets and the guild that negotiated the breakthrough contract. The AFM was the first union to obtain any form of supplemental compensation for motion pictures exhibited on television (in 1951), but its method of implementation—requiring the

Table 5.2. Development of Residuals, Domestic and Foreign Markets.

Market	Pioneer Union	Year First Negotiated
Theatrical films exhibited on domestic free TV	AFM	1951
Television shows rerun on domestic free TV	SAG	1952
Television commercial reuse	SAG	1953
Television shows exhibited on foreign free TV	WGA	1961
Theatrical films or TV shows exhibited in supplemental markets (domestic or foreign)	SAG	1971
Programs made for supplemental markets exhibited on free TV or theaters (domestic or foreign)	SAG	1980
Products made for basic cable exhibited in other markets	WGA	1988

Source: Compiled from basic agreements, union newsletters, and magazines.

soundtrack to be physically rerecorded—proved too unwieldy. Producers also viewed it as an unwarranted usurpation of their control of shop-floor production practices; they shifted musical recording work to nonunion sites outside the United States, and refused to extend residuals to other guilds. In 1952, SAG's strike against independent producers won a cash payment residual system (termed the Monogram model, after the first producer to surrender). At the same time, SAG obtained residual commitments from the fledgling television networks for the reuse of television programs and from advertisers for the reuse of television commercials. Residual compensation became an industrywide practice only in 1960, when the major studios surrendered in the face of bitter strikes by both SAG and WGA.

The principle of residuals was further tested in the early 1970s, when the supplemental markets of videocassette, cable, and pay-per-view emerged as important sources of revenue. Another round of strikes was fought before residual obligations were extended to those markets. In the late 1980s, when products made for supplemental markets began to appear on free television or in theaters, another contentious battle was fought to extend residual obligations to these transfers. Residuals for international distribution are a current bone of contention, given that 40 percent of a major studio's profit is likely to come from foreign sales and many products are now made for foreign supplemental markets with no domestic release. Indeed, foreign residuals were at the heart of the WGA's protracted strike of 1988, and residual payments are now required for foreign distribution.[11]

Although table 5.2 suggests that SAG has been the leader in extending residuals to new markets, the WGA holds that its rhetoric gives shape to the residual struggles, and SAG's strike power provides the muscle. This militancy has been necessary because of producers' strong resistance to residuals. Producers originally viewed residuals as a form of profit sharing, and expected that they would always be in at least a break-even position when products left their original markets for additional exhibition. Since the mid-1980s, however, almost no films or television shows have recouped their production costs in

[11] Canada is part of the U.S. domestic market for the purpose of residual calculations; Mexico (except for its TV stations that are owned by U.S. networks) is a foreign market (Lees and Berkowitz, 1982:125–26).

the original markets, and this pattern has engendered strong resistance among producers to any expansion of residual entitlements.

Administration of Residual Payments

There are considerable differences among the unions in the degree to which residual compensation is a collective versus individual entitlement. The least individualistic arrangements are those of IATSE (the International Alliance of Theatrical and Stage Employees), which specify that producers' payments go into the Motion Picture Industry Pension Plan and the Motion Picture Health and Welfare Fund, both of which benefit the union's membership as a whole. This arrangement is often seen more as a way to finance fringe benefits than as an augmentation of income (Gilbert, 1958), and the AMPTP denies that these payments are for the "additional use" of work (as specified in the SAG, WGA, and DGA basic agreements).

A middle range approach is found in the SAG (and AFTRA) contracts, which obligate producers to make lump sum residual payments directly to the union. The union divides those funds among the individual performers on each project according to a point system that was devised unilaterally by the union but written into the basic agreement. Residual entitlements are nominally proportional to the number of days each performer worked on the project, but the point system actually favors the lower-paid workers by limiting the number of points any performer can accumulate. SAG and AFTRA therefore maintain the principle of individual entitlement, but place collective controls on that entitlement via a union-administered redistribution of wealth.[12]

The most individualistic entitlements are found in the DGA and WGA basic agreements, which specify that residuals be paid directly to the individuals who contributed to the final product.[13] Residual entitlement is limited to those writers and directors who actually receive screen credit. Even the type of credit is relevant—the residual

[12]   Individual stars can still use their personal services contract as a vehicle to obtain residual compensation beyond the collectively defined entitlement (Mittleman, 1987).
[13]   However, there is precedent for exchanging the individual entitlement for a collective one: in 1984, the DGA abandoned demands for certain videocassette residuals in exchange for additional payments to its health and welfare funds.

Table 5.3. Percentage Distribution of Residual Payments to DGA, WGA, and SAG Members by Source.

Source of Residual Income	Year			
	1960	1970	1980	1990
TV reruns	100%	84%	82%	57%
Theatrical films exhibited on free TV	0	16	13	12
Supplemental markets[a]	0	0	5	32
Total residuals paid[b] (million nominal dollars)	$7.6	$24.9	$98.5	$337.9

Source: DGA, WGA, and SAG residual departments.
[a]Primarily videocassette rentals, cable TV, and pay-per-view.
[b]Excludes residuals for TV commercials.

payment warranted by a "created by" credit differs from that for a "written by," for example. The WGA and DGA contracts also specify grievance procedures to resolve disputes over screen credit, but the administration of this function is the purview of credit committees that are composed entirely of union members. These unions also function as clearinghouses that pass the checks on to their members after monitoring the producers' compliance.

*Residual Payments by Product Market
and Labor Force Segment*

The single most important factor in the growth of residual compensation has been the expansion of residual obligations to new entertainment markets. Table 5.3 details historical changes in the share of residual compensation from the principal entertainment markets over time. In 1954, aggregate residual payments totaled less than 1 million; by 1990, total annual residual payments for entertainment products had risen to more than 337 million.[14]

[14] We exclude residuals on television commercials here because they are not an entertainment product, nor are they regulated by the basic agreements between the unions and the AMPTP. (They are collectively bargained between the DGA, SAG, and AFTRA and an association of advertising agencies; because television commercials are written by employees of advertising firms, WGA members have no TV commercial residuals.) Despite this exclusion, it is important to note that commercials are the largest source of residual income for actors ($273 million in 1990).

Residual compensation grew quickly when residual rights for television reruns were introduced in 1954, and then again after obligations were extended (in 1960–61) to all theatrical pictures as obligations were extended to domestic cable television and foreign free television markets in the late 1970s. Since the mid-1980s, increasing videocassette sales and rentals and the expansion of premium cable channels (such as HBO and Showtime) have made the supplemental markets a major source of new revenues.

The importance of residuals to total compensation varies among labor market segments. Data for SAG members indicate an inverse relationship between an actor's total income and the proportion of that total contributed by residuals. Among feature film actors (nearly all of whom are highly paid under personal services contracts) the ratio of initial compensation to residuals is about six to one. Among television actors (who work under a mix of personal services contracts and minimum wage guarantees), initial compensation is about twice as large as residual income. In television commercials, in which nearly all actors receive minimum scale, residual compensation is four times as great as initial session fees. Although residuals are most important to actors in the lowest-paid segment, the total residual compensation from all markets is approximately equal to total initial compensation. Figure 5.1, showing the total compensation of actors in 1988 by source, demonstrates the importance of residuals to actors' total compensation.

But residuals' role in the operation of the labor market goes beyond that of a compensation mechanism. First, they cushion the impact of unemployment, especially among the neophytes who suffer long periods of unemployment between projects. For these workers, residuals generate a passive income stream between jobs, akin to an annuity. (Brian Walton, WGA executive director, explicitly calls residuals "a form of deferred minimum compensation"; quoted in Kaufman, 1988:1.) Second, residuals relate the control of creative resources to their ownership. We refer here to the conflict between creative workers' interest in preventing overexposure and the producers' desire to exhibit entertainment products in as many revenue-generating settings as possible. Residuals reconcile that divergence of interests by specifying cash compensation for the presumed devaluation of future work via present-day overexposure.

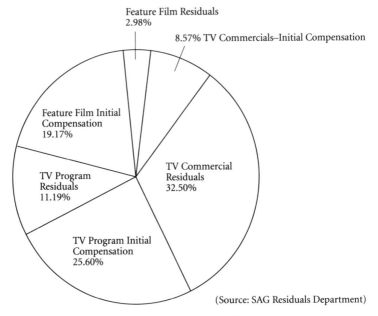

Feature Film Residuals
2.98%

8.57% TV Commercials–Initial Compensation

Feature Film Initial
Compensation
19.17%

TV Program
Residuals
11.19%

TV Commercial
Residuals
32.50%

TV Program Initial
Compensation
25.60%

(Source: SAG Residuals Department)

Figure 5.1. Income by Source, Screen Actors Guild, 1988.

Residuals and Collective Bargaining Practice

In the 1950s, residuals were seen purely as a mechanism to compensate workers for lost work and overexposure. Since then, however, they have evolved in such a way as to overshadow nearly all other aspects of the employment relationship. Their importance is evident in three ways.

First, residual entitlements are the issue over which MPTV unions are most likely to strike. In eighteen of twenty-one strikes by above-the-line unions since 1952, disagreements over residuals either were the major issue or figured prominently (see table 5.4). In most of these cases, strikers sought to extend the principle of residual compensation to new markets. Second, the pattern of residual entitlements has become nearly identical for all unions. Procurement of a residual entitlement by one union almost always stimulates the membership of other unions to press harder (usually successfully) for sim-

Table 5.4. Role of Residuals in Above-the-Line Unions' Strikes, 1952–90.

Union	Total Number of Strikes	Strikes in Which Residuals Were a Principal Issue
AFM	2	1
AFTRA	4	3
DGA	1	1
SAG	7	6
WGA	7	7

Source: Compiled by authors from various accounts in *Variety, Hollywood Reporter,* and *The Yearbook of Film and Television,* as well as from the unions' strike newsletters and other publications.

ilar standing.[15] Although each union negotiates independently with the AMPTP, the residual provisions of their contracts have become so similar that they represent the closest thing MPTV has to pattern bargaining. Finally, the contract provisions that deal with residuals are complex and finely detailed in most of the basic agreements. The residual formulas and procedural rules concerning the timing and methods of payment, regulations for transferring obligations, and so on make up the lengthiest and most complex articles in the WGA's basic agreement, comprising roughly one-sixth of the entire document.

Most important, residuals' emergence as the focus of MPTV labor relations has created a new relationship between unions and employers, demonstrating that fundamental shifts in labor relations can emerge organically from the collective bargaining process. This transformation was initiated when the MPTV unions assumed key responsibilities in residual administration, and has since evolved to incorporate more proactive forms of cooperation. We now examine this process and its broader implications for MPTV labor relations.

[15] In 1970, the WGA abandoned its quest for pay TV residuals in exchange for the right to abrogate the contract if any other unions later obtained such an entitlement. SAG won those residuals the next year, and WGA reopened negotiations and obtained similar rights. Such reopening clauses have become standard when a union concedes its claims for a new residual entitlement.

Impact of the Compensation System
on Labor Relations

Some of the discussion regarding Kochan, Katz, and McKersie's work has centered on what constitutes a true "transformation" (Block, 1990). Indeed, one might interpret the recent restructuring within a framework of traditional evolutionary adaption (Roomkin and Juris, 1990), and the development of MPTV's labor relations would support such an interpretation. But it is also true that evolutionary adaptation, driven by adversarial bargaining, has nonetheless allowed these unions to obtain a highly privileged status.

Accommodating technological change within the compensation system rather than the job security or work rules systems has impelled MPTV industrial relations along a unique pathway of transformation. The unions have taken on certain administrative functions that once were managerial tasks; in so doing, they have become indispensable to managing the labor process (Kleingartner and Paul, 1992). In this regard, MPTV's compensation mechanisms have been as significant as the quality of working life (QWL) circles, employee stock ownership plans (ESOPs), or union-dedicated board seats that Kochan, Katz, and McKersie (1986:146–205) offered as exemplars of their "strategic" transformation.

To show how such a situation has developed, we examine how two aspects of the residual system were institutionalized. Our description of that process draws from (1) synopses of annual events from the *Yearbook of Motion Pictures* (1945–92 editions); (2) a historical analysis of all basic agreements between the unions and AMPTP from 1948 to the present; and (3) interviews with key individuals who participated in contract negotiations.[16]

---

[16] Those who agreed to be interviewed were Warren Adler, DGA Assistant Executive Secretary; Leonard Chassman, SAG Hollywood Executive Director; Nick Counter, AMPTP Executive Director; Dee Dee Daniel, AFM National Contracts Administrator; John Mattler, American Film Marketing Association, Director of Planning; Gerry Schwartz, TPI/Residuals Vice President; and Chuck Slocum, WGA Director of Industry Analysis. At least two interviews were conducted with each to obtain their historical recollections of negotiations and perceptions of current practice.

The "Joint Administration" of Residuals

Although the transformation to flexible production was cohesively directed by the studios' management, it was also accompanied by unanticipated forms of opportunism that provoked an adaptive search for control. Whereas any number of regulatory mechanisms might have been devised, the task ultimately fell to the compensation system. At each stage, what had been seen as uncomplicated solutions were later revealed to be fraught with problems that required increasingly close attention.

The first instances of these problems surfaced in the late 1950s. An outdated conception of the production process was codified in early basic agreements, which required producers to pay residuals out of their exhibition revenues. In response, some producers vertically disintegrated their production and distribution functions into separate firms; by "selling" the product across firm boundaries, the "exhibition revenues" accrued to the distributor, who was not contractually liable. The guilds' reaction was to negotiate provisions into subsequent contracts that made producers' sales of distribution rights contingent on union approval. Approval was granted only if the sales agreement contained a codicil that also transferred the producer's residual obligation.

This change introduced a new problem—many distributors had no idea which particular workers had been employed on any given project. To administer the approval of distribution agreements and to ensure that residual payments reached the correct workers, the unions therefore had to become involved in the administration of compensation. Although the responsibility for payment rests entirely on producers and their assignees, the unions have come to play a major role in administering their disbursement.

SAG and AFTRA are the unions most deeply involved in administering residuals. Each union's residuals department devotes substantial effort to monitoring the number and type of exhibitions and verifying that payment is correct. When SAG's residuals department was established in 1953, it had one part-time secretary. By 1967, it had become the guild's largest department, with twenty employees handling seven thousand to eight thousand checks a month. In 1989, the department's thirty-five employees relied almost entirely on computer technology to handle approximately ninety-six thousand checks a month.

For WGA and DGA members, producers and distributors write residual checks that are payable directly to workers, but the checks are first routed through union headquarters to determine whether producers have met their obligations. The WGA's part in residual administration is especially important: its credit committee determines which among the many writers who work on the various stages of a teleplay or screenplay shall receive screen credit. This decision-making function, which is contentious because only writers with screen credit receive residuals, was taken on by the WGA to remove it from the purview of employer discretion.

After almost forty years, the many layers of union supervision have become so complex and deeply embedded that they cannot easily be altered. During 1988's bitter WGA strike, some employers argued that residuals are an assault on property rights and an unacceptable incursion into managerial prerogatives. The force of their arguments was muted by the reality that the industry has lived and thrived with residuals. DGA's simple monitoring role, SAG's contract approval and payroll functions, and WGA's adjudication of residual entitlements are all recognized by employers as elements of residual administration that rightly belong to the unions. Traditional incremental bargaining practice thus had an unplanned yet still transformative effect on MPTV's industrial relations system.

A Broader Form of Cooperation

Given their joint stake in the compensation system, unions and employers have sought to solve emerging problems within that context. This endeavor has ushered in a period of increased cooperation between the two.

Today, most entertainment products cannot show profits unless they are exhibited in several markets. Fortunately, the proliferation of outlets makes it possible for producers to employ a variety of distribution patterns, such as transferring movies produced for pay TV to theaters. Inevitably, some pattern will be used that does not obligate producers to pay residuals. Producers may not intentionally seek out markets for which there are no residual obligations, but their normal search for distribution revenues sometimes leads them to venues not contemplated in previous rounds of collective bargaining.

When a producer pioneers a lucrative distribution pattern and others follow, the unions' monitoring of market trends makes them aware of this situation very quickly. A problem arises because novel distribution patterns are profitable partly because they are free of residual obligations, whereas those very profits induce demand for residuals in subsequent rounds of collective bargaining. Because of their novelty, it is also difficult to assess new distribution patterns' ability to generate residual payments. This uncertainty creates another dilemma: if residual formulas are set too high, producers may be reluctant to utilize the new distribution pattern, and if they are set too low, they may violate norms of fairness that arise out of comparisons with other distribution patterns.

The typical response of an "untransformed" system of labor relations would simply be to adjust the residual formulas in subsequent rounds of bargaining, and this was the custom in MPTV throughout much of the period under discussion. In recent years, however, the WGA and AMPTP have used the collective bargaining process to create a means of experimenting together. Instead of a single residual formula, several formulas may be developed for novel markets. During a specified period, producers may choose their payment formula, and the AMPTP works with the unions to evaluate the new distribution pattern. After the experimental period, the union chooses the payment formula it prefers.

This simple compromise was made possible partly because the unions have developed responsibility for and competence in administering residuals over many years. Also, AMPTP members recognize that unions' monitoring helps employers obtain a fair share of revenues from distributors who might otherwise misrepresent their income. To a large degree, the unions' participation in the managerial process has helped the parties recognize their joint interest in the industry's health.

Accordingly, there is a growing tendency to engage in continuous bargaining and so avoid brinkmanship as contracts expire. At present, each union's basic agreement provides for the creation of standing committees of union and AMPTP representatives for discussion of important issues that arise between rounds of formal collective bargaining. These committees were originally constituted with purely deliberative powers, but they have, in certain circumstances, made some adjustments in the basic agreements without submitting the changes to formal votes by the wider memberships (Counter, 1992). Although the parties maintain an adversarial relationship, their successful experience in joint administration has highlighted their interdependence and made it difficult for either to do without the other.

Implications for the Future of Collective Bargaining

If labor relations have been transformed in the motion picture and television production industry without unions taking part in strategic planning or workplace control issues, one might ask whether the experience in this industry might be more widely applicable. After all, the MPTV unions have the same bread-and-butter interests as any AFL-CIO affiliate, despite their professional and elitist pretensions. What distinguishes them is that they have been able to protect their members' income directly, without necessarily protecting their jobs. This approach, which evolved out of incremental responses to technological change and production restructuring, has moved the MPTV unions to a central place in this industry's employment relationship.

The ability of other unions to achieve similar ends may well depend on whether they exhibit tendencies similar to those guiding MPTV's transformed system. Three of these are particularly important.

First, MPTV's above-the-line unions have demonstrated in practice their interest in the overall health of the industry. Although rhetoric to this effect usually surrounds the implementation of any cooperative institution, it is hard to find an arena of cooperation more closely connected to fundamental questions of equity and involvement than that of compensation. QWL programs are much farther from the vital nexus of the labor bargain, and the success of employees in directing the course of strategic planning through stock ownership plans or board seats has been mixed at best.

Cooperation in compensation administration requires unions to focus honestly and directly on employers' ability to pay and on the industry's health generally. In return, employers recognize unions as true partners in managing the employment relationship. Indeed, to the extent that MPTV workers have obtained an entitlement equivalent to a property right, one might argue that their standing is *superior* to that of workers who merely participate in strategic choice. This fact was clearly reflected in the comments of a leading AMPTP member at the height of the WGA's acrimonious 1988 strike: "The guild's viability was never and is not now an issue. If the guild didn't exist, we'd have to invent it."[17]

Second, these three MPTV unions have remained important for workers because they make possible the growth of individual careers. The segmentation of work that characterizes many emerging production systems creates conditions for profound divisions among workers, but these divisions need not necessarily be permanent. Many of the two-tier wage systems evident in other industries create rigid boundaries between classes of workers. Such agreements often undermine the principle of solidarity across subsectors of the labor market, and effectively separate the unions' "aristocracy" from those segments of the workforce that are a source of great bargaining power because of growing size. In the three-tier model, as workers move between labor market segments, they retain an attachment to the union irrespective of their career status or individual bargaining power, because the unions address the specific problems of each tier.

Finally, the MPTV compensation scheme also responds to the dynamism of the industry as whole. Traditional models of labor relations are predicated on continuous employment to effect the exchange of compensation and benefits. This imperative forced many unions to make job security a central tenet of their collective bargaining strategy, and ultimately hobbled their industries by constraining labor adjustment strategies. The MPTV unions have created an ongoing right to income and benefits that attaches to past rather than present employment, and so expands the scope of potential adjustment strategies in the face of dynamic competition.

Structural changes in the economy are putting pressure on labor relations systems to find new ways to moderate labor costs, increase

17 Sidney Sheinberg, president of MCA, quoted in Cieply and Margulies (1988).

flexibility, and sustain innovation, while increasing productivity and workers' skills. The system of labor relations we find in MPTV meets each of these challenges. Moreover, it contains certain features that other scholars have identified as critical to unions' survival in the post-Fordist era. Katz and Sabel (1985), for example, noted that unions must acquire rights that were once denied or thought irrelevant, but that now are near the vital core of the emerging production systems. And Miles's (1989) "new business unionism" calls for ways to attach workers' security to the industry as a whole rather than to the particular jobs they may occupy at any moment. The three-tier compensation system meets both of those challenges.

The experience of these three MPTV unions demonstrates how the incremental application of collective bargaining practices can initiate profound transformations in labor relations at other levels. The most important lesson here for unions in other industries may well be that it is not necessary to abandon traditional collective bargaining mechanisms or their traditional adversarial role to achieve a viable future.

CHAPTER SIX

Looking Ahead

Lois Gray and Ronald Seeber

The American entertainment industry and its system of labor-management relations is now at a crossroads. Its future will be determined to a great extent by emerging developments that could either hinder or facilitate expansion, depending on the course of affairs approaching the year 2000. The key trends to watch are technological, regulatory, and economic. All these will converge to influence the course of collective bargaining in the industry and the choices made by unions and employers.

Technological Developments

Technological innovations have always driven the entertainment industry to highs and lows and will continue to do so in the future. Indeed, technology has affected every facet of the entertainment business: the product itself, the end markets for the product, competition in the industry, costs and revenues, and labor-management relations.

All sectors of the entertainment industry are still struggling to adapt to technological developments that have been around for decades now. Meanwhile, emerging technologies have the potential of creating enormous new challenges. The movie business, for

instance, is undergoing its greatest period of change since the introduction of talkies as the digital revolution invades every phase of its
operations. The impending introduction of high-definition television (HDTV) could totally reinvent the broadcast industry and the
delivery of records and motion pictures may be completely transformed by satellites, fiber optics, and computers. Looming is the
struggle for control of the access to all video entertainment and electronic information entering the household. Companies that are ready
for the revolution when it comes stand to profit enormously. Others
could fall by the wayside.

Most of the important trends affecting the industry today—the
easing of federal regulations, the increased consolidation of ownership, and the transformation of labor-management relations—can
be traced to technological developments. Like the computer industry
with which it is converging, the recording, broadcast, and motion picture industries were born of technology and, it seems, are destined to
be ruled by it for all time.

Public Policy Issues

The entertainment industry, like many others, has undergone substantial deregulation in recent years. As new competitors have entered
the field, largely as a result of technological innovations such as cable
television and videocassettes, the rationale for imposing certain types
of regulation no longer make sense. On the other hand, there are
pressures for new types of regulations. Recent decisions of regulatory agencies and others to come in the near future could have vast
implications for the industry for decades.

When the Federal Communications Commission decided no longer
to enforce rules that prohibited movie companies from owning their
own distribution outlets (video chains, television stations, and movie
theaters), its decision allowed studios to own the means of distributing their products for the first time in forty years and provided the studios with a guaranteed outlet for any movie or program they produce.
The repeal of the Paramount decision is likely to result in greater domination of the market by a relatively few large conglomerates.

Another decision likely to result in greater vertical integration in the industry is the lifting of the financial interest and syndication rules barring networks from producing many of their own programs and profiting from reruns or syndication. Mergers between movie studios and television networks are under way as it becomes profitable for both parties to join forces.

Another recent regulatory decision with the potential for momentous impact on the industry allows local telephone companies to offer video services on their fiber-optic installations (a move that has dramatic implictions for cable television); this has already spurred mergers between telephone and cable companies. Pending are decisions whether and under what conditions to introduce HDTV. These technologies could produce big winners and big losers as they completely transform the playing field.

Economic Trends

The trend toward mergers, takeovers, and further conglomeration in the entertainment industry is likely to continue, in part so that the United States can keep pace with the media barons in the other parts of the world. Under new ownership, both the broadcast and film industries have recognized the financial gains to be reaped from vertical integration of their various operations while focusing on greater cost consciousness and efficiency. The emerging conglomerates, rather than maintaining direct control over all production and distribution facilities, as the old Hollywood studios did, operate largely through affiliated but separate companies that sometimes contract with outsiders to create the entertainment product.

This arrangement helps to explain how some independent producers have flourished in an economy increasingly dominated by large conglomerates. Because independents are not always bound by the constraints of union contracts, it is often more profitable for major studios to distribute independently produced films than to produce and distribute their own films.

Aside from conglomeration, the other major trend affecting the economic structure of the entertainment industry is globalization.

Privatization of television in Europe, resulting in huge new markets for domestic producers, along with an expanding number of coproductions and the acquisition of U.S. companies by foreign conglomerates have all helped to fuel the internationalization of the industry. Menacing on the horizon are trade barriers, quotas, and content laws enacted by other countries—which could halt or slow the growth of American entertainment exports—and rampant piracy, robbing producers and entertainers of the fruits of their labor. Technology which is wiping out the barriers that separate the electronic transmission of voice, data, text, and video has blurred the distinctions among broadcasting, cable TV, movies, recording, and even telecommunications and publishing, which have existed as separate sectors and are now in the process of converging into one global industry.

Impact on Labor-Management Relations

All of the factors discussed thus far—technology, deregulation, conglomeration, and globalization—have had a critical impact on labor unions and labor-management relations in entertainment. Robotic cameras, cart machines, computers, and other new kinds of equipment have eliminated thousands of jobs in television. A single projectionist now does the work that once required several; disc jockeys are being eliminated through satellite radio transmission; and movie stuntplayers are losing their jobs to computers that can graphically create special effects without the risk and expense of actually staging them in a studio or on location. As electronic synthesizers have replaced musicians, the rise of digital video synthesizers threatens to shrink the demand for middle-level photographers, actors, and directors.

Aside from eliminating jobs, existing and impending technological innovations (such as HDTV) have the potential to alter the labor relations status quo radically because of the way they affect union work rules, job categories, systems of compensation, and union jurisdictions. The bargaining strength of unions representing below-the-line workers has greatly deteriorated as the skill levels required to operate new equipment have decreased and as the functional lines between management and labor have blurred. In an industry in which materials and equipment have traditionally been the basis for work rules and union jurisdiction, the existence and identity of unions are at stake as equipment becomes obsolete or as certain jobs are eliminated outright. The decrease in required skill levels has also weakened the unions' power to strike because management has found it relatively easy to replace striking workers with no appreciable effect on production.

The proliferation of production companies and end markets for the entertainment product has created problems for unions, which previously had to deal primarily with a few large networks and studios. The growth of independent production companies that use cheaper nonunion labor has made it difficult for unions to make any contract demands that will result in increased costs for management and, in fact, has forced the unions to accept unpopular concessions in order to retain jobs.

At the same time, the emergence of entertainment conglomerates made up of affiliated but essentially separate companies has made it more difficult for unions to negotiate effectively. Similarly, because the unions are nationally rather than internationally organized, they are ill-equipped to monitor and deal with the increasing globalization of the entertainment business.

Clearly, unions are going to have to develop new strategies if they are to survive the changes sweeping their industry. A more international orientation, more inclusive membership policies, more flexibility in negotiations, and the setting aside of artificial jurisdictional boundaries are some of the strategies that have been proposed to reinstate the relative equilibrium that previously existed between labor and management in the industry.

Major Labor Relations Issues for the Future

The content and course of collective bargaining will be influenced by what occurs in the business, technological, and regulatory realms described above. Choices made by unions and employers will determine whether those changes are to be accompanied by a period of additional conflict or a new, yet uncharted course of cooperation on questions of mutual interest.

The critical issues for collective bargainers in the industry are all encompassed in the three broad themes of technology and job content; protection of creative rights; and the structure of employment.

Technological Change and Job Content

Technological change has led to a continual blurring of jurisdictional lines and the creation of new work that does not lie clearly in the domain of any union. Major battles loom as old work divisions become irrelevant and new types of work lead to competition among unions vying for the same piece of the pie. Peaceful and cooperative resolution of these jurisdictional disputes presents a significant challenge for AEEM unions in the future.

Moreover, even where technological change is not at issue, employers are seeking more flexibility in employment relationships in AEEM. This reflects a broader trend under way in the wider economy. Much of the movement toward nonunion film and television production is an attempt to circumvent not the above-the-line talent unions but rather below-the-line craft unions with their tight jurisdictions and work rules. Thus, it is clear that a critical issue for the bargaining table is the resolution of managerial desire for flexibility and traditional union desire to resist that push.

An issue related to job content is the acquisition of training for the new, technologically advanced work. Gradually the training of below-the-line employees has shifted away from an informal system of on-the-job training within the unions to more formal education outside the unions. If below-the-line labor organizations are to continue to serve a critical need in the industry, they need to gain control of the training, selection, and employment of employees in their jurisdiction. Otherwise, employers will rely on systems outside the control of the collective bargaining process to secure their supply of trained employees.

Residual Recovery and Protection of Creative Rights

For talent unions and producers, key issues are how to share in the income from multimedia distributions of the artist's product and how to protect the product from piracy and exploitation. Because technology has made it quite simple to steal an individual artist's work, a common goal for both artists and producers must be to maintain their stake in the product for a longer period of time. This is an area for potential collaboration.

On the other hand, sharing the income from new media markets has spawned much of the conflict in recent years between above-the-line unions and producers, and the pace of technological change points toward continuing difficult negotiations in this area as new media forms and methods of distribution arise.

The Structure of Ownership and Work

In the entertainment industry employment, which has always been high risk, is becoming even more casual. The live and recording sectors continue to be dominated by short-term contracts, and since the disintegration of the old studio system, in which everyone from actors to electricians was employed by the studio, the film industry has been characterized by short-term employment with individuals hired on a project-by-project basis. Television maintained for a much longer period the traditional employer-employee relationship and the notion of permanent employment with a single network or station. As the networks seek to move toward the casual employment model of the film, recording, and live performance sectors of the industry, the union response and the process of collective bargaining must rise to the challenge.

An accompanying trend, interwoven with the film-television convergence, involves the location of work. The film and television production industry has traditionally been centered in Los Angeles and, to a lesser extent, New York. As more inexpensive and mobile equipment allows production to shift to other sites, unions are being forced to decentralize their organizing efforts or risk representing an ever-diminishing proportion of the workforce. Thus, the collective bargaining structure historically set up to accommodate fixed employers, work sites, and unions must quickly shift to accommodate casual employment at a variety of locations.

While the issues cited above comprise a selective and subjective list, it is clear that most of the problems of the industrial relations system in AEEM are encompassed therein. Unions and managements face choices which will influence the future character and content of collective bargaining in the industry.

Issues for Unions

For the AEEM unions, the major issues to be confronted have to do with how and when to implement structural changes to accommodate new business trends. The unions continue to find themselves in a reactive posture, trapped by outmoded structures that render them unable to respond effectively to rapid changes at the studios and networks. Union structure has historically been linked to business and economic structure, different in every industry. We are at a point in time when union structures and bargaining structures are linked to business structures that no longer exist. Particularly for below-the-unions, choices made here will go a long way toward determining their future.

A related issue for unions is how to reacquire control of the job information network. Currently, people in the AEEM industry find out about jobs in the same way they acquire their skills—from a variety of means, often haphazard. If the unions could be perceived as a distributor of job information and a means of obtaining employment in the industry, they could regain some of the power lost in recent years.

Likewise, unions need to seek means to reacquire the training process by which individuals obtain skills necessary to employment. Many unions in other industries have wrestled with this problem, and through jointly funded training programs (e.g., the building and maritime trades and the auto industry) have reasserted themselves as partners critical to the creation and maintenance of skills.

A third issue for unions is the question of when and with whom to merge. Whether mergers occur will have a significant impact on collective bargaining in the industry. A fourth issue relates to the globalization of employers, creating the need for international collaboration among unions.

Issues for Employers

Employers in the AEEM industry are also at a crossroads. In order to compete in the global market, they must be able to predict and plan costs of production, attract and retain a skilled labor force, and keep abreast of technological change. Global leadership by U.S. production in this industry is ultimately at stake.

One choice is to continue down the nonunion path below the line and risk the eventual alienation of above-the-line unions. If employers pursue the nonunion model, unions could be forced to step up their defensive and adversarial campaigns. Employers, relying on the vagaries of a system uncontrolled by collective bargaining, face real risk in relying on that system to produce the necessary workforce. Alternatively, employers might choose to avoid confrontation and seek to cooperate with below-the-line unions in creating a more constructive environment in which there is a legitimate role for the unions. This could result not only in the creation and maintenance of a stable, skilled labor force but also in mutual efforts in the international area.

Question for Unions and Employers

Clearly, unions and managements have joint interests in finding ways to protect and share the proceeds of increasing productivity and market growth. Common ground could certainly be found in the cause of political action to advance funding for the arts and favorable legislation to protect intellectual property and to secure the access of U.S. products to the world market. These cooperative efforts could lead to more stable labor-management relations and could spur cooperative problem solving in other arenas.

Other industries have found that at certain times, joint union-management interests can outweigh factors leading to labor-management conflict. That has been the case in sectors of the U.S. manufacturing, construction, transportation, and communications industries, where employers and unions have found their integrative interests to outweigh their distributive interests in the face of external threats to their well-being.

Innovative Developments

In fact, movement toward labor-management cooperation is already under way in sectors of AEEM. In the aftermath of the devastating business and employment impact of the wave of strikes during the 1980s, both employers and unions expressed an awareness of the desirability of working out differences in the interest of promoting their common stake in industry survival and growth (see, for example, statements by Nick Counter and Jack Golodner in the foreword to this volume). In the broadcast industry, CBS and IBEW had led the way by establishing a system of periodic consultation to anticipate problems in advance of formal negotiations. Beginning in 1988, the AMPTP entered into "early warning" bargaining with IATSE, SAG, and the Directors and Writers guilds to resolve outstanding issues in motion picture production well in advance of contract expiration dates. A multiemployer, multilocal Cooperative Committee has been formed between AMPTP and IATSE and the Contract Adjustment Committee of the Writers Guild and AMPTP provides a continuing forum for bargaining during the term of the collective bargaining agreement (Counter interview). Unions and employers have also joined together in common efforts in international forums to protect American products against piracy.

Recommended Research

The arts and entertainment industry is a sector of our economy about which much has been written but very little is known. While there have been solid analyses of business structure and earnings prospects for entertainment firms, there are few recent publications analyzing employment and labor relations practices in this industry. We have outlined some of the key issues highlighting the implications of technological change. It is hoped that further research will deal with employment, compensation, and labor relations patterns. Among the questions with public policy implications are:

—The implications of growing part-time employment for income and job satisfaction.

—Results of a benefit structure in which individual pensions and health and welfare credits are fractionalized through intermittent employment and administration through multiple unions.

—Factors influencing the extent of unionization in the industry, pinpointing the reasons for the declining percentage of representation for below-the-line employees.

—Patterns in union contracts and grievances settlement as these reflect adaptation to technological changes.

—Results of the union-management consultations which are emerging in sectors of the industry.

While the arts and entertainment industry is, in many ways, unique in its employment and labor relationships practices, its experience in adapting to technological change should be of interest to public officials and leaders of other industries and unions which are facing similar challenges.

Bibliography

AFL-CIO Committee on the Evolution of Work. 1985. *The Changing Situation of Workers and Their Unions.* Washington, D.C.: AFL-CIO.

AFRA (American Federation of Radio Artists). 1941. *Official Bulletin,* April (2/8).

Aksoy, Asu, and Kevin Robins. 1992. "Hollywood for the 21st Century: Global Competition for Critical Mass in Image Markets." *Cambridge Journal of Economics,* vol. 16, pp. 1–22.

Andrews, Edmund. 1992. "Digital Radio: Static is Only between Owners," *New York Times,* May 6, sec. D, p. 8, col. 1.

———. 1993. "FCC Orders Cuts in Cable TV Rates, Eases Rerun Rules," *New York Times,* April 2, sec. A, p. 1, col. 6.

Bagdikian, Ben H. 1983. *The Media Monopoly.* Boston: Beacon.

Barnes, Peter W. 1987. "NBC to Seek Concessions from Union: Move Could Spur Networks' Cost Cutting," *Wall Street Journal,* February 20, sec. 1, p. 9, col. 1.

Baumol, William J., and William G. Bowen. 1966. *Performing Arts: The Economic Dilemma.* New York: Twentieth Century Fund.

Bension, Samuel. 1988. *The Producers' Master Guide 1988.* New York: Publications Manual, Inc.

Bernstein, Harry. 1989. "Hollywood's Craft Workers under Pressure to Take Cuts," *Los Angeles Times,* January 24, p. D1.

———. 1991. "Learning How to Flex Their Muscles," *Los Angeles Times,* January 4, pp. F14, F15.

Block, Fred L. 1990. *Postindustrial Possibilities: A Critique of Economic Discourse.* Berkeley: University of California Press.

Broadcasting. 1986. "The Trimming of the Guard at CBS," September 29, p. 34.
———. 1987. "G.E. Plans to Cut 700 Jobs at NBC," November 9, p. 84.
Brody, David. 1989. "Labor History, Industrial Relations, and the Crisis of American Labor." *Industrial and Labor Relations Review* 43 (1): 7–18.
Carter, Bill. 1989a. "Battling Studios on Profit, Networks Become Producers," *New York Times,* June 5, sec. D, p. 14, col. 1.
———. 1989b. "BBC Finds America is a Cable-Ready Market," *New York Times,* September 18, sec. D, p. 8, col. 3.
———. 1990. "NBC, Citing Nielsen, Sees a $200 Million Ad Shortfall," *New York Times,* June 7, sec. D, p. 19, col. 1.
———. 1992a. "CBS Discloses Plan to Begin Charging Fees to Its Affiliates," *New York Times,* May 31, sec. 1, p. 1, col. 1.
———. 1992b. "A Monopoly Once Moore, Nielsen is Still Unloved," *New York Times,* September 7, sec. 1, p. 41, col. 1.
Christopherson, Susan. 1992. "The Origins of Fragmented Bargaining Power in Entertainment Media." *Proceedings of the Forty-Fourth Annual Meetings* (New Orleans, January 2–5, 1992). Madison, Wis.: Industrial Relations Research Association, pp. 10–17.
Christopherson, Susan, and Michael Storper. 1986. "The City as Studio, the World as Backlot: The Impact of Vertical Disintegration on the Location of the Motion Picture Industry." *Society and Space* 4: 305–20.
———. 1989. "The Effects of Flexible Specialization and Industrial Politics and the Labor Markets: The Motion Picture Industry." *Industrial and Labor Relations Review* 42, no. 3 (April): 331–47.
Cieply, Michael, and Lee Margulies. 1988. "Writers' Rejection of Pact May Further Slow Industry," *Los Angeles Times,* June 24, sec. 1, p. 1.
Cooper, Marc. 1987. "Concession Stand," *American Film,* December.
———. 1988. "Labor Pains: Hollywood Unions Are on the Defensive: Can They Survive? Should They?" *Premiere,* September, pp. 86–89.
Counter, J. Nicholas III. 1992. "New Collective Bargaining Strategies for the 1990s: Lesson from the Motion Picture Industry." *Proceedings of the Forty-Fourth Annual Meetings* (New Orleans, January 2–5, 1992). Madison, Wis.: Industrial Relations Research Association, pp. 32–38.
Cox, Dan. 1994. "Study: IA Work Tied to Pic's Budget," *Daily Variety,* October 6, p. 1.
Cray, Ed. 1989. "Hollywood Unchained." *California Lawyer,* February.
Delugach, A. 1988. "Hollywood Finds a Gold Mine in Foreign Markets," *Los Angeles Times,* August 8, pp. 2, 4.
Dosi, G. et al. (eds). 1988. *Technical Change and Economic Theory.* London: Pinter.
Dunn, Donald. 1988. "This Year's Show Tune: Broadway Malady." *Business Week,* November 28, p. 81.
Economist. 1989. "There's No Bigness Like Show Bigness," March 25.

———. 1991. "A Survey of the Music Business," December 21, Special Supplement.

Fabrikant, Geraldine. 1988. "Network Affiliates Find New Buyers," *New York Times*, November 14, sec. D, p. 9, col. 2.

———. 1989. "U.S. TV Producers Seek More Foreign Partners," *New York Times*, November 13, sec. D, p. 13, col. 5.

Farhi, Paul. 1989. "Hollywood in the '80s: A Boffo Business Rolls On," *Washington Post*, March 26, pp. H1, H4.

Freeman, Mark. 1990. "Looking to 1995: Blurring of the Lines Between Producers, Syndicates," *Broadcasting*, January 22.

Gelman, Morris. 1967. "The Above-the-Line Unions." *Television* 24 (November): 40.

Gerard, Jeremy. 1988. "2 Moves at NBC Reflect Push for Efficiency," *New York Times*, November 21, sec. 8, p. 8. col. 1.

Gifford, Courtney D. 1994. *Directory of U.S. Labor Organizations, 1994–95 edition*. Washington, D.C.: Bureau of National Affairs.

Gilbert, Robert W. 1958. "'Residual Rights' Established by Collective Bargaining in Television and Radio." *Law and Contemporary Problems* 23 (Winter): 102–24.

Goldman, Kevin. 1992. "Reregulation Means Fights Over Fees to Broadcasters from Cable TV Firms," *Wall Street Journal*, October 7.

Goldstein, Michael. 1995. "Can Broadway Be Saved?" *New York*, May 29.

Goldstein, Richard. 1978. "Electronic Journalism and Union Rivalry: Is Litigation the Answer?" *Labor Law Journal*, March, pp. 137–48.

Gomery, Douglas. 1986. *The Hollywood Studio System*. New York: St. Martins Press.

Gomery, J. D. 1984. "Corporate Ownership and Control in the Contemporary U.S. Film Industry." *Screen* 25 (4–5): 60–69.

Gordon, David M., Richard Edwards, and Michael Reich. 1982. *Segmented Work, Divided Workers: The Historical Transformation of Labor in the United States*. New York: Cambridge University Press.

Greenhouse, Steven. 1989. "For Europe, U.S. May Spell TV," *New York Times*, July 31, sec. D, p. 1, col. 3.

Hofmeister, Sallie. 1994. "Rifts Shake and Rattle Warm-Music," *New York Times*, November 1, p. D1.

Hollywood Organizer. 1989. "Fighting Union Discrimination," May.

Huff, Richard. 1988. "NBC Enters Euro Market with Stake in Reuters Subsid," *Hollywood Reporter*, November 13.

Hummler, Richard. 1988. "Employment Hits a High for Equity, But Income Sets No Records," *Variety*, December 7, p. 93.

Izod, John. 1988. *Hollywood and the Box Office, 1895–1966*. New York: Columbia University Press.

Jones, Edgar. 1991. "The Interplay of Collective Bargaining Agreements and

Personal Services Contracts." *Loyola Entertainment Law Journal* 11, no. 1: 11–22.

Katz, Harry. 1992. "The Decentralization of Collective Bargaining: A Comparative Review and Analysis," manuscript, School of Industrial and Labor Relations, Cornell University, Ithaca, N.Y.

Katz, Harry C., and Charles F. Sabel. 1985. "Industrial Relations and Industrial Adjustment in the Car Industry." *Industrial Relations* 24: 295–315.

Kaufman, Dave. 1988. "WGA 1987 Resids Record $57 Mil," *Daily Variety*, January 11, p. 1.

Kleinfeld, N. R. 1990. "The Networks' New Advertising Age," *New York Times*, July 29, sec. 3, p. 1, col. 2.

Kleingartner, Archie, and Alan S. Paul. 1992. "Member Attachment and Union Effectiveness in Arts and Entertainment." *Proceedings of the Forty-Fourth Annual Meetings* (New Orleans, January 2–5, 1992). Madison, Wis.: Industrial Relations Research Association, pp. 18–31.

KMPG Peat Marwick. 1988. *Economic Impact of the Film Industry in California.* Report available from the California Film Commission, Hollywood, California.

Knowlton, Christopher. 1988. "Lessons from Hollywood Hit Men." *Fortune*, August 29, p. 78.

Kochan, Thomas A., Harry C. Katz, and Robert B. McKersie. 1986. *The Transformation of American Industrial Relations.* New York: Basic Books.

Kolbert, Elizabeth. 1993. "Television: As the Dust Settles in the Fyn-Syn War between Networks and Studios, Mutual Resentment Lingers," *New York Times*, April 12, D6.

Kubasik, Ben. 1987. "The Low Cost of News at CNN," *Newsday*, February 25.

Lees, David, and Stan Berkowitz. 1982. *The Movie Business.* New York: Vintage.

Lippman, John. 1991. "Cable TV Not Achieving Dream of Limitless Choice," *Los Angeles Times*, May 10, pp. A1, A20.

Lipset, Seymour Martin (ed.). 1986. *Unions in Transition: Entering the Second Century.* San Francisco: ICS Press.

Lipsky, David B., and Clifford B. Donn. 1987. *Collective Bargaining in American Industry.* Lexington, Mass.: D.C. Heath.

Lovell, Hugh. 1955. *Collective Bargaining in the Motion Picture Industry; A Struggle for Stability.* Berkeley: Institute of Industrial Relations, University of California.

Lowry, Brian. 1988. "NBC Expands Ties with Aussie Network," *Variety*, November 4.

———. 1989. "95% of NABET Membership Votes to Ratify ABC Pact," *Variety*, August 16.

Miles, Raymond. 1989. "Adapting to Technology and Competition: A New

Industrial Relations System for the 21st Century." *California Management Review,* Winter, pp. 9–28.

Miller, James. 1985. "How Much Is Not Enough?" In *Back to the Future: Prognostications on the Motion Picture and Television Industries.* Proceedings of the Tenth Annual UCLA Entertainment Symposium, Los Angeles, Calif., pp. 79–86.

Mittleman, Sheldon. 1987. "Residuals Under the Guild Agreements—WGA, DGA, IATSE, SAG and AFM: Accommodating the New Media." In *Reel of Fortune: A Discussion of Critical Issues Affecting Film and Television Today,* Proceedings of the Twelfth Annual UCLA Entertainment Symposium, Los Angeles, Calif., pp. 83–92.

Muhl, Lee. 1982. "The Sale and Acquisition of Rights for Theatrical Motion Pictures and Television Products." In M. Lauer and P. Dekom (eds.), *The Business and Legal Aspects of Representing Talent in the Entertainment Industry,* Proceedings of the Seventh Annual UCLA Entertainment Symposium, Los Angeles, Calif., pp. 371–424.

NABET News. 1965. "NABET Welcomes N.Y. Film Group into Union Fold," August.

Nelson, Richard R., and Sidney G. Winter. 1982. *An Evolutionary Theory of Economic Change.* Cambridge: Harvard University Press.

O'Donnell, Pierce, and Dennis McDougal. 1992. *Fatal Subtraction: How Hollywood Really Does Business.* New York: Doubleday.

Passell, Peter. 1989. "An Economist Looks at Broadway's Bottom Line," *New York Times,* December 10, sec. 2, p. 1, col. 2.

Peters, Anne K. 1971. "Acting and Aspiring Actresses in Hollywood: A Sociological Analysis." Dissertation, UCLA Department of Sociology.

Piore, Michael J., and Charles F. Sabel. 1984. *The Second Industrial Divide: Possibilities for Prosperity.* New York: Basic Books.

Prindle, David F. 1988. *The Politics of Glamour: Ideology and Democracy in the Screen Actors Guild.* Madison: University of Wisconsin Press.

Richter, Paul. 1989. "Studios Taste for TV Grows," *Los Angeles Times,* January 19, pt. 4, p. 1, col. 1.

Robb, David. 1988a. "Hope to Avert Teamsters Strike," *Variety,* September 28.

———. 1988b. "Teamsters Put on Walkin' Shoes," *Variety,* October 4.

———. 1994. "Labor Dept. Has Eye on Film Overtime Violations," *Hollywood Reporter,* October 6.

Roomkin, Myron, and Harvey Juris. 1990. "Strategy and Industrial Relations: An Examination of the American Steel Industry." In James Chelius and James Dworkin (eds.), *Reflections on the Transformation of Industrial Relations.* Metuchen, N.J.: Rutgers University, Institute of Management and Labor Relations Press and Scarecrow Press.

Ruttenberg, Friedman, Kilgallon, Gutchess and Associates. 1981. *A Survey of*

Employment, Underemployment and Unemployment in the Performing Arts, Washington, D.C.

Scott, A. 1984. "Territorial Reproduction and Transformation in a Local Labour Market: The Animated Film Workers of Los Angeles," *Environment and Planning D: Society and Space* 2 (3): 277–307.

Seltzer, George. 1989. *Music Matters: The Performer Musician and the American Federation of Musicians,* Metuchen, N.J.: Scarecrow Press.

Stevenson, Richard. 1989a. "Paramount Pictures' Success Key to Revamping at G&W," *New York Times,* April 11, sec. D, p. 1., col. 1.

———. 1989b. "Hollywood Takes to the Global Stage," *New York Times,* April 16, sec. 3, p. 1, col. 2.

———. 1991. "F.C.C. Rejects Producers' Bid to Delay Syndication Ruling," *New York Times,* April 9, sec. D, p. 15, col. 3.

Storper, Michael. 1989. "The Transition to Flexible Specialisation in the U.S. Film Industry: External Economies, the Division of Labour, and the Crossing of Industrial Divides." *Cambridge Journal of Economics* 13: 273–305.

———. 1991. "Technology Districts and International Trade: The Limits to Globalization in an Age of Flexible Production." Working paper, the Lewis Center for Regional Policy Studies, University of California, Los Angeles.

Storper, Michael, and Susan Christopherson. 1987. "Flexible Specialization and Regional Industrial Agglomerations: The Case of the U.S. Motion Picture Industry." *Annals of the American Association of Geographers* 77 (1): 104–17.

Tajgman, David. 1984. "A Primer of Labor Relations in the Entertainment Industry," *Industrial Labor Relations Report.* Spring.

Terry, Ken. 1993. "Around the World, They're Playing Our Songs." *Billboard,* May 8, p. M3.

Ulmer, James. 1988. "Despite Approval, Teamsters Dissatisfied with Pact Terms," October 31.

U.S. Department of Commerce. 1991. *U.S. Industrial Outlook,* January, pp. 32–1–7.

U.S. Department of Labor, Bureau of Labor Statistics. 1991. Telephone interview.

U.S. Department of Labor, Bureau of Labor Statistics. 1992. *Employment and Earnings* 39 (12), December.

U.S. General Accounting Office. 1991. "Strikes and Striker Replacements in the 1970s and 1980s." HRD-91-2. Washington, D.C.: USGAO.

U.S. Office of Technology Assessment. 1989. "Copyright and Home Copying: Technology Challenges Law."

Variety. 1988. "Union Will Seek to Curb Abuses by Studios in Film Pickup Deals," June 29.

Vogel, Harold L. 1986, 1994. *Entertainment Industry Economics: A Guide for Financial Analysis.* New York: Cambridge University Press.

Wasko, J. 1981. "The Political Economy of the American Film Industry," *Media, Culture and Society* 3 (2): 135–53.

Waters, Harry F., and Peter McKillop. 1988. "TV News: The Rapid Rise of Home Rule." *Newsweek,* October 17.

Weintraub, Bernard. 1992a. "Batman Is Back, and the Money Is Pouring In," *New York Times,* June 22, sec. C, p. 13, col. 1.

———. 1992b. "Budgets Bloat: Studios Worry," *New York Times,* June 25, sec. C, p. 13, col. 1.

Wharton, Dennis. 1989. "41% of Yanks Copying Music, Government Study Finds," *Variety,* November 1, p. 69.

Writers Guild of America. 1989. "The Status of Women and Minority Members of the Writers Guild, Report to the Guild Membership." Los Angeles: Writers Guild of America.

Zoglin, Henry. 1988. "The Big Boy Blues." *Time,* October 17.

Interviews

All interviews were conducted during 1989–1991.

Asner, Edward: Former President, Screen Actors Guild

Berman, James S.: President, Recording Industry Association of America

Bikel, Theodore: President, Associated Actors and Artistes of America

Chassman, Leonard: Hollywood Director, Screen Actors Guild

Coblenz, Walter: Producer

Counter, J. Nicholas III: President, Alliance of Motion Picture and Television Producers

D'Agostino, Louis: Business Representative, Local 644

DiTolla, Alfred W.: President, International Alliance of Theatrical and Stage Employees

Dolgen, Jonathan: President, Fox Television

Franklin, Michael: Former Executive Secretary, Writers Guild of America, West

Frasier, Cliff: Independent Producer

Fried, Robert: Vice President for Production, Columbia Pictures

Geffner, Leo: Attorney, International Alliance of Theatrical and Stage Employees

Gehan, Bernard: Vice President for Labor Relations, NBC

Gilliam, Reggie: Director of the Entertainment Division, International Brotherhood of Electrical Workers

Golodner, Jack: President, Department of Professional Employees, AFL-CIO

Goldstein, Richard: Attorney

Greenspan, Joan: Director of Industrial Department, Screen Actors Guild

Kent, Arthur: Former Local President, National Association of Broadcast Employees and Technicians

Krolik, Day III: Vice President, NBC

Mangan, Mona: Executive Director, Writers Guild of America, East

McGuire, Eugene: Executive Director for Personnel and Labor Relations, NBC

McGuire, John: Vice President, Screen Actors Guild

McLean, John: Vice President for Industrial Relations, CBS

Moffett, Kenneth E.: Assistant to the President, National Association of Broadcast Employees and Technicians

O'Neil, Frederick: Former President, Associated Actors and Artistes of America

Petrafesa, John: International Representative, International Alliance of Theatrical and Stage Employees

Prelock, Edward: Director of Legal and Contract Affairs, IBT Local 399

Raphael, Alan: Vice President for Industrial Relations, Warner Communications

Ruthizer, Jeffrey: Vice President for Labor Relations, ABC

Schoenfeld, Gerald: President, New York League of Theaters

Sirmons, James F.: Vice President for Labor Relations, CBS

Sprague, Steven: Assistant to President, American Federation of Musicians

Tajgman, David: National Labor Relations Board, Los Angeles

Turley, Thomas: Former Business Manager, NABET Local 15

Wolff, Sanford I.: Executive Director, American Guild of Musical Artists

York, Bruce: Executive Director, American Federation of Television and Radio Artists

Contributors

JOHN AMMAN, formerly a graduate assistant in the School of Industrial and Labor Relations, Cornell University, is a business agent for International Photographers, Local 644 of the IATSE, and for IATSE, Local 161.

LES BROWN is a media consultant.

SUSAN CHRISTOPHERSON is Associate Professor, Department of City and Regional Planning, College of Arts and Sciences, Cornell University.

LOIS S. GRAY is the Jean McKelvey–Alice Grant Professor of Labor-Management Relations, School of Industrial and Labor Relations, Cornell University.

ARCHIE KLEINGARTNER is the Founding Dean of the UCLA School of Public Policy and Social Research and Professor of Management and Policy Studies at UCLA.

ALAN PAUL is a doctoral candidate, Department of Geography, UCLA.

RONALD L. SEEBER is Associate Dean and Associate Professor, School of Industrial and Labor Relations, Cornell University.

Index

ABC (American Broadcasting Companies, Inc.), 5, 32, 64; ABC-TV, 55; ABC Video Enterprises, 55; and NABET, 136–37, 151. *See also* Capital Cities/ABC

Actors, 19–20, 91, 125–26. *See also* Talent unions

Actors Equity (AEA), 6, 38, 39

Advertising, 29, 33, 49, 58, 82; and cable television, 64, 69, 94–95; commercials, 38, 81, 168; in Europe, 75–76; and guaranteed ratings, 69–70; local *vs.* spot, 72; and major networks, 67; and residuals, 168, 170n14

AEEM industry, 2–14; defined, 2–3

AFL-CIO, 41, 153

Alliance of Motion Picture and Television Producers (AMPTP), 1, 13, 24, 124, 173; bargaining and labor relations, 42, 160–62; and job crossovers, 126; and labor-management cooperation, 49, 111; and residuals, 176–77

American Federation of Musicians (AFM), 5, 39, 41, 42, 47–48, 161; and residuals, 167–68

American Federation of Radio Artists, 166–67

American Federation of Television and Radio Artists (AFTRA), 7, 38, 41, 42; jurisdiction, 161; merger talks, 49; and news production, 142; and residuals, 169, 175–76

American Guild of Musical Artists (AGMA), 7, 39, 42

American Guild of Variety Artists (AGVA), 7, 39

American Motion Picture Export Association (AMPEA), 89–90

Association of Motion Picture Producers (AMPP), 115, 117

Association of Technical Engineers (ATE), 119

Audience, 1, 3, 66–68, 82

Audio Home Recording Act, 23

Automation, 71–74, 82, 131, 184

Basic Agreement, 126, 148–49, 163–66, 175; Article 20, 129, 139

Berlusconi, Silvio, 75, 76, 80

British Sky Broadcasting (BSkyB), 60

Broadcasting, 2–3, 28–34; deregulation, 30–31, 51–52; employment in, 71–72; independent, 90–91; international, 74–80; live, 80–81; operating costs, 31,

Broadcasting (*cont.*)
33; ownership, 33; revenues, 33–34, 48,
64; and skills, 120. *See also* Cable television; Radio; Television

C. Itoh and Company, 80
Cable television, 6, 29, 54, 60, 82, 91, 132;
audience, 66–68; end markets, 94–95;
and news programming, 32; and regulation, 31, 52; revenues, 69; size of,
68–69; subscriber fees, 64, 69, 94–95,
132
Canada, 74–75, 78–79
Capital Cities/ABC, 52, 55, 64, 67, 133.
See also ABC
CBS, 5, 32, 49, 132–33; and affiliates, 69;
and IBEW, 119, 151–52
CBS Records (Columbia), 53
Christopherson, Susan, 131
CIO, 119–20. *See also* AFL-CIO
CNN (Cable News Network), 53, 138
Collective bargaining, 4–8; and compensation, 174–78; future of, 178–80; joint
consultations, 5, 10, 47; structure,
34–42; study of, 3–5; unions,
40–41(table). *See also* Unions
Communications Act of 1934, 51–52
Communications Workers of America
(CWA), 152–53
Compensation, 25, 34; and cooperation,
176–78, 189–90; flat rates, 140; and
labor relations, 174–78; minimum pay
rates, 13, 163–64; personal services
contracts, 13, 164–66; three-tier model, 157, 162–65, 179. *See also* Employment; Residuals
Computers, 43, 46, 73–74
CONUS, 137–38
Counter, Nick, 24
Craft unions, 4, 9–12, 25, 34, 38–39,
113–55, 161; Basic Crafts, 41, 115, 123,
126; membership, 106–7

DBS, 60–61, 66, 75, 76, 82, 85
Directors Guild of America (DGA), 41,
42, 123, 156, 161; minimum pay rates,
163; and residuals, 169–70, 176
Disney Corporation, 27, 80, 100, 130, 131

Distribution, 26–28; false independents,
130; joint ventures, 129; in motion
picture industry, 25–28; negative pick-
ups, 25, 92, 100, 129–30; oligopolistic
control of, 88–89; and ownership,
94–97, 99; and production, 92–93; and
residuals, 176–77; and technology,
94–97

Economics, 8; ancillary markets, 24, 28;
and live performing arts, 17–18; operating costs, 31, 33; production costs,
16–18, 77, 93, 124; trends, 15–34,
183–84
Employment: benefits, 11, 103–4, 126,
136, 144, 152, 154–55, 190; double
time, 127–29; job content and working
conditions, 44–45; labor standards,
139–42; loosening ties of, 102–5; minimum conditions, 6, 48; nonunion
workers, 139–47; per diem, 134–37,
152; QWL programs, 174, 178; roster
system, 103–4, 117, 145, 149–50;
seniority categories, 136–37; skills
acquisition, 107–8; staff reductions,
71–73; structure of, 187–88; and subcontracted production, 103, 139; and
technology, 42–44, 50; workforce composition, 105–8, 111–12. *See also*
Compensation; Freelancers; Residuals;
Unions
Entrepreneurial culture, 24, 106, 108–11
ESPN, 55, 64, 66, 68, 95
Europe, 74–80; France, 76, 77, 79; Germany, 76; Italy, 75, 76; United Kingdom, 76
Exports, 8, 9, 16, 22, 30, 85, 95

Federal Communications Commission
(FCC), 8, 12, 30–31, 52, 83–85, 95–97;
early regulations, 118–19; and trans-
mission standards, 63
Financial interest and syndication rules
(fin-syn), 31, 60, 83–85, 92, 95–97; and
unions, 138–39
Financing, 16, 27, 88–89, 100
Fox Broadcasting, 33, 58–60, 65, 84, 131
Freelancers, 134, 152, 154; broadcast

Freelancers (*cont.*)
technicians, 73; news groups, 137–38; television technicians, 141–42. *See also* Nonunion workers

Globalization, 30, 86, 88, 97–98, 183–84; and unions, 153–54
Group W, 80, 138

HBO (Home Box Office), 54–55, 95
High-definition television (HDTV), 61–63, 82, 182
Home video, 26, 82

Imagine, 100–101
International Alliance of Theatrical and Stage Employees (IATSE), 11–12, 38–39, 41, 42, 48, 113, 118–55; Local 644 (East Coast Camera), 114, 147, 149–50, 153; Local 659 (Camera), 114, 145, 149–50; locals, 114, 143–50; membership, 117–18, 120, 143, 144–46; national contracts, 149–50; New York Production Locals (NYPL), 147–48; organizing film projects, 143–44; and residuals, 169; special contracts, 146–49; strategies for change, 142–43; Studio Mechanics Caucus, 146
International Brotherhood of Electrical Workers (IBEW), 6, 12, 41, 42, 114, 119, 151–53; and CBS, 151–52; jurisdiction, 131; membership, 120–21
International Brotherhood of Teamsters (IBT), 5, 38, 110, 416; and WGA strike, 126–29

Japan, 62–63

League of New York Theaters, 41, 48
Lewis, Drew, 57
Live performing arts, 2–3, 17–18; and bargaining, 39–40; unions, 39–40

Markets: ancillary, 89, 104; end markets, 91, 93; export, 8, 9, 16, 22, 30, 95; front end *vs.* back end, 78; multiplication of, 94–97; and regulations, 95–97; video, 89
MCA Inc., 79, 98, 100

Morgado, Robert, 22
Motion picture and television production (MPTV), 157; collective bargaining in, 160–66; framework for analysis, 157–60. *See also* AEEM industry
Motion Picture Health and Welfare Fund, 104, 169
Motion picture industry, 2, 3, 23–28; economic factors, 23–28; and independent filmmakers, 122–24; organizational structure, 90, 114–18; and outsourcing, 129–30; steps in production, 24–25; and technology, 43–44; theaters, 96, 130–31
Motion Picture Industry Pension Plan, 169
MTM Productions, 79, 93
MTV (music television), 22, 95
Murdoch, Rupert, 17, 30, 58–60, 65, 84
Musicians, 43, 47–48, 184

National Association of Broadcast Employees and Technicians (NABET), 12, 38, 42, 44, 113–14, 151–53; jurisdiction, 131; locals, 136, 147, 150–51; membership, 120–21; and NBC, 134–35
National Association of Broadcasters, 71, 81
National Labor Relations Act (NLRA), 119, 141, 164n6
NBC (National Broadcasting Corporation), 5, 32, 44, 46; and automation, 73, 74; and IATSE, 148; and NABET, 134–35, 151; Red and Blue networks, 119
Negative pick-ups, 25, 92, 100, 129–30
Networks: affiliate stations, 32, 69, 90; Big Three, 32–33, 52–53, 57–58, 118, 132, 133, 141; program costs, 70–71; virtual, 33
News programming, 31–32, 53, 71; and automation, 73–74; nonunion, 141–42; and technology, 137–38
Nielsen ratings, 29, 32, 63, 66, 69–70
Nonprofit organizations, 18, 20–21
Nonunion workers, 158; film technicians, 124; labor conditions, 139–47; and news programming, 141–42. *See also* Freelancers

Olinsky, Mel, 73
Organizational structure: and collective
  bargaining, 34–42; contractual integration, 130–31; and distribution, 88;
  and employment, 187–88; in motion
  picture industry, 90, 114–18; and ownership, 187; and production, 92–93,
  98–102; of television, 90 91; of
  unions, 114–21, 188; vertical disintegration, 88, 91–93, 98–99, 110–11; vertical integration, 10–11, 17, 26, 88,
  90–91, 130–31; virtual integration, 11,
  91, 99–102
Ownership: and broadcasting, 32–33;
  conglomeration, 33, 183–84, 185; consolidation, 17, 182; and distribution,
  94–97, 99; foreign, 8–9, 33, 79–80;
  globalization, 16–17; mergers, 84–85,
  133–34; oligopolistic, 87–92; property
  rights, 108–9; takeovers, 17, 33

Paramount decision, 26, 91, 95, 116, 130,
  160, 182. See also Regulation
Paramount Pictures, 27, 80, 130–31
Parretti, Giancarlo, 80
Pay-per-view, 82
Piracy, 9, 23, 27–28
Producers Guild (PGA), 41, 42
Production: collaboration, 109; costs,
  16–18, 77, 93, 124; and distribution,
  92–93; flexible, 110–12, 158, 175; independent producers, 92–93, 122–24,
  160; labor costs, 25; nonunion, 158;
  organization of, 92–93, 98–102; path,
  91–92; postproduction technology,
  125–26; and residuals, 175; subcontracted system, 91–92, 93, 103; and
  unions, 113–55
Profits, 64, 69; box office revenues, 19,
  27, 124, 160
Projectionists, 43
Property rights, 106, 108–9
Public policy, 9, 10, 12, 51, 82, 182–83.
  See also Federal Communications
  Commission; Financial interest and
  syndication rules; Regulation

Qube, 56–57

Radio broadcasting, 2, 28, 43–44
Ratings. See Nielsen ratings
RCA, 81, 133
Reagan administration, 51–52, 83
Recording industry, 2–3; economic factors, 21–23; and home taping, 22, 23;
  unions, 41
Recording Industry of America (RIA), 41
Regulation, 89–90, 182; adaptation to,
  111; and children's programming,
  30–31; and deregulation, 30–31,
  51–52, 54, 182–83; early, 118–19; and
  marketing, 95–97
Reif, Jessica, 67
Residuals, 13, 45, 46, 48, 103, 106,
  166–73, 173n15; administration of
  payments, 169–70; and collective bargaining, 172–73; development of,
  167(table); and distribution, 176–77;
  foreign, 168; history, 166–69; joint
  administration of, 175–76; Monogram
  model, 168; percentage distribution of,
  170(table); point system, 169; by product market, 170–72; recovery of,
  186–87. See also Compensation

Schools, 108–9, 139
Screen Actors Guild (SAG), 7, 38, 39, 41,
  42, 156; income by source, 172(figure);
  jurisdiction, 161; merger talks, 49; and
  residuals, 168–69, 173n15, 175–76;
  and strikes, 45, 46, 110
Screen Extras Guild (SEG), 39, 110, 123,
  161n4
Screen Writers Guild, 165n7
Sherman Anti-Trust Act, 26, 116
Solomon, Michael Jay, 77
Sony Corporation, 53, 79
Strikes, 45, 46–47, 121; NABET, 134–37;
  and residuals, 172–73; and solidarity,
  110; and technology, 134–35; timing
  of, 144. See also Writers Guild of
  America
Studios: acquisition of, 125; independent, 27; mini-major, 160–61; top sev-
  en, 87, 96
Studio system, 12, 26, 88, 110, 115, 125,
  161

Syndication, 31, 81, 124, 132; barter syndication, 58, 65; domestic, 77

Talent unions, 9, 11, 13, 34, 105–6, 156–80
Teamsters. *See* International Brotherhood of Teamsters
Technology, 9–10, 16, 26–27; beta-cart, 72; camcorders, 131–32; and collective bargaining, 3–4, 8; and compensation, 174; developments, 181–82; digital, 23, 61; distribution, 94–97; and employment, 42–44; fiber optics, 30, 61; and filmmaking, 26–27; full service systems, 61; and labor-management conflict, 46–47; miniature equipment, 82; minicam, 46, 132; and news production, 137–38; and strikes, 46–47, 134–35; and television, 71–74, 131–32; and theater, 20; trend projections, 13–14; union responses to, 47–49; and unions, 122; VCRs, 124; voice sampling, 43
Telephone companies, 30, 33, 61, 85
Television, 2, 24, 28; and automation, 71–74; color, 81–82; eras of, 80–82; foreign ownership, 79–80; Hispanic, 65; independent, 29–30, 33, 57, 132; in-house production, 102, 103, 138; internationalization of, 79; networks, 5; operating margins, 67; outsourcing, 137–38; pilots, 70–71; production costs, 77; programming expenses, 31–32; public, 65; reruns, 70, 171; satellite, 54–56, 82; stations, 29–30, 132; and strikes, 5; structure, 90–91; and technology, 10, 33, 131–32; UHF band, 55, 56, 57; VHF stations, 58. *See also* Broadcasting; Cable television; Networks; News programming
Theater, 18–20, 39–41
Time Warner Communications, 17, 22, 61, 80, 131
Tisch, Laurence A., 53, 64, 133
Turner, Ted, 53, 55, 65

20th Century-Fox Film Corporation, 58, 59, 79, 84

Unions, 4, 35–37(table), 41; above-the-line, 9; and Basic Agreement, 115–17; below-the-line, 9; and broadcast television, 118–21; in era of prosperity, 121–22; future directions, 154–55, 184–91; international issues, 153–54; interunion conflicts, 45–46; and job identity, 109–12, 142, 186; jurisdiction, 34–38, 45–46, 107, 119, 131, 161–62; membership, 7, 38, 39, 158–60; and motion picture industry, 114–18; regional jurisdiction, 114, 116; structure of, 114–21, 188; and technology, 122; work rules, 48. *See also* Craft unions; Talent unions; *individual unions*
United States vs. Paramount, 26, 91, 95, 116, 130, 160, 182
Universal Pictures, 98, 100

Van Deerlin, Lionel, 51–52
Vertical disintegration, 88, 91–93, 98–99, 110–11
Vertical integration, 10–11, 17, 26, 88, 90–91; return to, 130–31
Videocassettes, 30, 168, 171
Videotape, 81, 141
Virtual integration, 11, 33, 91, 99–102
Vogel, Harold L., 24, 25, 27, 28, 29

Walton, Brian, 171
Warner Communications, 27, 56–57, 77, 80
Wolzien, Tom, 74
Women, 106
Writers Guild of America (WGA), 41, 42, 45, 123, 133, 156; jurisdiction, 161–62; membership, 105–6; minimum pay rates, 163; personal services contracts, 164–65; and residuals, 168, 169–70, 173n15, 176; strike, 1, 2, 45, 126–29, 176